HARTFORD

An Illustrated History of Connecticut's Capital

Glenn Weaver

Picture Research by Melancthon Jacobus

"Partners in Progress" by Marvin G. Thompson

Produced in Cooperation with the Connecticut Historical Society

Windsor Publications, Inc., Woodland Hills, California

PREVIOUS PAGE: Harriet Stark Eastman painted this *View of Hartford* from the east side of the Connecticut River in 1846 or 1847. The craft at the center of the picture is a "horse-powered" ferry. To propel the vessel, a horse walked along a treadmill connected to paddle wheels. (CHS)

PAGE SIX: This Kellogg brothers lithograph from the mid-19th century is the cover of a piece of sheet music entitled "Foot Guard Quick-Step." The subject is the First Governor's Foot Guard, assembled in front of the State House. (CHS).

Windsor Publications, Inc.
History Books Division
Publisher: John M. Phillips
Editorial Director: Lissa Sanders
Administrative Coordinator: Katherine Cooper
Senior Picture Editor: Teri Davis Greenberg
Senior Corporate History Editor: Karen Story
National Sales Manager: William Belger
Marketing Director: Ellen Kettenbeil
Production Manager: James Burke
Design Director: Alexander D'Anca
Art Production Manager: Dee Cooper
Typesetting Manager: E. Beryl Myers

Staff for *Hartford: An Illustrated History of Connecticut's Capital*
Editor: Rita Johnson
Designer: Laurie Handler
Picture Editors: Jana Wernor, Jim Golding-Mather
Sales Manager: Michele Sylvestro
Editorial Assistants: Clareen Arnold, Susan Block, Patricia Dailey, Phyllis Gray, Karen Holroyd, Judith Hunter, Doris Malkin, Susan Wells
Production Artists: Beth Bowman, Ellen Hazeltine
Typographers: Shannon Mellies, Barbara Neiman

Library of Congress Cataloging in Publication Data
Weaver, Glenn.
   Hartford: an illustrated history of Connecticut's capital.
   "'Partners in Progress' by Marvin G. Thompson."
   Includes index.
   1. Hartford (Conn.)—History.   2. Hartford (Conn.)
—Description.   3. Hartford (Conn.)—Industries.
I. Connecticut Historical Society.   II. Title.
F104.H3W43 1982   974.6'3   82-17606
ISBN 0-89781-052-X
©1982 by Windsor Publications. All rights reserved.
Published 1982
Printed in the United States of America
First Edition

To
Thompson R. Harlow,
Librarian and Director of
the Connecticut Historical Society
from 1940 to 1980

Contents

Settlement in the Wilderness

~HARTFORD, *MASSACHU-SETTS?* CONNECTICUT WITHOUT HARTFORD, THE CITY THAT HAS CONTRIBUTED SO MUCH TO THE STATE'S character, traditions, and prosperity?

Only 11 years after the landing of the Pilgrims, the nucleus of America's renowned Insurance City was restive in Newtown, Massachusetts, on the north bank of the Charles River and on the future site of Harvard University.

There, in one of the Massachusetts Bay Colony's more affluent towns, its inhabitants enjoyed the services of the skilled craftsmen essential to material comfort in a small community and also those of two learned clergymen: the Reverend Thomas Hooker, the pastor of the church, and the Reverend Samuel Stone, the teacher, as the assistant minister was then called.

But all was not well in this little palisaded village. The low-lying land was not particularly fertile, and the town's restricted territory was inadequate to its farming and grazing needs. Furthermore, Hooker had become involved in a theological controversy with the Reverend John Cotton of the Boston church. Cotton insisted that faith went before good works. This was sound Calvinist doctrine, but Cotton saw fit to make Hooker his foil by charging that the Newtown pastor had made too much of teaching. Nor could Hooker accept Cotton's idea that only the "regenerate" could be admitted to the church and, ultimately, to the franchise. Both Cotton and Hooker had what were regarded as excellent credentials—academic and spiritual—and the 17th-century historian William Hubbard observed that "nature did not allow two suns to shine at the same time."

The parting of the ways came soon, for on March 15, 1634, the Massachusetts General Court granted the Newtown people permission "to seek out some more convenient place." The Newtown leaders investigated several sites within the territory assigned to the Bay Colony by the Charter of 1628. None was found satisfactory, and attention turned to the Connecticut River Valley. In July of 1635, six Newtown men journeyed westward to a place the Indians called Sukiaug, at the confluence of the Connecticut and Little rivers.

Although the Dutch had already established a trading station (1633), The House of Good Hope, on the south bank of the Little River, there were overwhelming considerations in the site's favor. Some five miles to the north, the Plymouth Colony also had established a trading post that year. Close by, people from Newtown's neighbor, Dorchester, were already beginning the settlement that would become Windsor; and five miles to the south, John Oldham had begun what was to become Wethersfield. Thus, there would be friendly neighbors among the English. The Dutch settlement would be of little cause for concern, as that was intended solely as a trading operation. Furthermore, the Indians were peaceful and were eager to work out an arrangement in regard to possession of the land and for trade in furs and corn.

During the summer of 1635, the Newtown people were able to sell out to a group of Englishmen led by the Reverend Thomas Shepard. A complete transfer of property was arranged, and the new community, set up by Shepard's people, was, in February, 1636, decreed by the Massachusetts General Court to be the Town of Cambridge.

Meanwhile, during the late summer of 1635, 12 men had gone to Sukiaug to make the first preparations, and in October of that year a larger band of some 60 Newtown men, women, and children followed. Fall was in the air, and the first need was to provide shelter for the winter. On a site just upstream from the Dutch fort, these pioneers set themselves to the construction of dugout huts along the steep riverbank.

Winter came early, and it was severe. By mid-November the Connecticut River had frozen over. Food became scarce, and the chilled little band barely survived on roots, acorns, and small game. Thirteen men decided to return to Massachusetts. Of these, one died on the way back to Newtown, but the other 12 made it safely, certainly to be much berated by Thomas Hooker.

Those who remained kept busy. On Sunday all attended religious services, and on all other days, weather permitting, home lots were surveyed and mapped in anticipation of the arrival in the spring of the larger body. For themselves, these original settlers laid out lots along the south bank of the Little River. For those yet to come, lots were plotted on the north bank. A large central common (now State House Square) or Meetinghouse Yard was set off some quarter of a mile to the north. Also included in the surveying project was the laying out (on paper, at least) of the first streets. Between stints at surveying, all able-bodied men in the settlement worked at

An artist depicted the journey of Thomas Hooker and his congregation as they traveled cross-country from Newtown in 1636 on their way to found Hartford. Mrs. Hooker, who was ill, was carried in a litter. Actually the covered wagon was not invented until over 100 years later. Courtesy, Connecticut Historical Society (CHS)

John Winthrop, Sr. (1588-1649), top, was the first governor of the Massachusetts Bay Colony. His son, above, John Winthrop, Jr. (1606-1676), served as governor of Connecticut in 1636-1637, 1657, and 1659-1676. From Cirker, Dictionary of American Portraits, *Dover, 1967*

putting up a crude palisade for protection against both the Indians and the Dutch.

The settlement had been made far below the southern boundary of Massachusetts, as had the Dorchester and Oldham settlements. They were actually "squattings," made outside any effective jurisdiction. Realizing the precariousness of their situation, the leaders of the three communities sought some sort of legal foundation. Some suggested that they seek recognition by the Plymouth Colony, as, according to one reading of that colony's land patent from the Council for New England, the settlements would fall within Plymouth territory. When it was agreed that this grant was of questionable validity and that Plymouth itself was little more than a squatting colony, attention turned to the Warwick Patentees.

On March 19, 1631/2, the Earl of Warwick, president of the Council for New England, had transferred certain loosely defined New England lands to a group of English Puritan gentlemen and nobles, including Lord Saye and Sele, Lord Brook, and Lord Rich. Anticipating a civil war in England, the patentees were hopeful of setting up a refuge in the New World, should the Puritans in the Mother Country come under serious disadvantage. John Winthrop, Jr., had been sent to America in late 1635 with the title of governor and with instructions to erect a fort at the mouth of the Connecticut, and here was where the interests of the Connecticut River settlements, the patentees, and the Winthrop family converged.

John Winthrop, Sr., then deputy governor of the Bay Colony, prevailed upon the governor, Sir Henry Vane, to make an accommodation. A plan was devised whereby the river settlers would recognize Winthrop, Jr., as governor for one year, and the Connecticut people would maintain an informal relationship with Massachusetts.

On March 3, 1635/6, the Massachusetts General Court commissioned eight men to carry on the functions of government in the new settlements, allowing them to hold courts of law, adopt local ordinances, and declare war. These magistrates were to serve for one year, and after that the "plantation" would be free to adopt any form of government it would choose. Of the eight magistrates—Roger Ludlow, William Phillips, William Pynchon, Henry Smith, John Steele, William Swaine, Andrew Ward, and William Westwood—five met in Newtown to swear in Samuel Wakeman as constable.

All was now ready for the final move from Newtown on the Charles to Newtown on the Connecticut. On May 31, 1636, about 100 men, women, and children started westward by land, taking with them some 160 head of cattle.

Each head of family proceeded to his designated land, where a small dugout or similar makeshift was provided. And as it was still not yet midsummer, all began setting up more comfortable structures. Within the year, the last of the dugouts had been filled in, and soon householders were adding second rooms, lean-tos, and even second stories.

While these simple homes were being built, the mansion under construction for entrepreneur George Wyllys must have seemed something of an anachronism. That Wyllys was a personage was evident in the fact that his lot (bounded by present Main, Charter Oak, Governor, and Wyllys streets) was roughly four times the size of the largest of the others. Wyllys was of gentle birth and had been lord of the manor of Fenny Compton in Warwickshire. He was also one of the wealthiest men in all New England, and although a freeman of Newtown, Massachusetts, he was so involved in the Indian trade on the Maine coast that he was unable to accompany the settlers to the new Newtown in 1636. He did, however, signify his intention to move to the colony (which he ultimately did in 1638) by commissioning his steward,

ABOVE: *The first meetinghouse was a very plain structure, both inside and out. (CHS)*

ABOVE RIGHT: *There were no photographers present when the Newtown congregation arrived, but the dedication of Hartford's new stone bridge in 1908 was occasion for a reenactment. President W. Douglas Mackenzie of the Hartford Theological Seminary took the part of Thomas Hooker. (CHS)*

William Gibbons, to build a replica of his English manor house. With the assistance of 20 indentured servants, Gibbons, beginning in the summer of 1636, erected a splendid nine-room residence, set off by formal gardens and surrounded by stables, barns, and various other outbuildings. The Wyllys mansion was unquestionably the most elegant in New England.

Although the more modest homes were hardly as comfortable, most of them, too, were soon surrounded by barns, sheds, shops, and "necessary houses." Within the simple dwellings were equally simple furnishings—chests, benches, tables, and beds, some brought from England, and some homemade. Pewter substituted for silver, and wood for chinaware. Especially lacking were chairs. Usually there was one for the master; the rest of the family had to be satisfied with benches or stools.

Next, having provided shelter for both man and beast, all hands turned toward completion of the meetinghouse. This framed structure was 36 feet by 23 feet, with thatched hip roof, board shutters, and a door of heavy plank. Inside, it was totally without ornament, and its only furnishings were a pulpit and a series of rough benches. The first meetinghouse soon proved to be too small, and in 1638 it was replaced by a larger structure, located just west of the first one, which was then given to Thomas Hooker for use as a barn. The new meetinghouse was made more commodious by the addition of a gallery in 1646.

The congregation had been in existence since 1632, and there was no problem in keeping the society (as congregations then were called) afloat. All residents, members or not, were at first required to attend the two Sunday services as well as the Thursday lecture. Attendance was never a problem, but the question of where one would sit within the meetinghouse was quite a different matter. Each New England congregation was expected to "seat the meeting" every few years, when a committee would reassign seats "according to the dignity of the family." The first seating took place on March 13, 1640/1, and although we do not have any contemporary record as to the results, it may be assumed that there was probably a mixture of joy and gloom, according to where one placed on this primary indicator of social standing.

When the magistrates turned to making an arrangement with the Indians, Sequassin, the Sukiaug Chief, granted lands extending from present Manchester to six miles west of the Connecticut River. Although the Indians were not familiar with the English concept of landholding, and although the purchase price was small, the agreement apparently met with their satisfaction.

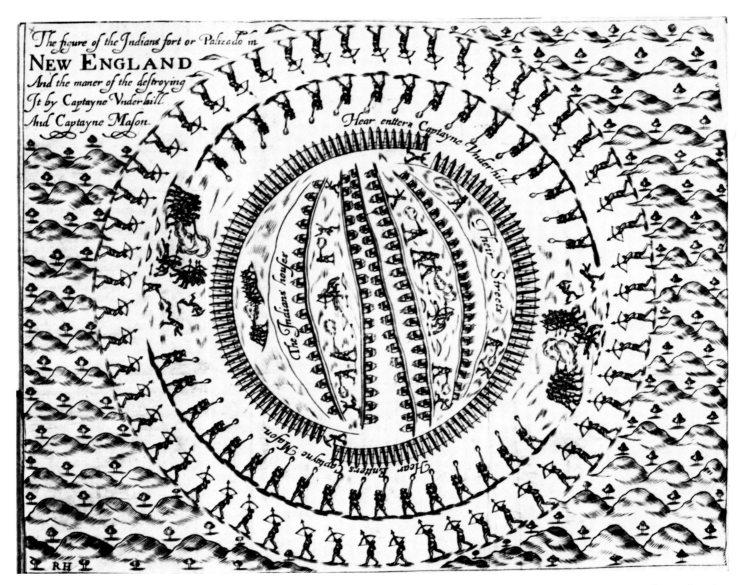

In 1637 Captain John Mason was sent from Hartford in command of troops who faced the task of clearing out the Pequot fort at Underhill, near Mystic. This was the plan for capturing the Indian stronghold and "the manner of destroying it." (CHS)

During the first year, all functions of government were carried out by the magistrates and the constable. Even the influence of John Winthrop dwindled rapidly, and the magistrates seemed oblivious of the fact that there was indeed still a governor.

On February 21, 1636/7, the magistrates changed the name of Newtown to Hartford, after the English home of the Reverend Samuel Stone. The name of Dorchester was also changed, to Windsor, and that of the Oldham settlement (Watertown) to Wethersfield.

The magistrates had also given much care to the matter of defense. A trainband (or militia corps) was organized for each of the settlements, and Major John Mason of Windsor was appointed to drill all males over 16 years of age at the monthly training day.

From the beginning the magistrates, or the commission, had existed as both a legislative body and, as they had tried several small cases under Massachusetts law, as a judicial body. But the commission and Winthrop's nominal term as governor were to expire on March 3, 1636/7, and a new arrangement would have to be made. On

March 28, 1637, the magistrates outlined a new plan of government whereby the inhabitants would elect a new body of eight magistrates (later to be called assistants), and each of the towns would send their committees, or deputies, as they would be known, to comprise a General Court for the entire plantation.

On May 1, 1637, the elected delegates assembled in the meetinghouse at Hartford as the first Court of Election. One of its first acts was to define the franchise: "admitted habitation" (i.e., the enjoyment of privilege within the town) would demand no religious test—all that would be required was a minimal property holding. The first General Court also fixed the price of Indian corn, declared wampum to be legal tender, awarded a monopoly for the fur trade, and declared war against the Pequot Indians.

The Pequot War grew out of a series of small clashes between the Pequots and the English, the culmination of which was the attack in February, 1636/7, upon Wethersfield. Connecticut's declaration of war was something of an accommodation to the Sukiaug Indians, a minor tribe subject to tribute to the larger and fierce Pequots. Also, the war represented the first instance of cooperation among the several New England colonies, as troops were sent from Connecticut, Massachusetts, and Plymouth.

Connecticut raised a force of 90 men, under command of John Mason, and, with Stone as chaplain and "Dr." (a courtesy title) John Olmsted as surgeon, Hartford alone sent 61. A band of Sequassin's braves accompanied the whites.

The Pequot War was brief but bloody, consisting of little more than the burning of two Pequot villages, one on the Mystic River, where some 600 Indian men, women, and children were slaughtered as they attempted to flee the Puritan firepower, and the other at present Southport, where, in "the Great Swamp Fight," the Mystic-massacre scene was repeated. Those who survived were taken as slaves. The adult males were sold in the West Indies, and the children and adult females were divided among the victorious military leaders.

The Sukiaugs were grateful to the English for the Pequot defeat, and in appreciation they ceded the portion of the North Meadows that had been retained by them according to the agreement of 1636 and moved their village to the South Meadows. This land was then divided into field lots for the returned Hartford veterans, and this low-lying section was long known as Soldiers Field.

The Pequot War left the colony with a debt of £620, and it was at this point that the General Court imposed its first general tax. Although Hartford's share of £251.2 might seem excessive by modern standards, there was an acceptance of the tax as an investment in a corporation in which dividends ultimately were to be realized in the form of additional grants from the town's still undivided lands.

In this, the Hartford homeholders were not to be disappointed. As Hartford's town government was being set up with the selection of townsmen (later selectmen) and the beginnings of town meetings in 1639, one of the principal functions of government at the local level was that of dividing and apportioning landholdings from what was still held in common by all members of the town.

One of the first divisions beyond the original town lots was made for the Adventurers, those heroes of the settlement's start—John Barnard, Richard Goodman, Stephen Hart, Matthew Merriam, James Olmsted, William Pantry, Thomas Scott, Thomas Stanley, John Steele, John Talcott, Richard Webb, and John Westwood. This tract, roughly in the vicinity of present Albany Avenue and Garden Street, was intended for the planting of field crops. Then, too, there was the Soldiers Field grant, also intended for farming purposes beyond what one could carry out on

Known as King Philip, this Indian was the second son of Massasoit. He later became Sachem of the Wampanoags, and he was greatly feared by the colonists when he ranged up and down the Connecticut Valley. (CHS)

his home lot. Other divisions followed, and in most cases all holders of home lots were entitled to outlying lots in each new division.

Perhaps the best interpretation of the rule of division was given by William DeLoss Love in his *Colonial History of Hartford* (Hartford, 1914, p. 122) as having been "according to one's estate, social standing, occupation, family, public service, convenience, and ability to improve the land."

Ever since the arrival of Hooker and his party, there had been a steady stream of newcomers from Massachusetts and from England. All who demonstrated that they were of good character were given lots, as old roads were extended and new ones were laid out, although newcomers were given home lots of one acre, half the size of the original lots.

In 1639 a Body of Proprietors was created to determine who had a right to share in the undivided lands. Those found to have such a claim were those who had shared the financial burden of the plantation's founding and who had paid taxes on real or

ABOVE: Members of the Hartford Canoe Club, in appropriate costume, portray the Indians who may have "greeted" the Hooker congregation. (CHS)

ABOVE RIGHT: In 1636 Hooker's congregation crossed the Connecticut River several miles upstream from this spot, but for purposes of the bridge pageant, the group was rafted over from East Hartford. (CHS)

personal property on a regular basis. This was simply to say that those who had participated in the earlier land division had closed the doors against the newcomers. Although later arrivals had no legal claim to land—even to a home lot—those possessed of talent in the skills and crafts then wanting in the community were given land "by the town's courtesy."

Obviously, the possession of land was a mark of status. It must be remembered, too, that land was essential to survival, as the community was entirely dependent upon itself for food and clothing, necessities that could be provided only by field and flock.

On each house lot there was a kitchen garden, and often there was an orchard. Each household had its own cattle that were branded and kept in the common cow yard; hay was cut in common from the meadows under the direction of the hay ward, and sheep were kept in the common flock by the town shepherd. Indian corn was the chief field crop, although there were small plantings of English wheat, rye, and peas. But even corn was in short supply during the early years, and much of that consumed by the settlers had to be purchased from the Indians. This crop, too, was soon recognized by the General Court as legal tender (or "commodity money"), and thus its value was fixed by law. In 1638, corn was priced (or fixed) at 5s. per bushel. In 1642, it fell to 2s. 6d., which remained the standard for several years.

In this early economy, every person farmed, few of them full-time but all of them part-time. Whatever one may have listed as his primary occupation, farming was his second, and whether he actually worked with his hands or whether he employed the services of servants or slaves, each householder, from the Reverend Thomas Hooker on down, farmed. While these part-time farmers were engaged in this subsistence type of agriculture, each was busily pursuing his primary "calling." John Barnard was a maltster; John Bidwell and Gregory Wolterton were tanners; Nicholas Clark was a carpenter; Nicholas Disbrow was both carpenter and cabinetmaker; John Cole was a cooper; Philip Davis was a tailor; Thomas Lord was a

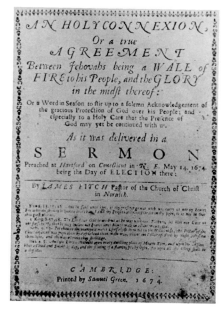

blacksmith; and George Grove and John Baysey were weavers.

Each of these artisans held a variety of public offices. John Baysey, for example, rose from chimney viewer in 1649, surveyor of highways in 1652, constable in 1656, and fenceviewer in 1667, to townsman in 1669. Others held such posts as hay ward, juror, and rate and list maker (for purposes of taxation). In addition, each man took his turn at nighttime street patrolling, and each served in the trainband. Also, as every householder was required to keep both a fire ladder and fire bucket in readiness, these men constituted a volunteer fire department. And each was obligated to two days of service a year for repairs on the town roads.

Larger industrial undertakings that employed journeymen workers in addition to the master were sawmills, quarries, gristmills, and brick kilns. The sawmill, or saw pit, was a simple operation carried on by two men, and from the beginning of settlement several pits were producing boards and beams for houses and barns. Late in 1637, a brick kiln was opened on the site of the present railroad station. Foundation

ABOVE: This sermon was the first of the famous series of election sermons delivered to the General Assembly at the opening of the annual session in 1674. From Clark, A History of Connecticut, 1914

ABOVE LEFT: This photograph, taken circa 1904, shows the general area of what was once Thomas Hooker's house and land. (CHS)

stones were quarried at the falls of the Little River not far from the brickyard.

Matthew Allyn built the first mill, which stood along the Little River. When Allyn moved to Windsor in 1644, he turned the mill over to his son, John. The younger Allyn had several partners in succession, and the Allyn partners formed other partnerships after John Allyn's death. The mill operated well into the 19th century, during which it was known as Imlay's Mill.

The town mill, called Hopkins' Mill for Edward Hopkins, the first operator, was built in 1640 and cost the town £120. Members of the town were assessed shares according to the size of their landholdings. These shares passed from hand to hand, and controlling interests were purchased by the individuals by whose names the town mill came to be known—"Brent's Mill" for Bela Brent, and later, "Todd's Mill" for Ira Todd.

These larger industries—milling, brickmaking, and quarrying—employed journeymen at wages, and thus a working class existed in Hartford from the very beginning. Quite early the matter of wage earning came before the Connecticut General Court, and in 1640 it passed "The Order Concerning Artificers and Laborers for Wages." When the men intended to be covered by the act began charging what were reported as exorbitant wages, the General Court on June 7, 1641, ordered that carpenters, plowwrights, wheelwrights, masons, joiners, smiths, and coopers should receive no more than 20d. for a day's work between March 10 and October 11, nor above 18d. for the remainder of the year. Hours of labor for these men were fixed at 11 for summer and 9 for winter. This was an early example of wage control, and its unworkable nature was demonstrated in its repeal on March 20, 1649/50, at which time the ceiling price on corn was also removed.

Nothing in Hartford during these early decades even remotely resembled a retail shop or general store. In 1643, the General Court granted authority for a weekly market in Hartford. This market, held in an open building on the southeast corner of Meetinghouse Yard, was something of a combination of English cattle fair, 20th-century flea market, and roadside vegetable stand. Two years later, Hartford was granted authority to hold two fairs each year. The fair differed from the market only in that it was conducted on a larger scale and was attended by buyers and sellers from other towns.

Although Hartford's early artisans were able to care for the day-to-day needs of the people, it was imperative that there be an external trade—both with the Indians and with the larger European world of commerce. Henry Stiles of Windsor got trade with the Indians off to a bad start when he exchanged some sort of firearm to the Indians for a quantity of corn. The General Court of April 26, 1636, ordered Stiles to make recovery "in a faire & legall waye, or else this corte will take [it] into further consideration." Stiles was unable to recover the weapon, but the incident prompted the Court to declare that any person who traded with the Indians "any piece or pistol or gun or powder or shott" would be dealt with severely.

In 1638, William Whiting and Thomas Stanton were given the Hartford monopoly on the Indian trade in corn and beaver skins. Two years later, Edward Hopkins was given license to trade with the Indians in Massachusetts, and, as corn soon became an exportable commodity, Hopkins and Whiting were given the sole privilege of sending corn to Plymouth and the Massachusetts Bay.

Whiting was then Hartford's leading merchant and was engaged in trading operations from the Piscataqua to Virginia. Whiting died in 1647, leaving the remarkably large estate of £2,854. His inventory revealed that he had then in his possession several hundred pounds' worth of furs and tobacco, a large supply of uten-

This two-story building with belfry is the second meetinghouse, pictured in 1640. The structure was built in 1638 next to the first meetinghouse, and a gallery was added in 1646 to further increase its size. (CHS)

sils intended for the Indian trade, and a sizable stock of hardware, clothing, spices, and miscellaneous household articles.

Thomas Stanton came to the colony from Virginia in 1639. Stanton always kept up his Virginia connections, sailing on numerous occasions to the First Colony in the interests of the tobacco trade, often in partnership with other Hartford men. Stanton's father-in-law, Thomas Lord, Hartford's first blacksmith, may have been a minor partner, but it was the blacksmith's son, Captain Richard Lord, who formed partnerships first with Stanton and later with Samuel Wyllys, the son of George Wyllys. Captain Richard Lord built Hartford's first warehouse, in which he stored grain, soap, salt, lime, and a great variety of what might be called general hardware. Lord died in 1662 and left an estate of £1,539. The captain's son, Richard Lord, Jr., was even more expansive, as he traveled frequently between Hartford and England. His estate came to a princely £5,786.

Samuel Wyllys had his own particular business interests, including part ownership in several sugar plantations in Antigua. Edward Hopkins was both an exporter of corn and beaver skins and an importer of English goods. Samuel Wakeman, perhaps the last of the first generation of Hartford merchants, was shot and killed in 1641 in the Bahamas, where he had gone in the hope of purchasing cotton. One of the most interesting early Hartford merchants was Thomas Olcott, who traded in tobacco with Virginia, transshipped the tobacco to Boston, and brought English goods back to Hartford. Olcott prospered in this form of triangular trade, and at his death in 1654 he left an estate of £1,466. 8s. 5d. His widow carried on the business for another 40 years and made her own small fortune as a sort of informal banker, lending money on mortgage security.

This early trade operated under considerable disadvantage. The sandbar at the mouth of the Connecticut River provided only 12 feet at high water. This limited the river traffic to vessels of 60 to 80 tons, and in extremely dry weather a sandbar at Middletown made that town the head of navigation for the small sloops and pinnaces in which Hartford's trade was carried on.

In Hartford these small vessels could sail up the Little River, perhaps as far as present Main Street, but quite early a landing place was established on the Connecticut, just south of the foot of present State Street. Here were built the earliest warehouses, and from this point was operated the ferry across the river.

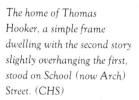

The home of Thomas Hooker, a simple frame dwelling with the second story slightly overhanging the first, stood on School (now Arch) Street. (CHS)

Of Puritans, Dutchmen, and Regicides

~WHILE HARTFORD WAS BEING TRANSFORMED FROM A CRUDE FRONTIER SETTLEMENT TO A SELF-SUFFICIENT AGRICULTURAL village, Connecticut was undergoing the metamorphosis from plantation to colony. A General Court had been set up and was operating under the English Common Law, Massachusetts precedent, and a nominal authority of the Warwick Patentees. There was, however, no single document of constitutional force to limit and regularize the functions of government.

No one was more aware of this than Thomas Hooker, and on May 31, 1638, Hooker preached the famous sermon in which he declared that the foundation of governmental authority must always lie in "the free consent of the people." Hooker's words have often been misconstrued to the extent of making him a "democrat," but Hooker's "people" were not the people of the 20th century—far from it. To Hooker, "the people" were responsible, property-holding males.

It would be easy to think that Hooker's sermon provided the inspiration for the constitution that was to be drawn up, but work had already been begun on the Fundamental Orders, and Hooker was giving a preview of what was to come. The document was largely the work of Roger Ludlow of Windsor, the only man in the river towns with training in the law. The document was adopted on January 14, 1638/9, although it is uncertain whether ratification was by the magistrates and committees, by the freemen, or by all adult males.

The Orders provided for a form of government not much different from that already in operation. Two regular meetings of the General Court were to be held each year, one in September for the enactment of legislation and another in April, the so-called Court of Election, at which were to be chosen magistrates and colony secretary, treasurer, governor, and deputy governor. John Haynes was elected the first governor, and Roger Ludlow the deputy.

At about the same time that Haynes was elected governor, he purchased a lot across the Little River from George Wyllys' lot, and there he erected a handsome mansion of his own. Although not so elegant as that of Wyllys, it was an L-shaped structure that formed two sides of a "great court," as Haynes described it, the rectangular enclosure completed by attached barns, outhouses, stables, sheds, and a brew house.

Relations between the Hartford people and their Dutch neighbors had always been quite strained. Although the Dutch had never made any claim to the land north of the Little River, they were incensed when the earliest lots were extended to the very walls of the Dutch fort.

Actually, their House of Good Hope was a rather imposing facility, surrounded by a fortification of logs, reinforced at the corners with brick and stone. Inside, there were a two-story blockhouse, several sheds, a kitchen garden, and a cherry orchard — all within an enclosure of little more than an acre. Outside the wall there was a small burial ground.

At first, the two communities had largely ignored each other. When the Hartford people began planting fields near the Dutch fort, however, the Dutch tried to drive them off, and the Hartford men beat them with cudgels. Gysbert Opdyck, the Dutch commissary in charge, protested to Governor Haynes, and although Haynes met with Opdyck, no agreement could be reached. The following spring it was the Dutch who began to plow the land in question, whereupon Constable Thomas Hosmer appeared on the scene with 12 armed deputies. Although no blows were struck, the shouting of the Hartford men frightened the horses, which, breaking their traces, ran away. When they had gathered their animals, the Dutch finished planting the field of corn. That night the Englishmen replanted the same field, and the question might well be raised as to who was fooling whom.

From that point on, the situation deteriorated rapidly. Dutch horses strayed into Englishmen's fields, and Hartford homeholders impounded the strays. Englishmen were accused of stealing cattle from the Dutch, and the Reverend Samuel Stone reportedly took a cartload of meadow hay that had been cut on Dutch lands.

In the spring of 1641, the English built a fence to separate their own lands, or their own lands as they saw them, from those of the Dutch. The Dutch promptly tore it down, and the English retaliated by again attacking a Dutch plow team. However unbelievable these childish actions of otherwise staid Calvinist gentlemen might seem, blood had been shed at the last encounter, and Governor Edward Hopkins promptly called a halt to the antics. From then on, the English policy would be one of restraint.

ABOVE: *Thomas Hooker's statement of the reason for the emigration from Massachusetts to Connecticut is surrounded by four Connecticut seals. Clockwise from upper left: seal of 1784, seal of 1622-1787, seal of 1711-1784, and English seal of colonial days. From Clark,* A History of Connecticut, *1914*

ABOVE RIGHT: *George Wyllys (1710-1796) served as Colony State Secretary from 1735-1796. His father, Hezekiah, held the office from 1712-1735, and George's son, Samuel, served from 1796-1810. This service of almost 100 years from a single family is an example of Connecticut's "steady habits." From Cirker,* Dictionary of American Portraits, Dover, *1967*

For almost a decade thereafter there was an unsteady truce. Although the English took no further physical action, they did lodge complaints that the Dutch were urging Hartford servants to run away from their masters, receiving stolen goods, and performing marriages for couples whose unions had not been permitted by the Hartford authorities.

When the English Civil War broke out in 1642, the four New England Puritan colonies—Massachusetts, Plymouth, New Haven, and Connecticut—fearing that the Mother Country would no longer be able to provide for colonial defense, formed the Confederation of New England. The purpose of the Confederation (set up in 1643) was to promote the shared religious ideals, to improve commerce, and to provide for defense against both the Indians and the Dutch.

On September 19, 1650, commissioners from the Confederation of New England met with Dutch representatives in Hartford and signed a treaty that set the boundary line between New Netherland and Connecticut and confirmed the Dutch right to operate the House of Good Hope without interference from the English. But even the Treaty of Hartford did not provide for a working relationship between the two groups, and the situation was further aggravated with the outbreak in 1652 of the First Dutch War between England and Holland.

By 1653 Governor Peter Stuyvesant was again protesting "scores" of English depredations against the Dutch fort and its inhabitants. Late in June of that year, Captain John Underhill, acting for Providence Plantation, and without the blessing of either Connecticut or the Confederation of New England, seized Fort Good Hope. This was an embarrassment to Connecticut, and on April 6, 1654, the Connecticut General Court ordered the sequestering of the entire Dutch interest in Connecticut.

The Dutch had presented a threat from the outside, but there were also internal threats—moral threats—to Hartford's well-being that were, in their way, even more serious.

Much has been made of the fact that only a small portion of the people in any of the Puritan colonies were active church members, but the fact remains that all who came knew the rules of the game in advance, and most of them, initially at least, must have had some intention of abiding by them.

Connecticut Puritans were convinced that God would punish the sins of a colony by its destruction, and that punishment of the offending individual had to be both swift and vigorous. All New England statute books had long listed adultery, sodomy, and bestiality as capital offenses, and in each Puritan colony, executions for one or more of these crimes were carried out. Whippings were common, doubtless because of the small expense involved and because they provided examples of the wages of sin. Lesser offenses were punished by fines. Imprisonments were both rare and brief.

It would seem that few moral offenses were committed by the responsible adults of the first generation. There were, of course, exceptions, such as the prodigious example of promiscuity by the wife of proprietor Nicholas Disbrow, who was convicted in 1640 of "wanton dalliance" with three men. One of the three was none other than Nicholas Olmsted, one of the original settlers. For his part, Olmsted was fined £20 and ordered to stand in the pillory in Meetinghouse Yard.

"Single fornication" seems to have been the most common offense, and its extent must have been even greater than the available records would indicate. Only such cases were brought to light as those involving the birth of bastard children or couples who had their first child less than seven months after marriage. At times, the cases involving fornication seemed to dominate the docket. In the earlier years the punishment was invariably whipping, even though marriage followed, and there was always, of course, the public confession in the meetinghouse, after which the guilty parties were admonished and sometimes excommunicated.

The "natural" offenses against morality were bad enough, but with witchcraft what was involved was not the natural, but the supernatural. In 1655 Nathaniel Greensmith and his wife arrived in Hartford. Neither was very popular from the beginning, and charges of witchcraft were soon brought. Both were found guilty. The wife was hanged in Meetinghouse Yard in late 1662, and the husband met a similar fate on January 25, 1662/3. The trial and execution attracted wide attention throughout New England, and it might be noted that Hartford's first witches were executed exactly 30 years before the more famous, or infamous, witchcraft trials at Salem, Massachusetts.

The most stable influence during these unstable times was, of course, the church. The "Congregational Way" presented an entirely new concept of "the church"—not The Church as "the Body of Christ," but "the church" as the covenanted body of all believers. Thus, the church was made up of those who through their conversion experience had first covenanted with God and then covenanted with other covenanted believers.

The church was totally autonomous, dependent only upon itself and holding no relationship to any other congregation. Having rejected the Anglican doctrine of Apostolic Succession, it was autonomous to the extent of ordaining its own officers, including the minister, the ruling elder, and the deacon, and both admitting to its fellowship those who had "owned the covenant" and excommunicating those who had broken the covenant with God and the congregation. Both men and women were admitted to membership, and soon the women were outnumbering the men, although, despite their superior numbers, women were allowed neither to hold office nor to speak at meetings. Newcomers to the town were admitted by letter of transfer

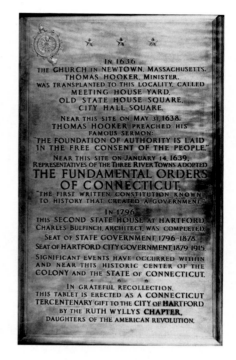

The Fundamental Orders are commemorated by this plaque, placed on the wall of the Old State House in 1935. (CHS)

from another congregation—and no questions asked. Even servants, free or bond, were admitted, provided the master would serve as spiritual overseer.

Hooker was less given to hellfire-and-damnation sermons than were the other ministers in the river towns, nor did Hooker seem to place any particular limits as to the exact nature of the conversion experience. Perhaps Hooker was satisfied that all were required by law to attend meeting, and, with the penalty for absence being 5s., the pews were always filled. Hooker preached in the morning, and Stone gave the afternoon discourse. Psalms were droned out, and prayers were fervent, long, and homemade. Sunday was a holy day but not a Holy Day, and, as the Congregationalists had completely rejected the Church year, Christmas, Easter, and the lesser Christian feasts and fasts were ignored.

During the summer of 1647 the Connecticut Valley was struck by an epidemic, the nature of which is not precisely known. The General Court took what measures it could, ordering that all meat offered for sale be inspected carefully, and also putting an end to the practice of throwing garbage upon the streets to be devoured by the town hogs. Despite those official precautions, there were several fatalities in Hartford, and among the victims was Thomas Hooker, who died on July 7.

With the passing of Hooker, church leadership fell to Samuel Stone, who proved immediately to be a difficult person with whom to deal. When Elder William Goodwin married Hooker's widow, the congregation split into two factions—those who sided with Stone and those who favored Goodwin. The division at first was one of personalities, but doctrine, too, was soon to widen the breach, and the particular point was the conversion experience and admission to the church.

The Massachusetts congregations had adopted the "Half-Way Covenant," whereby those who had not had the conversion experience were admitted to a sort of halfway membership—at least to the extent of having their children baptized, even though they were not themselves admitted to the Holy Communion. Stone accepted the principle, but a considerable portion of the congregation found it unacceptable.

It was on the matter of the selection of a colleague minister for Stone that most of the congregation's infighting occurred. A series of young candidates (all Harvard men) presented themselves to preach trial sermons: Jonathan Mitchell (1649); Michael Wigglesworth, later to write the famous poem *Day of Doom* (1653 and 1654); John Davis (1655); and John Cotton, Jr. (1659). In the case of Wigglesworth, Stone even refused to allow the congregation to vote on his candidacy. The possibility of having the younger John Cotton in Hartford was too much for Elder Goodwin, and he led a small group of the dissidents to settle in Hadley, Massachusetts.

Even this did not end the turmoil, and the General Court, in 1657 and again in 1659, appointed a Council of Ministers to investigate. The second Council suggested that the Hartford church adopt the Half-Way Covenant.

By 1660 there was sufficient harmony within the congregation to elect John Whiting, the son of Hartford's Major William Whiting, as colleague minister to Samuel Stone. When Stone died in 1663, Joseph Haynes, a son of the former governor, was selected as Stone's successor. The two young men proved to be a quarrelsome pair.

Haynes and a majority of the congregation insisted upon admitting according to the Half-Way Covenant. Whiting and an equally determined minority held to the "visible saints" idea, firmly insisting, with logic on their side, that there could be no such thing as a Half-Way Christian. On February 12, 1669/70, Whiting led 31 of his followers in organizing Second Church.

Thomas Hooker's grave has never been found, but some believe he was buried in a part of the Ancient Burying Ground near the pulpit end of Center Church. (CHS)

The separation was certainly not an amicable one. The Town Meeting cut off Whiting's salary, and the Proprietors refused to provide land for a meetinghouse; nor would the First Church allow the Second to use their building for worship. In 1672 the Town Meeting voted that taxes collected on the South Side be used to pay Whiting's salary, but on the matter of land there was no accommodation, and the congregation was obliged to purchase the first South Meetinghouse lot at the corner of present Sheldon and Main streets. The Second Congregation worshiped at first in private houses, but within a few years a South Meetinghouse was erected, an almost exact replica of that of First Church.

While these horrendous religious disputes were tearing the Hartford community apart, an old familiar name—that of John Winthrop, Jr.—was being tossed about. Although Winthrop lived in New London and also had a house in New Haven, Hartford leaders felt that were Winthrop to be attracted to Hartford, he would provide the leadership needed to bring calm to the troubled community. Hartford was also well aware of Winthrop's reputation as a medical practitioner, and were he to be induced to come, the community's medical needs would be well served.

Hartford's physicians had come and gone. Dr. Olmsted had long since left for Norwalk, and for several years no medical service was available. Following the epidemic of 1647, however, the General Court made efforts to provide for medical service and to license physicians, and in the course of the Court's discussions, the magistrates had consulted with Winthrop, who had come to Hartford on occasion to treat a patient or two.

Under Connecticut's licensing law, the General Court, in 1652, appointed Thomas Lord of Hartford as Colony Physician, setting his fees at 12d. for a home call in Hartford, 5s. for Windsor, 6s. for Wethersfield and Farmington, and 8s. for Middletown, plus a stipend of £15 from the colony treasury. In 1655, the Court licensed Daniel Porter, granting him a stipend of £6 and allowing him to charge 6s. for each call. Jasper Gunn was licensed in 1657, although probably with no colony stipend. But none of these men enjoyed a reputation comparable with that of Winthrop.

The first bait was offered in 1651, when Winthrop, probably with his consent, was elected Assistant. Although reelected each year following, he probably did not attend a single session of the General Court until the spring of 1653. Winthrop evidenced little interest in the official business of the colony, but the Hartford leaders persisted, and in 1657 he was actually elected governor. But Winthrop was coy. The General Court offered him the house and lands of the late Governor Haynes, but it was only after two delegations had met with him personally that Winthrop finally accepted, and even then it was with apparent reluctance.

In November of 1657 Winthrop moved his family to Hartford, but the move was not a total break, for Winthrop still maintained his houses in New Haven and New London, as well as his extensive sheep-raising operation on Fisher's Island.

In 1660 the Cromwellian Period came to an end in England, and Charles II was restored to the English throne. Winthrop was then acting as chief executive of his colony, devoting one or two days each week to the practice of medicine, overseeing his various commercial enterprises along the Connecticut shore, and carrying on the extensive scientific correspondence that established him as an authority on mineralogy, geology, mathematics, astronomy, chemistry, alchemy, and the occult "sciences"—a reputation that would result in his election to the Royal Society created by Charles II.

Winthrop had always had doubts regarding the legal status of the colony, particularly since the Fundamental Orders had been a self-entered-into arrangement, not a document emanating from the Crown. Others were of the same persuasion, and in 1662 Winthrop was sent to England to secure a Royal Charter, one, it was hoped, that would provide for a form of government essentially that laid down in the Fundamental Orders. Winthrop's mission was a total success, for the Connecticut Charter of 1662 deviated from the Orders in very few details. Furthermore, the Charter attached the neighboring colony of New Haven to the river towns.

The Charter was read publicly in Hartford on October 9, 1662, in what has been described as an "audience of the Freemen." The document was then given for safekeeping to young Lieutenant John Allyn.

The publication of the Charter fixed Hartford as colony capital. Winthrop stressed that the document implied that Hartford would be the seat of government, but this insistence was hardly necessary, for colony affairs had always centered about Hartford. It had already become the legislative center as the place of meetings of the General Court. When the Court of Assistants (the upper house of the General Court acting in judicial capacity) assumed the functions of a Superior Court, it, too, always met in Hartford. The town's importance as a legal center was fixed in 1666, when the colony was divided into four counties and Hartford was designated as Shire Town, or county seat, of Hartford County.

Hartford would remain the capital of the colony until 1701, when legislative sessions would begin to be shared with New Haven: the April session meeting in Hartford and the October session in New Haven. This arrangement would prevail until 1873, when Hartford would again become the sole capital. Hartford, little Hartford, with a population of a mere 4,000 inhabitants in 1662, thus became the scene of much coming and going and the stage upon which high drama regarding the success or failure of the small Puritan colony was to be played.

In 1662 a Royal Commission, sent by King Charles II to investigate conditions in the several New England colonies, arrived in Hartford. The commission had already been to the Bay Colony, where they had been treated in a most discourteous fashion. In Hartford, however, it was quite different, and John Allyn, their official host, did all that was possible to make their stay pleasant.

Soon thereafter Hartford received several less welcome visitors, Edward Whalley and William Goffe, two of the judges who had condemned Charles I to death, and in search of whom Charles II had sent a party of royal officials. The Regicides had come to Boston immediately upon the restoration of Charles II. When the pursuit became too hot, they moved southward, stopping at several places including Hartford along the way to New Haven, where, joined by another of the judges, John Dixwell, they were concealed, according to legend at least, in a cave on West Rock. The Regicides were never captured. Goffe went to Hatfield, Massachusetts, changed his name, and lived there until his death, although he may have resided for several years in Hartford, using the name of Mr. Cooke.

In 1675 King Philip's War broke out. The intent of Philip, the son of Massasoit, was to unite the North American Indians in the destruction of all English settlements. The war in southern New England lasted for less than two years, but these were busy times in Hartford. Military officers from the New England colonies met on several occasions in First Church Meetinghouse. Major John Talcott, Jr., was in command of Connecticut's several hundred volunteer militiamen, and the Reverend John Whiting served as chaplain.

In 1687 Hartford was visited briefly by a most distinguished and awesome gentleman, Sir Edmund Andros, Governor of the Dominion of New England. During his short stay, Connecticut underwent the most severe crisis in the colony's histo-

Appointed governor of the Dominion of New England, Sir Edmund Andros, under order of King James II, formally assumed control of Connecticut at Hartford on October 31, 1687. Andros demanded that the Connecticut Charter of 1662 be surrendered, and he suffered humiliation after it was "ghosted" away. From Cirker, Dictionary of American Portraits, Dover, *1967*

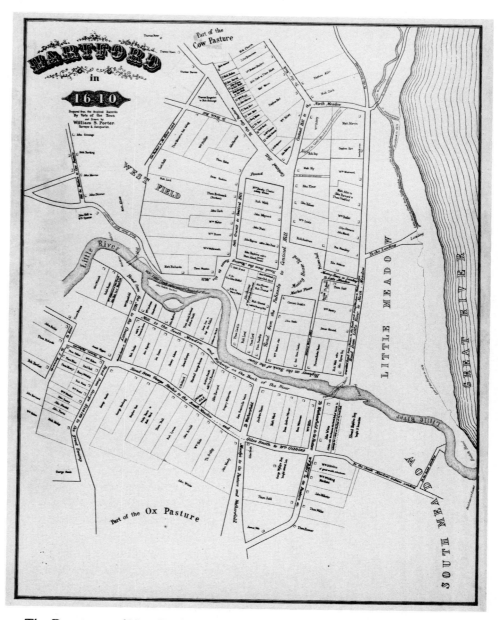

In 1640 spacious lots with surrounding fields and pastures were given to Hartfordites who demonstrated "good moral character." Courtesy, Geer's City Directory

ry. The Dominion of New England was the creation in 1686 of King James II, and its ostensible purpose was to improve trade and provide more adequately for defense. Originally, the Dominion included Massachusetts, Plymouth, Rhode Island, and Connecticut. Two years later, New Jersey and New York were added. Massachusetts had, because of her open persecution of Anglicans and her rough treatment of the several Royal Commissions that had visited that province, lost her charter in 1684; Plymouth was still a "squatter settlement" with no constitutional basis for existence whatever; and now the creation of the Dominion legally voided Connecticut's Charter of 1662 and Rhode Island's Charter of 1663.

Orders were sent to each of the New England colonies declaring that the old colony governments no longer existed, that the elected colony officials were to cease performing their regular duties, and that the provincial general courts were not to function. Instead of the colony assemblies, there would be a Council whose members would be appointed by the Crown and whose function would be to legislate in all matters, including that of taxation, for the entire Dominion. Although this was contrary to both English law and tradition, there was little that Connecticut could do but wait.

The blow came in October, 1687. On the 18th of that month, Andros, then in Boston, received orders to incorporate Connecticut formally into the Dominion. The following day, Andros wrote to Fitz-John Winthrop in New London, ordering the late governor's son to join him in Hartford. Robert Treat of Milford, Connecticut's elected governor, was sent neither an order nor an invitation to be present until three days later.

On October 26, Andros, with a retinue of 75 men, set out from Boston. On the morning of October 31, Andros crossed the Connecticut River on the ferry at Wethersfield. There he was met by a delegation of Connecticut officials, and, escorted by the Hartford County Troop of Horse, all rode to Hartford, where several companies of militiamen presented themselves for review in Meetinghouse Yard. Andros then proceeded to the Assembly Room on the second floor of First Church Meetinghouse.

Upon taking the governor's seat, Andros read the Royal Proclamation. Next he announced the appointment of Fitz-John Winthrop, Robert Treat, and John Allyn to the Dominion Council and proceeded to administer the oath of office, which the three took freely and with no apparent hesitation. Then, several persons who had been at odds with the old government were sworn in as judges, although, as if to soften the blow somewhat, Andros also renewed the commissions of all judges and justices who had been appointed at the last session of the General Assembly.

Finally, Andros demanded that the Charter of 1662 be surrendered. John Allyn, the colony secretary, obligingly placed the Charter on a table in the middle of the room. One by one, the old Connecticut statesmen rose to give their reasons why the Charter should not be returned, and after each plea, Andros, without showing the slightest sign of impatience, gave a lengthy counterargument. The debate continued until long after the early autumn sunset, and candles were brought in and lighted. As Andrew Leete of New Haven, the last speaker for the cause of Connecticut rule, began his argument, he fell into a faint, or feigned a faint, falling upon the table and dashing the candles to the floor.

When the candles were relighted, the Charter was gone. Tradition has it that the document was spirited from the room by Captain Joseph Wadsworth and hidden in the hollow of the huge oak tree that stood on Samuel Wyllys' yard. Perhaps it was placed in Wadsworth's strongbox. But whatever the truth of Hartford's famous legend, no amount of persuading on Andros' part could induce any of those in the room to go out and search for the document. Hence, Mr. Secretary Allyn was obliged to conclude the official account of the day's proceedings with the entry that Andros "took into his hands the Government of this colony." The government, yes: the Charter, no.

Andros returned to Boston, never again to set foot in Hartford, the place of his great humiliation. Nor was Andros long to remain in power. When news of the Glorious Revolution of 1688/9, which overthrew King James II, reached Boston, the authorities there put Andros on the first vessel sailing for England. Thus ended the Dominion of New England.

Connecticut immediately returned to the form of government provided in the Charter, and amazingly there was no retaliation against those who had supported Andros and the Dominion. Robert Treat was reelected governor at the next election, and his successor in that office was none other than Fitz-John Winthrop.

A large mural in the Supreme Court Chamber of the State Library building depicts the men who stood around the Charter (as the story goes) before candles were snuffed out and the document was whisked away and hidden in the hollow trunk of an oak tree. (CHS)

Connecticut's defiance of Sir Edmund Andros was an almost ludicrous incident—considering that the inhabitants of a small colony in a small village on the very edge of European civilization had defied the representative of the English Crown. Another impudent demonstration against royal authority would come during King William's War, an "American sideshow" to the larger European war known as the War of the League of Augsburg.

In this, the first of four "Inter-Colonial Wars," the New England colonies were asked to participate, and participate they most certainly did. Connecticut voted troops for both border defense against the French and the Indians and a proposed expedition against Canada. And, as she would do in each subsequent conflict, Hartford came forth with her full quota of militiamen. In 1689 Hartford troops were sent to reinforce Albany, New York, and in 1693 Hartford men were transported by water to help protect the inhabitants of eastern Massachusetts.

Hartford's participation in King William's War was neither dramatic nor extensive, but from the beginning of hostilities in 1689, every precaution was taken on the home front. Both town and colony authorities designated four strategically located Hartford dwellings as "fortified houses": Bartholomew Barnard's place on Centinel Hill (present Main and Morgan streets), Samuel Wyllys' mansion on Charter Oak Hill, James Steele's place on present Washington Street, and the dwelling of John Olcott on the Windsor Road. Fortunately, refuge never had to be taken in the fortified homes.

Now for the impudent incident. Early in the war, Governor Benjamin Fletcher of New York had been ordered by the Lords of Trade to assume control of the Connecticut Militia and to coordinate the operations of the troops of the two colonies. On October 13, 1693, Fletcher arrived in Hartford, prepared to publish his commission, assume command, and raise troops. The Assembly had already decided against placing all Connecticut militiamen under Fletcher's command, but the olive branch was extended by the Assembly's offering both men and money for the defense of the New York frontier.

The Hartford County Militia Regiment was holding its drill in Meetinghouse Yard, and Fletcher asked the officers to line the troops in formation. The officers complied, and Fletcher ordered an aide to read the official order to the assembled men, whereupon Captain Joseph Wadsworth ordered the drummers to "beat the drum." When the long drumroll had finally ceased, Fletcher again tried to have the order read. Once again the drums drowned out the aide's voice. Fletcher returned to New York, having actually accomplished most of his mission, but he certainly was not a happy man.

King William's War ended in 1697 with the Treaty of Ryswick, but the ensuing period of peace was a brief one, for in 1701 the colonies were called upon to participate in Queen Anne's War, the American phase of the War of the Spanish Succession.

This time the war actually came close to home, for the Indian allies of the French had been sent on the warpath, and there was again concern that Hartford might be attacked. Once more the fortified houses were placed in service, and the town's two "great guns" were put in working order. Hartford County's Council of War met frequently, and on several occasions Hartford hosted meetings of military leaders from neighboring colonies. Hartford men saw service in the guarding of Deerfield, after its burning by the Indians in 1704. Hartford men also participated in expeditions against Montreal, Quebec, and Port Royal on the Acadian Peninsula. This long and tedious conflict ended with the Treaty of Utrecht in 1713.

From Puritan to Yankee

~DURING THE 18TH CEN-
TURY HARTFORD CHANGED, GRADUALLY OF COURSE,
FROM A SMALL AGRICULTURAL VILLAGE TO A SMALL
New England city. Hartford would remain small in com-
parison with Boston or Newport, Rhode Island, but it
would become a city nonetheless, and there would be
growing pains. During the century Hartford would
acquire what urban historians have called "the appurtenances of urban living." There would be schools,
taverns, shops, and improved transportation and communication, and the central village—or the "downtown"—would take on much of the appearance, at least,
of a small city.

There had been education in Hartford from the
beginning. Among the earliest women in Hartford were
those who conducted "dame schools." Acting upon the
prevailing English assumption that elementary education
should be provided in the home, they added the
children of others to their own to be taught reading,

writing, and arithmetic. Likewise, the ministers took older boys into their studies to teach them the Latin and Greek needed for admission to Harvard College.

These early teachers were supported entirely by fees paid by the students' parents. In 1642, however, the Town Meeting voted £30 per year "for ever" to be "settled upon the schools." Accordingly, in April of 1643, William Andrews was engaged to "keep the school" with a grant of £16 from the town, in addition to what he would collect in tuition fees, and Andrews and his 16 pupils were ensconced in a small schoolhouse erected on present Sheldon Street. Andrews taught the traditional grammar-school subjects, but in 1650 a Connecticut law required every town having 50 families to maintain an elementary school. In keeping with the law, Andrews added the three R's to his curriculum.

In the 1650s William Gibbons and John Talcott left small bequests (each of £5) toward keeping the school, but much larger encouragement was given by the will of former Governor Edward Hopkins, who died in England in 1657. When the estate was finally settled, Hartford received £400 for the maintenance of a Grammar School, and Hartford trustees accordingly erected a building on what is now Main Street. Here for many years was conducted the Hopkins Grammar School, where both grammar-school and elementary subjects were taught.

The Grammar School was relieved of its lower grades when a Connecticut law of 1690 ordered the setting up of free schools for the teaching of Latin, Greek, reading, writing, and arithmetic. Each school was to be open for at least six months of the year, and the master was to receive a salary of £66 to be paid one-half from colony funds and the remainder from the county. From that time on, elementary education was provided by the town common school and by numerous proprietary operations.

It was perhaps the success of the Grammar School that turned Hartford's leaders to thinking of a college. What was to become Yale University was founded in 1701 as The Collegiate School. It had been opened in Saybrook, and then followed a series of moves and divisions in the student body as the school's trustees tried to find a permanent location. In the spring of 1716, when it seemed that agreement was impossible, the trustees voted to allow the students to "go to other places for instruction, 'til the next Commencement." Under this temporary arrangement, the Hartford trustees, the Reverends Thomas Buckingham and Timothy Woodbridge, attempted to locate the troubled institution in the Hartford area, and their appointment of the young Elisha Williams of Wethersfield as tutor set their plan in motion.

On October 17 the trustees, with Woodbridge and Buckingham dissenting, voted to fix New Haven as the permanent location. Four of the students remained at Saybrook. Ten or so students went to New Haven. Another 14 placed themselves under Elisha Williams at Wethersfield, and among the students who assembled there in late October was Isaac Buckingham, son of the Reverend Thomas Buckingham. The Wethersfield arrangement called for instruction in Williams' home; the students boarded with families in the neighborhood.

On November 20, 1716, the Hartford Town Meeting, prodded by Woodbridge and Buckingham, voted to offer £1,000 to the Collegiate School, should the trustees decide on a Hartford location.

Meanwhile, the "seaside" trustees proceeded to erect a college building in New Haven, but Buckingham and Woodbridge persisted in their obstructionism at every step. When the trustees invited Elisha Williams to move to New Haven as senior tutor, the Hartford ministers persuaded Williams not to accept. And when commencement was held in New Haven on September 17, 1717, and four A.B. degrees were granted there, a lone student, Isaac Burr, was given a diploma at Wethersfield by Timothy Woodbridge. Also, when all of the students were ordered to meet at New Haven in October, Woodbridge's will again prevailed: the Wethersfield group chose to remain with Williams.

On September 11, 1718, commencement was again held in New Haven, and 10 degrees were awarded. At that same time, the two Hartford trustees were holding their own commencement at Wethersfield, where Woodbridge distributed five diplomas as presiding trustee.

"Yale in Wethersfield" came to an end in June 1719, when the Wethersfield students finally took up residence in New Haven. Woodbridge and Buckingham had been defeated in their efforts to bring Yale to Hartford, but they enjoyed something of a moral victory in 1719 when both were elected as Hartford's representatives to the lower house of the General Assembly. Connecticut law forbade the seating of clergymen, and therefore neither was allowed to serve. Nevertheless, the election indicated that the reverend gentlemen and their efforts had the full support of Hartford's electorate. Another direct result of the college controversy was the vote in 1719 of the General Assembly to build a new State House in Hartford as compensation for the town's loss of the Collegiate School.

During the colonial period of American history, the tavern was the center of the community, much more so than the meetinghouse, for here men from all levels of society gathered to discuss public affairs, transact business, and exchange bits of news. Here were held the ordination balls given at the time of the installation of a new minister, and here, in the earlier days, was held an occasional meeting of the legislature or a court session. Here, also, were entertained such visitors from outside the community as would not be invited to share private entertainment.

The taverns were the scenes of much drinking, but one must remember that our colonial forebears were a drinking folk who could hardly have imagined sitting down to a meal without a pint of beer or cider. The Puritans enjoyed drinking, but they certainly detested drunkenness, which they regarded as the abuse of "God's creature," and here was where problems always arose.

Several of Hartford's earliest settlers had sold spirits to the Indians, and this prompted the General Court, in 1643, to forbid the sale of liquor to white or Indian by any unlicensed person. A law of 1647 forbade drinking more than one-half pint of wine at a sitting and spending more than one-half hour in a tavern. The Connecticut Code of 1650 forbade the playing of shuffleboard in the taverns. A law of 1656 added cards and dice to the proscribed amusements, and to complete the list, an act of 1686 added singing, dancing, and riotous conduct.

In the beginning, liquor was dispensed from private homes, and it was not until 1644 that the first inn was opened in Hartford. The commissioners of the New England Confederation had accepted an invitation to meet in Hartford in December of that year. The commissioners made clear, however, that they did not wish to hold their deliberations in the meetinghouse, nor did they care to accept any sort of private accommodations. On June 3, 1644, the General Court decreed that each town should maintain an inn, and, as to Hartford, during the meeting of the commission, John Steele, Andrew Bacon, and James Boosey would be a committee to secure an appropriate building to function as a public house. That chosen, just east of Meetinghouse Yard, was the home of Thomas Ford. Ford opened his home to the commission and continued to keep an inn until 1660.

Sometime before that date, Jeremy Adams opened a second inn on what is now the Travelers Block on Main Street, and it was here that Governor Andros spent the night of October 31, 1687. Legislative sessions were held here until the completion

Children in colonial Hartford learned their first lessons from a "hornbook" like this one. The paper on which the alphabet and Lord's Prayer had been printed was covered by a sheet of transparent horn to protect it from fingerprints and anything else that might soil or damage it. The wooden frame, with handle, was about four and one-quarter inches long. (CHS)

of the State House in 1720. Adams' place was also the official headquarters on Hartford County Militia training days. When Adams died in 1683, the business was taken over by Zachary Sandford. Members of Sandford's family operated it as the Black Horse Tavern until after the Revolution.

Other inns or taverns in early Hartford were those of Jonathan Gilbert (opened in 1663, "near Meeting House Lane"), Hezekiah Collier (opened in 1760, "just north of the Court House"), Frederick Bull (City Coffee House, successor to Collier's inn), Samuel Pelton (1747, "on the West Side of the square"), David Bull (1757, "The Bunch of Grapes," on the Pelton location), Cotton Murray (the "Globe," also on the west side of Main Street), and Joseph Mygatt (1656, near the present State Capitol). There were also several short-lived operations near the River Landing, as from time to time the ferryman was allowed to operate an inn in his own home.

Most of Hartford's early inns and taverns were eminently respectable. The one exception seems to have been that kept by Disbrow Spencer near the Landing. In defiance of the law, Spencer permitted gambling and even encouraged it, perhaps in the interest of taking a kitty from the players. On October 11, 1703, a brawl resulted from a card-game dispute. Several were injured, and those participants who could be identified were fined. Three years later, Spencer challenged one Henry Merry to a duel, and the two met on the Landing. Someone, however, had alerted the constables, who appeared on the scene and prevented the contest. Both were fined for disturbing the peace.

The existence and continued success of so many places of public accommodation were a reflection of Hartford's growing commercial importance. By the 1720s, what is now Main Street was becoming the center of a considerable market trade, as many new shops were being built. The old home lots were being divided and subdivided, and the newer mercantile buildings were being constructed side by side, usually with party walls separating the one from the other. And as these new structures were transforming the appearance of Hartford's retail center, there was always encroachment upon the public street, as each builder attempted to gain a few feet by pushing the front of his new building farther toward the public thoroughfare. The practice came to an end in 1758, when the Town Meeting ordered all property holders in the central part of the town to provide sidewalks.

But this new regulation did not stop encroachment upon the Ancient Burying Ground, a tract bounded originally by present Main, Pearl, Lewis, and Gold streets. The Burying Ground was "ancient" in that it was laid out in 1640, after several burials had been made in Meetinghouse Yard. At present Main and Gold streets, First Church's third meetinghouse was built in 1739, and after that one business building after another was erected between the meetinghouse and Pearl Street with a total disregard for the graves over which the structures were placed.

By the middle of the 18th century, the neighborhood of Meetinghouse Yard had at least a score of small shops catering to the retail trade, but they were a far cry from the 20th-century supermarket. The equipment was rudimentary. Walls were shelved for the display of small items, bins held grains and powders, and goods shipped in barrels or buckets were merely left in the opened containers. Each shop had a ledger desk that served as the office.

A sampling of ledgers kept by Hartford's 18th-century shopkeepers would reveal sales of nails, gunpowder, flints, cord, wire, brimstone, salt, axes, mohair, drugs, tiles, paper, pots, pans, needles, knives, indigo, logwood, earthenware, thimbles, buckles, buttons, thread, soap, looking glasses, pewter dishes, pepper, molasses, rum, raisins, mace, tea, sugar, flour, various grains and vegetables, lace, gloves, Sile-

John Spencer kept a tavern in Hartford on the road that led north to Windsor. This artifact from his tavern was painted with a facsimile of the Pennsylvania State Seal. (CHS)

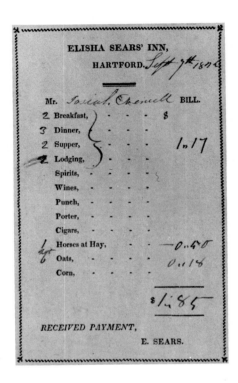

sian linen, dimity, dorsetteens, and Italian crape.

These items were supplied from what in the colonial mercantile hierarchy was known as the inland merchant—the wholesaler, of whom there were perhaps a dozen in Hartford. The inland merchant, in turn, bought his goods from the "sedentary" or importing merchant who had direct trade with London or Bristol. Goods passed through the hands of such London exporters as Champion and Hayley, to Boston sedentary merchants like Thomas Hancock and his more famous nephew John, to an inland merchant such as Joseph Pitkin of "east-of-the-river" Hartford, to a shopkeeper "near the Meetinghouse," to Goodwife Smith who lived on the South Side along the road to Wethersfield.

In payment, the shopkeeper, of course, preferred money: Spanish silver dollars, Portuguese gold johnnies, or other French, Spanish, German, or Arabian coins that had come to Connecticut via the West India trade; English shillings, pence, or farthings; stray Massachusetts pine-tree shillings (last minted in 1684); Connecticut coppers (struck at Simsbury early in the century); bills of exchange; or the bills of credit of Connecticut and neighboring colonies. The great difficulty was that money of whatever sort was scarce throughout the colony.

Hartford customers regularly paid the shopkeeper with the products of the farm and forest: hogs, sheep, pork, beef, deerskins, tobacco, firewood, butter, cheeses, birch brooms, feathers, beeswax, grain, turnips, or malt. The shopkeeper passed these items on to the inland merchant, who in turn sent them to the sedentary merchant engaged in the West India or London trade. Customers also could perform such tasks as carting, carpentry, or mason work, and many availed themselves of the opportunity.

But above all, there was credit, and it was, in fact, by a form of credit known as "money-barter" that all 18th-century business was carried on, and all payments in money, goods, or services were merely part of this larger scheme. A bushel of grain was a matter of shillings; a paper of pins was a matter of pence. The goodwife needed her paper of pins on a certain day, and its purchase would not wait until grain had been harvested. Credit made possible the immediate sale. The credit that eased the purchases of the housewife was also enjoyed by the artisans of 18th-century Hartford, and the cabinetmaker, the tailor, or the wheelwright traded with the shopkeeper on the same terms.

Each shopkeeper employed a simple method of bookkeeping in his day-to-day business. An itemized record of purchases and payments was kept in a large ledger. There was a double spread (folio) for each customer. On the left-hand page were recorded sales to the individual, giving the value of the items in terms of pounds, shillings, and pence. Goods were given to customers as they were requested. On the right-hand page credits were entered, as payments were made in money, produce, or services. "Balancings" were made at the end of each year to determine in whose favor the balance stood, but there was still no need for an immediate cash settlement, for with the money-barter system, the process simply was repeated in the next year. Hartford throughout the colonial period never produced a single successful sedentary merchant, although Hartford's external trade was moderately successful in the West India trade and in that with the major ports of Boston and New York.

Few 18th-century Hartfordites cared to invest their capital in shipping. In 1680 Governor William Leete reported to the Lords of Trade that only one vessel listed Hartford as its home port, and Governor Joseph Talcott's report of 1730 was no more encouraging. As late as 1776 only seven Hartford merchants had interests in sailing vessels of any description.

SAMUEL C. CAMP, City Hartford,
Inn-keeper, Sign of the double headed EAGLE,
State-Street.

	Dols. Cts. M.
Stage Fare,	
Days Boarding,	
Breakfast, -	
Dinner, - -	
Supper, - -	
Lodging,	
Madeira Wine, -	
Port Wine, -	
Porter, -	
Punch, - -	
Grog,	
Horse-keeping, -	
Oats, - -	
Servant's Bill,	
Dols.	4 19

Received payment,
Saml. C. Camp.
Decr 27. 1806

*ABOVE AND OPPOSITE:
"Entertainment for Man and
Horse" was provided by
Hartford tavern-keepers, who
rendered itemized statements
listing food, wine, and grog
for the traveler, and hay, oats,
and corn for his horse.*
(CHS)

There was, however, something of an exception in the case of vessels built in the small shipyard that had operated on the North Meadows from as early as 1730. The sloops and brigs built there were usually sold to shippers from other ports, although occasionally one would be loaded with Connecticut products and sent directly to an English or Irish port to be sold along with its cargo.

But even though Hartford men preferred to leave the 18th-century shipping business to others, Hartford was becoming quite busy. Improvements at the Landing Place had been begun as early as the 1670s, and as Centinel Hill was cut down, much of it was carted to the riverside, where it was used as landfill. In 1720 Samuel Thornton erected the first wharf, the only one built before the Revolution. Most merchants simply used the common Landing Place, and when vessels were too large to dock at either the wharf or the Landing, business was conducted on deck. Close by the Landing, warehouses were erected in rapid succession, and by mid-century there were 20 or more. Also to be found were smiths, coopers, carters, tavern keepers, and all who catered to the river trade or Hartford's wholesaling enterprises. New streets were opened between the river and Meetinghouse Yard in what a century before had been the Great Meadow, and King Street (present State Street) connected what could be regarded as the retail district with the wholesale district.

Given the nature of Hartford's trade, and perhaps because of Hartford's position as provincial capital, the several 18th-century wars had a profound effect upon the town's prosperity—or lack of it. King William's War (1689-1697) had been a small war, as far as Connecticut was concerned, but Queen Anne's War (1701-1713) was a much larger conflict. Hartford's inland merchants prospered during the war through sales of foodstuffs and other supplies to both the British Army and the colony government, but the most significant economic development during these war years was Connecticut's first issue of colony bills of credit in 1709.

These bills were wallet-size promissory notes issued by the colony in order to pay its debts in advance of the collection of taxes. Although they were a form of government borrowing, these bills of credit performed the function of money as they passed freely from hand to hand before redemption.

The economy took a sharp upward swing in 1741, when Great Britain and France again went to war in what was known in America as King George's War. As had happened during the earlier conflicts, the price of imports from Britain rose by about 30 percent, while locally produced commodities increased at a much slower rate. Hartford's merchants benefited slightly by British Army purchases, which were always paid for in coin, and housewives profited when British troops were billeted in Hartford homes (again for cash) during the winter months. But this hard money did not circulate locally for long, for the Hartford retailers, pressed by the English exporters, "put the squeeze" on every Hartford recipient of British silver.

Hartford's economic hopes rose in 1745, when poorly trained New England militiamen, supported by the British Navy, captured the supposedly impregnable French fortress at Louisbourg on Cape Breton Island, east of Nova Scotia. This almost unbelievable victory sent eager New England merchants to the island in the hope of expanding the Nova Scotia trade. Their hopes were dashed when in 1748 the Treaty of Aix-la-Chapelle returned Cape Breton Island to the French.

Almost a hundred Hartford men participated in the Cape Breton expedition. Hartford was immensely proud of her part in the Louisbourg victory, and news of the event was celebrated on July 8, 1745, with a huge ox roast in Meetinghouse Yard.

The signing of the peace treaty did nothing to end the economic uncertainty, for by the summer of 1748 the price spiral had peaked, and prices began to fall rapid-

The names of the first settlers of Hartford are cut into two of the sides of this obelisk, which stands in the Ancient Burying Ground. (CHS)

ly. Debts could not be collected at any level, and, for the first time in almost 40 years, Boston merchants were reluctant to accept Connecticut bills of credit, which Thomas Hancock declared to be worth little more in Massachusetts than oak leaves. By this time it was obvious to all that although war led to temporary economic prosperity, the long-range effect was one of impoverishment and depression. Connecticut trade was to remain sluggish until the outbreak of the French and Indian War.

Hostilities began on the Monongahela River in present Pennsylvania in the summer of 1754, but it was not until the following spring, with the prospect of large numbers of British regulars being sent to the colonies, that the full economic effect would be felt in Hartford. Beef and pork, two staples produced locally, rose rapidly in price.

Although no battles were fought in Connecticut, Hartford became a strategic center during the French and Indian War. Each spring the General Assembly voted several thousand troops for service in the Lake George region of upper New York. Hartford was the staging point for the march to Albany and the point at which supplies were gathered and sent overland by cart.

The French and Indian War years were years of activity for those who had both influence and capital, for between 1755 and 1758 the imports were double those of 1744-1748, and the increase was due largely to the shipment of military supplies. In 1757 a crop failure in Great Britain and Ireland forced the British to permit the colonists to ship provisions to the British Isles, and beef, pork, wheat, flour, and other commodities sold at higher prices than ever before. But despite the steady flow of army supplies through Hartford during the French and Indian War, no fortunes were made. Even John Ledyard, the leading merchant, engaged in no fewer than eight partnerships for this purpose but was little better off at the close of the war than he had been at the beginning.

European travelers and British officers who had served in America during the war expressed amazement at the "lavish" scale of living in both the seaboard cities and the larger inland towns such as Hartford, and they were quick to note that even those of modest station enjoyed many more creature comforts than their counterparts in England or on the European continent. Certainly the standard of living had advanced far above that of the pioneer stage, and this was reflected in the home. Chairs had long since taken the place of stools and benches, and chinaware had replaced pewter and wood on most tables. The clothing of the people was both comfortable and serviceable, although the fashion was a few years behind what was being worn in England—and perhaps a season or two behind the latest of Boston or New York.

Benjamin Franklin, writing about the British North American colonies in general, noted that an "almost general mediocracy of fortune" prevailed among the people, meaning that there were few individuals with notable wealth and an almost total absence of abject poverty, and he could easily have applied his generalization to the population of Hartford. Students of the colonial period of American history accept the £2,000 estate as the minimum for the well-to-do and the £5,000 figure as representing real wealth. Significantly, during the quarter century before the outbreak of the Revolution, there were in Hartford few of the former and none of the latter. Actually, Hartford was not a particularly wealthy town. The tax list for 1761, for example, gave the entire town's property value at £39,821 11s. 6d., a figure that placed Hartford as number 10 among Connecticut's towns.

The "mediocracy of fortune," however, did not mean that there was a "mediocracy" of status, for 18th-century society was a totally deferential one in

ABOVE: Buildings along the bordering streets have encroached upon the Ancient Burying Ground, but the major portion of the cemetery remains intact. Although the weather has damaged some of the brownstone markers, the grounds are maintained as a city park. (CHS)

ABOVE RIGHT: The southeast corner of the Ancient Burying Ground was chosen as the site of the third meetinghouse, built in 1739. Apparently any graves that obstructed construction were disregarded. (CHS)

which each person had his place, knew his place, and was usually content with it.

At the top of the 18th-century social structure were what were called the "better sort"—in Connecticut known as "the Standing Order." These individuals, representing from 5 to 10 percent of the Hartford population, included the higher colony officials, the clergy of the Congregationalist establishment, the large landholders, and the more important merchants. It was also the "better sort" who held the judgeships, filled the higher militia ranks, and accepted the necessary, albeit onerous, commissions as justice of the peace. Some of them, although far from all, were members of "proprietary" families: those who, as descendants of early Hartford landholders, still maintained their rights to the common and undivided lands. Among these families were the Allyns, the Bunces, the Goodwins, the Hayneses, the Olmsteds, the Pitkins, the Seymours, and the Wadsworths.

Some 80 percent of Hartford's free, white population fell within what was called the "middling sort"—self-employed shopkeepers, artisans, and small farmers, all property holders or substantial renters, and all the owners of tools of production.

At the bottom of the social scale were those of the "meaner sort," the property-less workers for wages on the farm or in the shop. This group, which comprised roughly 10 percent of the population, was a fluid one, for in the 18th century, with skilled workmen in great demand and short supply, it was easy for someone who had mastered his craft to start up his own business and thus move into the ranks of "middling sort." Furthermore, many of those working for wages were young, unmarried

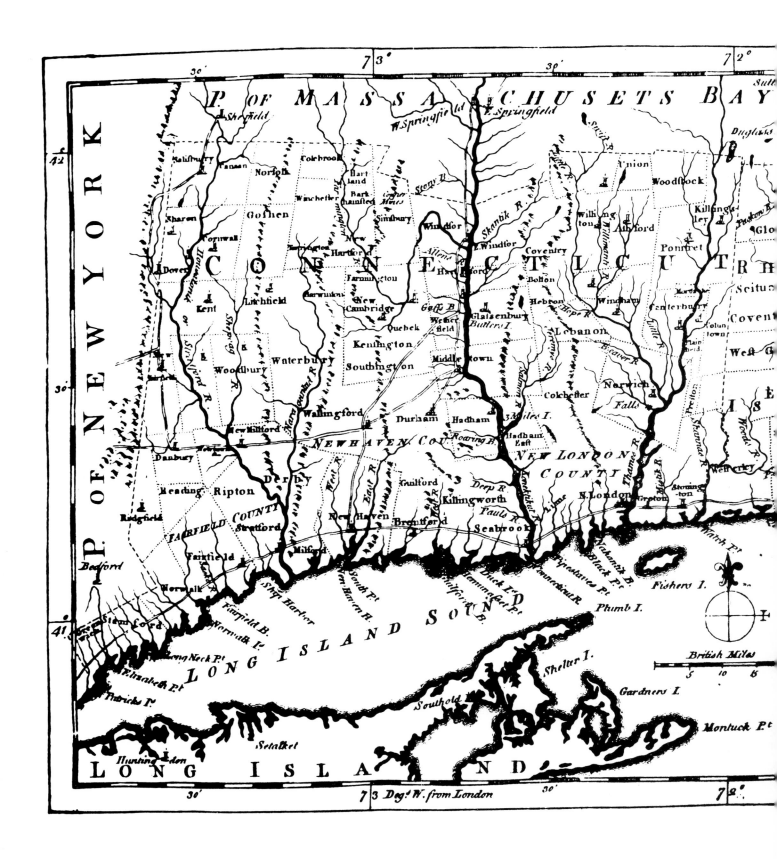

men from families of much higher station than their immediate situation would suggest; and they, too, would leave this lower group as they acquired land or opened shop in competition with a former employer.

Although there was little open snobbery, each individual had constant reminders of his place on the social scale. Only the "better sort" were addressed as "Mister" or "Madam." The "middling sort" were "Goodman" or "Goodwife." Those of the "meaner sort" were simply addressed by their first names. Seating in the meetinghouse was still "according to the dignity of the family," and children in the Grammar School were "placed" in similar fashion.

In the grave and at the ballot box, however, all were equal. On March 3, 1640, the Hartford Town Meeting appointed Thomas Woodford as sexton of the church, with the additional obligation to "attend the making of graves for any corpses deceased . . . [and to receive as compensation] . . . when such graves have been made[,] for the lesser sort, 2s. 6d., for the middle sort, 3s., and for the higher sort, 3s. 6d." The vote, however, had nothing to do with the location of any particular grave. Burials were made in the Burying Ground without distinction as to class or family. The rich were buried beside the poor, and so it was with bond or free, or with white or black. As there were no family plots, graves were dug at random as long as the land held out. When the city block, or what had not already been encroached upon by First Church Meetinghouse, the school, or the shops along the main street, had been filled with graves, bodies were laid one on top of another in several layers for almost two centuries. Although the records are incomplete, it is estimated that there were some 6,000 burials.

In voting, too, there was something of a "mix" as far as social class was concerned, and although political status was somewhat connected with social status and minimal wealth, these were not the only criteria. In 1706 the Connecticut Assembly adopted the qualifications for voting that prevailed until after the Revolution.

To be "admitted" to a town and thus be allowed to vote for local officers, a man had to be of legal age, hold property to the extent of £40, and be acceptable to the ecclesiastical authorities and a majority of the town's voters. To become a freeman, one had to—besides being admitted to the town—give "additional proof of civil conduct and conversation," be approved by the town selectmen, and, finally, be accepted at the annual Open Meeting of the Freemen. The limited available data would suggest that about 63 percent of Hartford's adult males, or about 75 percent of all heads of families, had attained the status of freeman and were thus eligible to vote

This 1758 map shows the division of Connecticut's early counties and townships. From Clark, A History of Connecticut, *1914*

in colony-wide elections and to hold any sort of colony office.

Not all of those living in colonial Hartford could make this transition—or, for that matter, any transition at all. Slavery had been brought to Hartford with the earliest settlers, as Edward Hopkins and others brought blacks with them from Massachusetts, and the Pequot War added the new element of Indian slavery. Virtually all well-to-do families owned a slave or two, although few owned more than three. The exception was the Reverend Timothy Woodbridge, who was noted for the large number of blacks listed among his personal property.

Hartford's slaves seem to have been treated fairly well. Usually they worked side by side with their masters, whether in the field or in the shop. Madam Sarah Knight, who traveled through Connecticut in 1704, although she did not pass through Hartford, noted the familiarity—to her an offensive familiarity—between master and slave, and she was shocked to observe that it was the custom for Connecticut slaves to eat at the same table as their masters.

Slaves were exempted from military duty, but this was a mark of servility, as it was a denial of the right to bear arms. Slaves were permitted to be away from their homes only with the master's permission and were subject to a 9 p.m. curfew. Although slaves were allowed to accumulate small personal property, they were forbidden to sell goods of any sort to whites.

Even the few free blacks were subject to restrictions. All blacks were required to carry identification passes, and free blacks were not allowed to enjoy social contact with slaves. Free blacks, furthermore, could not serve on juries, although they could (and did) testify in court. Blacks were not allowed to hold any sort of public office, nor could they become admitted inhabitants of the town.

A census of 1761 shows that of Hartford's population of 3,938, there were 109 persons listed as black. In 1774, when Hartford's population stood at 4,881, there were 150 blacks, quite a small figure when compared with New London's 552, Stonington's 456, Groton's 360, or even Colchester's 201.

Hartford never had a formal slave market such as those of Boston or Newport, but the slave trade was carried on in Hartford from the earliest days until the Revolution. Eighteenth-century advertisements for the sale of slave babies or teenage blacks more than suggest that Hartford's slaveholders had little regard for the sanctity of slave marriages or the black family. Nor would the repeated advertisements for runaway blacks convince many that Hartford's slaves were content with their lot. Only once, however, did the slaves act in concert and in open revolt, and that incident occurred in 1658, involving both blacks and Indians. Few of the details of the affair are known, but it is certain that several houses were destroyed.

In 1702 a mulatto slave named Abda ran away from his owner, Thomas Richards, and sought the protection of Captain Joseph Wadsworth of Charter Oak fame. When the town constables demanded that Wadsworth surrender the fugitive, the captain refused to turn Abda over, and, with the help of Wadsworth, the slave sued Richards for damages of £20 sterling for being held in bondage. Abda's defense was that his father was a Caucasian, but this was to be his undoing. When Governor Gurdon Saltonstall and the Council heard the case, the governor decreed that because Abda's mother was a black slave, Abda, too, was a slave, as "all persons born to Negro bondswomen" were legally slaves. Abda was returned to Richards. This decision remained for many years the legal foundation of slavery in the Nutmeg State.

About the middle of the century the custom of Negro Election Day, or "'Lection Day," began, when each May Hartford's blacks elected the black "governor."

The Reverend George Whitefield (1714-1770) was the itinerant English evangelist who led the "Great Awakening" in Connecticut. From Cirker, Dictionary of American Portraits, Dover, *1967*

Pictured here are the signatures of nine generations of Hartford Wadsworths. The Wadsworths were leaders in Hartford's military, religious, economic, and cultural life. From Goucher, Wadsworth *or The Charter Oak, 1904*

Each slave was fitted out in his master's cast-off finery. The day began at 10 a.m. with a reception, then came the election, and finally the inauguration. The remainder of the day was spent in feasting and the enjoyment of games.

Although Negro Election Day did nothing to mitigate the slaves' rest-of-the-year situation, and although there were those who condemned the practice as having a demoralizing effect upon the participants, the attitude on the part of the masters was not a consciously patronizing one, and the office of black "governor" was a coveted honor for both the master and the slave.

Hartford's white population was almost unbelievably homogeneous. In the summer of 1659 one "David the Jew," and that was how he was known, appeared in Hartford as a small-time peddler. His stay was short, however, as he entered a house while the owners were absent and was fined 20s. and sent out of the community. The Town Meeting used the occasion to pass an ordinance allowing only such transients as should be "concented to" by the Meeting to remain in town. Whether it was by force of this ordinance or merely by chance, Hartford's white population remained almost completely English until long after the Revolution.

Religiously, too, there was a remarkable homogeneity, and Hartford's civil and religious leaders did all in their power to maintain the Congregationalist status quo. During the 1650s and 1660s several Quakers had been driven from the town, and in 1767 one William Edmundson, a professed Quaker, was ejected from First Church Meetinghouse with such force as to injure his arm seriously. John Tiley, a member of First Church, made history in 1745 when he declared himself to be a Baptist and was thereupon excommunicated.

Quakers and Baptists were easy for the established Congregationalists to handle, but with the Anglicans it was different. Anglicanism was the established religion in the Mother Country, and it was, after all, because of the Puritans' differences with England's bishops that the New England colonies had come into being in the first place. Connecticut had always been somewhat timid in taking an open stand against the Church, and the Church of England had come into Connecticut through the back door when the first Anglican mission was organized at Stratford in 1707.

Perhaps hoping to keep in favor with the British authorities, the General Assembly in 1708 passed an "Act of Toleration" that gave immunities to certain non-Congregationalists. Although the law recognized the legal existence of Anglicanism, the Connecticut authorities still collected the ecclesiastical taxes for the support of meetinghouse and minister and embarrassed the Churchmen by causing "public days of humiliation and prayer" to fall upon the great feast days of the Christian Kalendar. An act of 1727 permitted the Anglicans to pay the ecclesiastical taxes to the support of their own church, although only such parishes as had a "resident minister" could claim the exemption. As the Anglican missionaries invariably served a number of towns, the parish of the missionary's residence alone seems to have benefited.

Anglicanism was attractive to many Connecticut people. The Great Awakening, the great revival of religion that reached its high point in the winter of 1740-1741, had split the Congregationalists into two mutually hostile factions: the "New Lights," who favored the emotionalism of the revival, and the "Old Lights," who opposed it. It was this division that allowed the Church of England to gain a first foothold in Hartford.

The Great Awakening began in Northampton, Massachusetts, with the revivalistic preaching of Jonathan Edwards in 1734. During the next few years there were revivals of religion throughout central Massachusetts and eastern Connecticut. Several New England ministers, hearing of the evangelistic successes of the Reverend

The first State House, completed in 1720, replaced Jeremy Adams' inn as the headquarters for legislative meetings. Freemen spent election days defining terms and delineating the functions of city officers. From Hartford, Connecticut, 1889

George Whitefield in the middle colonies, invited the famous revivalist to tour New England in the fall of 1740. Whitefield accepted the invitation, and in September he was officially welcomed to Connecticut by Governor Talcott and several of the leading clergy.

Through September and October, Whitefield traversed lower New England, from Newport to Boston, thence to Northampton and down the Connecticut River Valley, preaching to "large and affected congregations." Wherever the evangelist appeared, crowds of hearers, often in the thousands, were entranced by his magnetic personality and astounded by the novelty of extemporaneous preaching. And there were visible signs of "conversion"—cryings out, convulsions, and faintings. Whitefield played the game by his own rules, for into whichever town he went, he decided for himself which of his host pastors were "converted" and which were not. Those of whom he approved, he praised; those of whom he did not, he condemned. For the time, only those who were the objects of Whitefield's censure were unhappy.

Whitefield arrived in Hartford on October 22, 1740, and, despite the fact that the minister, the Reverend Daniel Wadsworth, was notably hostile to Whitefield's methods, preached in Hartford's First Church. Evidently, Whitefield gave an especially heavy dose of hellfire, for he recorded in his journal: "I did not spare them." One must wonder whether Wadsworth was among those not spared.

Whitefield had his imitators, and soon the colony was flooded with itinerant preachers, few of them with more than a modicum of theological learning. These, too, made converts and split congregations.

The colony was in a state of religious turmoil, and in 1741 the Hartford Association of Ministers adopted a resolution questioning the propriety of the emotional conversions. In 1742 the General Assembly passed a law forbidding an itinerant preacher from entering a pulpit except by invitation of the minister.

In May, 1742, the General Assembly tried two of the itinerants, James Davenport and Benjamin Parry, as dangerous to the peace of the colony. During the trial, Davenport addressed a large crowd from the steps of First Church Meetinghouse and almost provoked a riot when his followers attempted to free him and his codefendant. Forty militiamen were called out to keep order. Both defendants were found guilty of the charge, and Davenport was declared to be a madman. Following the verdict, Davenport was marched through files of militiamen to the Landing Place, where he was put on a boat and sent into exile on Long Island.

Whitefield and the others had made converts in Hartford, and these had been admitted to full membership in both First and Second churches. But as has been the case throughout the history of revivalism, many of the converts lapsed, and the long-range effect of the Awakening was a deadening of spirituality in both congregations. Membership fell off rapidly, and by the early 1770s First Church had only 15 male members in full communion.

The Anglicans had offered a peaceable and orderly alternative to the squabbling Congregationalist factions, and parishes were set up in Simsbury (1740), Wallingford (1741), and Middletown (1749). But despite the fact that several of Hartford's newer families had come directly from England and were members of the Church, Hartford's Congregationalist authorities stood firm. In 1761, however, the Reverend Thomas Davies of Litchfield County began holding Prayer Book services in private homes. Davies was soon joined by the Reverends Samuel Peters of Hebron and Jeremiah Leaming of Norwalk, who on one occasion secured use of the State House and attracted a crowd of more than 300, mostly Congregationalists who had come out of curiosity.

Benjamin Boardman (1731-1802) served as pastor of the Second (South) Church in Hartford from 1784-1789. (CHS)

Early in 1762 an Anglican parish was organized as Christ Church, and in October of that year land was purchased—just north of present Christ Church Cathedral. Building stones were gathered, but they were soon confiscated by several leading Congregationalists headed by Deacon Samuel Talcott, Jr., of First Church. The Anglicans sued for the recovery of their property, but without success. Soon came the Revolution, and public sentiment turned against the Church of England as being the religion of the enemy. It was not until 1792 that Christ Church, by this time called the Episcopal Church, was able to complete its building. At the time of the cornerstone laying, Prince Brewster, the chief mason and a loyal parishioner, took up his ceremonial trowel and declared: "I lay this stone for the foundation of an Episcopal Church, and Sam Talcott and the gates of Hell shall not prevail against it."

CHAPTER

IV

Hartford and the Revolution

~NEWS THAT THE PEACE
OF PARIS OF 1763 HAD BROUGHT THE FRENCH AND
INDIAN WAR TO AN END WAS RECEIVED JOYFULLY IN
Hartford. There were bonfires and fireworks, and the
bell in First Church steeple sounded for an hour. In each
of the meetinghouses sermons appropriate to the occasion were preached, and Almighty God was thanked
most heartily for the victory.

But the Peace of Paris did not mark the beginning of a
new and happier age for the colonials. While it is true that
the French menace to the north had been removed, the
British adopted a new tone in their relations with the colonies. Although the officials at Westminster had no intention of asking the colonies either to help pay for the cost of
the war or to reduce Britain's almost overwhelming
national debt, there was general agreement that the colonists should pay one-third of the support of several regiments of British troops to be stationed in British North
America, ostensibly for the protection of the inhabitants.

In March, 1764, Parliament passed the Sugar Act with the twofold purpose of raising revenue to defend the colonies and of putting an end to the molasses smuggling in which the colonists had long been engaged. The most serious provision, as far as the colonials were concerned, was the reduction of the duty on non-British West Indian molasses from 6d. to 3d. with the understanding that henceforth the duty would actually be collected.

When the British authorities undertook the strict enforcement of the Sugar Act, merchants, distillers, and farmers experienced new misfortunes when it was no longer possible for them to dispose of their agricultural products to those who traded with the West Indies. Nor was it long before the colonists—already short of media of exchange—felt the effects of decreased circulation of specie.

Hartford was not Boston, nor even New London, and given the small amount of the Hartford region's agricultural surpluses involved in the West Indies trade, the Sugar Act might have caused nothing more than a ripple, had not Hartford's first newspaper been started just as the act was going into effect.

On October 29, 1764, Thomas Green printed the first issue of the *Connecticut Courant*, in which he noted:

> ... it behooves the colonies to represent their grievances in the strongest point of light, and to unite in such measures as *will be effectual* to obtain redress. The northern colonists have sense enough, at least the sense of *feeling;* and can tell where the *shoe pinches.*

The *Courant* always would be anti-British—at first, mildly so, and later, vehemently. The *Courant* would soon become one of the largest-circulation newspapers in the colonies, the only paper to be distributed widely in northern Connecticut and western Massachusetts, and as such it would play a significant part in the shaping of public opinion in the back country.

One year after the passage of the Sugar Act, Parliament passed the Stamp Act, which provided that legal instruments drawn up in the colonies were to be executed on paper that bore a stamp of value from 2d. to £6, depending on the importance of the particular instrument, and that all almanacs, calendars, dice, newspapers, pamphlets, and playing cards were to carry the stamp also.

The Stamp Act aroused more opposition than had the Sugar Act, as it operated directly upon a larger—and more articulate—segment of the population. These lawyers, printers, and merchants complained bitterly that there was no silver with which to pay the stamp tax (as required by the act), as the effect of the Sugar Act had been to cause all specie to disappear from circulation.

Once more, the *Courant* spoke out. Publisher Thomas Green took particular delight in reporting in his pages the rough treatment of New Haven's Jared Ingersoll, the Stamp Distributor for Connecticut, as he set out from New Haven for Hartford to advise the governor and Council that he had accepted the position. On September 23, 1765, the *Courant* described Ingersoll's reception in Hartford:

> Last Wednesday Afternoon a large Company of able-bodied Men, came to Town (on Horseback) from the Eastern Part of this Government, and informed those who were willing to join them, that they were on their Way to New Haven to demand the Stamp Officer of this Colony to resign his Office ...
> On Thursday Morning, the whole Body, (including a considerable Number from this town) [Hartford] set off, on their intended Expedition, and in about an Hour met Mr. Ingersoll, at the Lower End of Weathersfield, and let him know their Business,—he at first refused to comply, but it was insisted upon, that he should resign his Office of

Stamp Master, so disagreeable to his Countrymen;—after many Proposals, he delivered the Resignation, mentioned below, which he read himself in the Hearing of the whole Company; he was then desired to pronounce the Words, *Liberty and Property,* three Times, which having done, the whole Body gave three Huzza's; Mr. Ingersoll, then went to a Tavern, and dined with several of the Company:

After Dinner, the Company told Mr. Ingersoll, as he was bound to Hartford, they would escort him there, which they did, to the Number of almost Five Hundred Persons on Horseback. After they arrived in Town, Mr. Ingersoll again read his Resignation in Public, when three Huzza's more were given, and the whole Company immediately dispersed without making the least Disturbance.

When the Stamp Act went into effect on November 1, 1765, a special edition of the *Courant* quoted newspapers in New Jersey, New York, Rhode Island, and Massachusetts against the Stamp Act. Then the *Courant* ceased publication for five weeks, ostensibly to avoid the hated tax, but as the stamped paper from England had not yet arrived in the colonies, it must be assumed that Thomas Green was simply making a gesture.

Eastern Connecticut, where the New Lights had dominated for 20 years, was the poorer section of the colony. It was in that radical section of the province that the extralegal organization known as the Sons of Liberty made its first appearance in the summer of 1765. Ingersoll was hanged in effigy in Lebanon, Windham, Norwich, and New London, and it was these Liberty Boys who had led in the humiliation of the Stamp Master in Wethersfield.

Governor Thomas Fitch and the conservatives were appalled by the action of the Sons of Liberty. William Pitkin, Sr., the deputy governor from east-of-the-river Hartford, did not express himself on the matter. Pitkin was not an active "Son," although William Jr. was.

Fitch issued a proclamation that condemned the tumults. The General Assembly voted to send three members to the Stamp Act Congress meeting in New York that fall, and at the same time it adopted a resolution condemning the riots, even though some of the members had themselves taken part.

Under the terms of the Stamp Act, Governor Fitch was required to take an oath to support the act. Fitch was fearful of British action against the colony if he defied the law, and yet he realized that a large portion of Connecticut's population did not believe he should take the oath. In late October the governor came to Hartford and asked the members of the Council to administer the oath. After a long debate, all of the "eastern" Assistants refused to take part in or even to witness the oath-giving ceremony and withdrew from the chamber.

On the day the act was to go into effect, a large crowd gathered at the Hartford State House and buried a copy of the Stamp Act and symbolically buried Governor Fitch with it. The "eastern men," who always had opposed Fitch, now had a winning issue to use against him, and the governor and the four Assistants who had cooperated with him were marked for political death.

On March 15, 1766, a colony-wide Sons of Liberty meeting was held in Hartford. William Pitkin, Jr., the clerk of the meeting, publicized the proceedings in signed notices in the newspapers. People other than Sons of Liberty were allowed to attend the first part of the meeting, which set up a Committee of Correspondence to write to Sons of Liberty in other colonies; but after this business was concluded, all spectators were asked to leave. Some Sons proposed to give the freemen "a lead" in the upcoming election. Even some of the Sons were shocked by this open interference in the election proceedings and answered that the general warning of the

Stamp Act officials were hanged in effigy during the winter of 1765-1766. From Grafton, The American Revolution, *1975*

The Hartford Courant *occupied this building on State Street in 1880. Established in 1764, the* Courant *enjoys prominence and respect throughout Connecticut today. From* Hartford, Connecticut, *1889*

election was lead enough, and that any other politicking would be "unconstitutional" and "fraught with the worst sorts of mischief." Nevertheless, the Sons endorsed William Pitkin and Jonathan Trumbull for governor and deputy governor.

The last edition of the *Courant* before the May voting day carried the news that the Stamp Act had been repealed by Parliament. Nevertheless, William Pitkin won the election by a landslide, bringing into office with him Jonathan Trumbull as deputy governor and the New Light, radical majority in the Assembly, which would remain in control through the Revolutionary period.

On May 23 Hartford celebrated the repeal of the Stamp Act, but the festivities were marred by an accident that left 6 persons dead and more than 20 injured. As the *Courant* reported the incident on May 26, 1766:

The morning was ushered in by the ringing of bells; the shipping in the river displayed their colors; at 12 o'clock 21 cannon were discharged and the greatest preparations making for a general illumination.

But sudden was the transition from the height of joy to extreme sorrow. A number of young gentlemen were preparing fireworks for the evening in the chamber of the large brick school house, under which a quantity of powder granted by the assembly for the purposes of the day, was deposited.

Two companies of militia had just received a pound a man, by the delivery of which a train was scattered from the powder cask to the distance of three rods from the

45

house where a number of boys were collected who, undesignedly and unnoticed, set fire to the scattered powder which soon communicated to that within doors and in an instant reduced the building to a heap of rubbish.

The Stamp Act was dead, but Thomas Green, from his small office above James Mookler's barbershop just north of First Church Meetinghouse, continued to keep the fires of dissatisfaction aglow. Evidently he had hit the right editorial note, for his circulation grew rapidly. What had begun as a one-man operation was expanded in 1767, when Green apprenticed young Ebenezer Watson to the printers' trade. Watson must have been a quick learner, for soon Green took him into partnership, and when, in 1768, Green began a second newspaper in New Haven, Watson became the de facto publisher of the *Courant*. Watson, too, would berate the British on the slightest provocation, and he certainly had the knack of needling his Hartford readers into action by comparing what he regarded as Hartford's inaction with what was going on in other places.

In 1767 Parliament levied the so-called Townshend Acts, which imposed duties on lead, paper, tea, and painters' colors, all articles whose production in the colonies Britain had always discouraged, and the colonists, deferring to British wishes, had never seriously attempted. The colonials regarded this as a low blow, and response from the commercial centers was forthcoming. Boston and New York merchants adopted nonimportation agreements immediately, and in July, 1769, New London, Wethersfield, Norwich, Middletown, and New Haven merchants agreed not to import any English goods until the Townshend Acts were repealed. Oddly, no similar, supposedly binding, written agreement was made in Hartford, despite the "Indignation Meeting" held on October 13, 1770. During the nonimportation period, Hartford retailers were still receiving regular supplies of British tea.

Parliament removed all of the Townshend Duties except that on tea on April 12, 1770. But the repeal was greeted with no enthusiasm in Connecticut, as nonimportation had had a most positive effect on the provincial economy by creating a favorable balance of trade for the New England colonies.

On July 9, 1770, the New York merchants voted to end their nonimportation agreement, and the reaction in Connecticut was immediate, as most of the colony's merchants and farmers had benefited from the favorable balance of trade. Hartford merchants joined their fellows from all parts of the colony in a large gathering held in New Haven on September 13, and at that meeting it was agreed to continue nonimportation in Connecticut and to break off all commercial relations with New York.

But even more important than the effect of the repeal of nonimportation was the effect of the Boston Massacre, which had occurred on March 5, 1770. Bostonians had questioned the necessity of a military presence from the start, and the soldiers became the object of harassment. One such unfortunate incident occurred when small boys began to throw snowballs at the company of British regulars drilling in front of the Boston State House. A trigger-happy sergeant gave the order to fire, and five lives were lost.

Although there was the to-be-expected cry of "brutality," Boston took the "massacre" calmly, and, with John Adams as the lawyer for the defense, a court trial resulted in the acquittal of five of the British soldiers, with two others receiving a penalty of a slight (symbolic) branding on the hand.

Actually, the "massacre" was more of a sensation in Hartford than it was in Boston, for the ever-anti-British Ebenezer Watson burst forth in the March 19 issue of the *Courant* with a tirade that magnified the incident out of all proportion:

The town of Boston affords a recent and melancholy Demonstration of the destructive consequences of quartering Troops among Citizens in a Time of Peace, under a Pretence of supporting the Laws and aiding Civil Authority; every considerate and unprejudic'd Person among us was deeply imprest with the Apprehension of these Consequences when it was known that a Number of Regiments were ordered to this Town under such a Pretext, but in Reality to inforce oppressive Measures; to awe and controul the legislative as well as executive Power of the Province, and to quell a Spirit of Liberty, which however it may have been basely oppos'd and even ridicul'd by some, would do Honour to any Age or Country.

The flare-up over the Boston Massacre died down quickly, as had the indignation over New York's rescinding of her nonimportation agreement. Business went on as usual, and little was heard in Hartford about the alleged enormities of the British, as even Ebenezer Watson took a milder tone. This was a period of calm, but it was also the calm before the storm.

The storm came in 1773. Parliament, hoping to revive the fortunes of the East India Company, which had contributed so much during the recent war and now found itself in serious financial straits, permitted the company under the so-called Tea Act to sell its tea to colonial consignees without having it pass through the hands of middlemen. Although the tax of 3d. per pound was retained, the effect of the Tea Act was not at all what either the company or Parliament had expected. The retail price of tea was actually lower than it had been for many years, and this should have delighted the colonial consumer. But now what was to happen to the tons of tea the Boston merchants had smuggled in from Holland at a greatly inflated price?

Paul Revere's famous engraving of the Boston Massacre shows British soldiers firing on a defenseless group of citizens. From Grafton, The American Revolution, *1975*

The merchants decided to resist, and they turned to the Boston Sons of Liberty and a group of "town toughies," who, disguised as Indians, boarded the ship carrying the first consignment of tea and dumped the cargo into Boston Harbor. The company and Parliament were incensed, and the latter responded quickly with a series of acts known in the colonies as the "Intolerable Acts." The most significant to this account was the one declaring the port of Boston closed until restitution should be made to the East India Company.

Even before the Boston Tea Party of December 16, 1773, the *Courant* was attacking the British again, and Watson, completely distorting the purpose of the act, poetically urged the Bostonians to resist:

> Parliament an Act has made
> That will distress and ruin trade,
> To raise a tax as we are told,
> That will enslave both young and old;
> Look out poor Boston, make a stand,
> Don't suffer any Tea to land.

When news of the Tea Party reached Hartford, the *Courant* applauded the action as that of free-born men against their oppressors. Hartford's Sons of Liberty raised a "liberty tree" in Meetinghouse Yard, and a large crowd attended the ceremony. But there were probably few in Hartford who realized that the Tea Party marked the point of no return in British-Colonial relations. By the British insistence that the destroyed tea be paid for and the Bostonians' insistence that it would not, each side had jockeyed itself into a position from which there was no possible retreat.

Hartfordites were sympathetic with the Bostonians, and upon receiving news of the closing of the port, an informal committee raised several cartloads of foodstuffs to aid what the *Courant* described as the starving Bostonians.

This British cartoon from 1774 shows tea being forced upon a tarred and feathered tax collector. Hartfordites applauded the disregard for Royal authority. From Grafton, The American Revolution, 1975

ABOVE RIGHT: These 20 and 40 shilling notes are examples of Connecticut currency from the mid-1770s. By 1781 paper notes were virtually worthless. From Clark, A History of Connecticut, 1914

The port of Boston was not reopened, but the excitement in Hartford soon abated. Yet Watson's columns continued to put the British in the worst possible light, and the constant barrage of aspersions did much to drive more deeply the wedge between the radicals and the conservatives in Connecticut, something that was reflected in the name of "Whig" being taken by the former and the name of "Tory" being assigned to the latter.

Hartford's small group of Anglicans formed the nucleus of Hartford's Tories, and the Whig Congregationalists did all they could to make life uncomfortable for them. The Reverend Samuel Peters, who came to Hartford to hold Prayer Book services, was often the object of a discourtesy seldom encountered by a man of the cloth. The cleric's brother, Jonathan Peters, fared even worse, for that unfortunate gentleman was sent out of town on a rail, while the delighted Whigs chanted, "A Tory, a Tory, a cursed, damned churchman!" Ebenezer Watson was soon joined in his anti-British propagandizing by the Reverend Nathan Strong, who had become minister of First Church in 1774 and in his sermons preached John Locke's "right of revolution" under the guise of classical Calvinism.

On April 18 and 19, 1775, Massachusetts militiamen and British regulars shed the first blood of the American Revolution at Lexington and Concord. Hartford's response was instantaneous, and four companies of militiamen were sent to the Bay Colony as soon as word of the Battle of Lexington had reached Hartford.

On June 30 George Washington passed through Hartford on his way to Cambridge, Massachusetts, to assume command of the New England militiamen, who had been adopted by the Continental Congress as the Congressional Army. During his brief stay Washington was the guest of Colonel Jeremiah Wadsworth. In the summer, companies of volunteers from Virginia, Maryland, and Pennsylvania tarried briefly in Hartford on their way to participate in the siege of Boston. After the British evacuation of that city in March of 1776, many of these same troops passed through Hartford on their way to the defense of New York City.

Hartford was the staging point for the Ticonderoga Expedition when in early May, 1775, General Samuel Holden Parsons gathered men and provisions. And as the scene of military action moved into the province of New York, caravans of as many as 100 ox teams set out from Hartford to Poughkeepsie. In 1778, when Colonel Henry Champion of Colchester gathered his herd of beeves to be driven overland to Valley Forge, many of the animals were obtained in Hartford.

Morale was high in Hartford, and here the clergy did much to help. The Reverend Nathan Strong was in his element, for now he no longer needed to disguise his hatred of Britain and the Church of England. But no less ardent in support of the revolt was the Reverend Nathan Perkins of West Parish (now West Hartford), who, in a sermon preached to a company of volunteers about to leave for Cambridge, declared that "We must resist unto blood ... or be slaves."

BELOW: *The colonies rallied against the British, increasing their resistance after the Boston Tea Party in December 1773. From Grafton,* The American Revolution, *1975*

RIGHT: *It is said that when Washington and the French commander Rochambeau met in Hartford in September* 1780, *they planned what became the final, decisive engagement of the Revolutionary War—the Battle of Yorktown. The meeting is memorialized on this plaque affixed to a boulder beside the Old State House. Courtesy, Society of the Descendants of the Founders of Hartford*

THIS TABLET COMMEMORATES THE HISTORIC FIRST MEETING OF GENERAL GEORGE WASHINGTON AND GENERAL COMTE DE ROCHAMBEAU, COMMANDER-IN-CHIEF OF THE FRENCH ARMY IN AMERICA, WHICH TOOK PLACE SEPTEMBER 20, 1780.

ON THAT OCCASION, AND IN A SUBSEQUENT MEETING THE FOLLOWING MAY, WAS DEVELOPED THE STRATEGY WHICH RESULTED, AT YORKTOWN, IN VICTORY AND INDEPENDENCE FOR THE AMERICAN COLONIES.

ERECTED BY THE CITY OF HARTFORD, SEPTEMBER 20, 1946, IN GRATEFUL REMEMBRANCE

"UPON THEIR APPEARANCE IN THE CITY, THEY WERE RECEIVED WITH IMPOSING CEREMONIES. THE GOVERNOR'S GUARDS, AND A COMPANY OF ARTILLERY, WERE ON DUTY UPON THE OCCASION"

ABOVE: *Hartford men participated in the capture of Fort Ticonderoga on May 10, 1775. British artillery captured at the fort would later serve the Continental Army well. From Grafton,* The American Revolution, *1975*

When the Continental Congress created Committees of Observation to carry out the policies of the Congress and to see that no British goods be allowed to enter the colonies, such a body was created for Hartford County. There were, at the outbreak of the Revolution, 153 merchants and shopkeepers who advertised the sale of imported goods, and the affairs of each had to be investigated carefully. Hartford's Whigs were quick to accuse, and almost a third of Hartford's merchants and shopkeepers appeared before the committee. Fortunately, most of them were found not to have violated any of the numerous regulations that were in effect.

An early sufferer from the effects of the war was the *Courant*. With the end of all importation from Britain, the printer soon ran out of the high-quality paper the *Courant* had always used, and the August 21, 1775, issue appeared on wrapping paper. The printer urged the women of the community to save linen and cotton rags for papermaking, as a paper mill was already under construction east of the river. The September 11 issue consisted of two pages rather than the usual four, and it contained an apology for the poor quality of newsprint.

Work on the paper mill proceeded slowly, and by the end of the year the *Courant* was forced to suspend publication for a month. Several issues were printed on inferior paper until March, when production at the mill began.

On January 27, 1778, the paper mill was destroyed in a fire that Hartford Whigs insisted had been set by Tories. The Connecticut General Assembly came to the rescue by authorizing a public lottery to raise money for a new mill, and in four months the new plant was in operation.

During the Revolution, Hartford suffered from a severe monetary inflation. In 1775, for example, the *Courant* cost 6s. a year. By 1779 a year's subscription had gone to 30s., which, the printer noted, "our Customers must judge to be very reasonable, especially considering the great Difficulty, Risque and Expense of procuring

Jeremiah Wadsworth (1743-1804), a prominent Hartford merchant during the Revolution, was sometimes called "Hartford's First Citizen" because of his leadership in banking, insurance, and civic affairs. From Cirker, Dictionary of American Portraits, Dover, 1967

BELOW: This mahogany box was made for Jeremiah Wadsworth by Samuel Kneeland of Hartford, circa 1786. It was designed for the safe storage of Wadsworth's Oriental punch bowl. (CHS)

Printing Material." Price, however, had no effect upon the *Courant's* circulation. In 1775 there had been some 700 subscribers, while in 1778 there were about 800.

Ebenezer Watson did not live to enjoy the success of his paper, as he died of smallpox in September of 1777. His widow, Hannah, continued the business without interruption and soon took on as a partner 20-year-old George Goodwin, who had begun working on the *Courant* as a nine-year-old errand boy. On February 11, 1779, the Widow Watson married her next-door neighbor, Barzillai Hudson, a mason by trade and commandant of the county jail at Hartford. The following month the husband became a partner in the firm of Hudson & Goodwin, which published the *Courant,* assumed an interest in a second paper mill, and soon ventured into book publishing. Throughout the Revolution, the *Courant* steadfastly supported the Patriot cause, and its readers were first introduced to some of the more important documents of the times through its pages. Starting on February 19, 1776, the *Courant* devoted most of the space of four issues to a complete serialization of Thomas Paine's *Common Sense.* The *Courant* also reprinted all of the Declaration of Independence, considerable portions of the Articles of Confederation, and much of the Treaty of Paris of 1783.

Because of its inland location, Hartford was a relatively safe place for the incarceration of both Tories (or Loyalists, as they soon came to be called) and prisoners of war. Following the capture of Fort Ticonderoga, more than 50 prisoners were consigned to the Hartford jail. The August 5, 1776, issue of the *Courant* noted the arrival in Hartford of "a motley mess" of 20 or 30 Tories, and the following year prisoners taken at Princeton, New Jersey, also arrived. Of this group, the officers were permitted to go to Middletown each Sunday to attend Anglican services. Two of them were assisted in an attempted escape from Hartford jail by the Reverend Roger Viets, the Anglican rector at Simsbury. The parson was placed under house arrest for the remainder of the war.

Actually, life for the prisoners was reasonably comfortable. Officers were sometimes assigned to private homes rather than to the jail, and usually they were free to walk the streets during daylight hours.

Not all of Hartford's prisoners were so fortunate. On March 19, 1777, Moses Dunbar was hanged for treason, having admitted to accepting a commission in Fanning's King's American Loyalist Regiment. The execution took place on what was then known as Gallows Hill, today the site of Ogilby Hall at Trinity College. On November 10, 1778, David Farnsworth and John Blair were executed for both spying and passing counterfeit money, and on March 21, 1781, Alexander McDowell was hanged for desertion.

Hartford provided no military leaders during the war, but in the more pedestrian line of military supply Hartford excelled. Jeremiah Wadsworth was the leading Hartford merchant during the latter years of the war. He never concealed the fact that the greatest fortune made in Hartford to that time had come from his supplying the French troops, first in Newport and later as they marched toward Yorktown, Virginia, and that he always insisted he be paid for his produce and services in gold.

John Morgan, John Chenevard, and John Caldwell, known as "the three Johns," sometimes operated with Wadsworth and sometimes in competition. Several of the numerous Bull family also had State contracts, and the fact that they operated from Bull's Tavern, the best in town, gave them an advantage. Lesser figures were Ashbel Welles, Amassa King, Hezekiah Merril, and Daniel Olcott. All of these traders were identified at some time and in some way with Wadsworth's activities,

TOP: *The Marquis de Lafayette was among the distinguished military men who met with General Washington and Governor Trumbull in Hartford on September 20, 1780. Courtesy, Library of Congress*

ABOVE: *The Webb House in Wethersfield, where Washington and Rochambeau were entertained at their first meeting in 1781, was known as "Hospitality Hall." From Clark, A History of Connecticut, 1914*

although it is doubtful that they shared fully in the profits. Nevertheless, this was a cadre upon which Wadsworth was to depend later as he advanced bold plans for the improvement of Hartford's economy.

Military supply had brought money into Hartford, and the money circulated freely. But Hartford was also the center of considerable monetary speculation during the war and was referred to by contemporaries as the "Grand Focus" of Continental bills of credit for all of New England. Much money was in circulation, but all of it—except for Wadsworth's gold coins—was depreciated. It has been estimated that Hartford had as many as 70 individuals who were more than nominal security holders.

During the closing years of the war, much occurred in Hartford that would long be remembered. On May 19, 1780, Hartford experienced the "Dark Day," when at about 10 a.m., following a thunderstorm, darkness fell, causing many to think the end of the world was at hand. The General Assembly was in session, and one member, fearing it was indeed the Day of Judgment, moved that the Assembly be adjourned. Another member, old Abraham Davenport of Stamford, took a different view, declaring that either the Day of Judgment was at hand or it was not, and that in either case, nothing could be done about it. Davenport declared that if "the Day" were really at hand, he would prefer to be found by his Creator doing his duty. He therefore moved that candles be lighted and that business go on. The world, as the reader probably knows, did not come to an end, and it was soon learned that the darkness was caused by a forest fire to the west.

The Lord did not make his Second Coming to Hartford, but General Washington did. On September 20, 1780, Washington, along with General Henry Knox, the Marquis de Lafayette, the Comte de Rochambeau, and Admiral de Ternay, met with Governor Jonathan Trumbull at the home of Jeremiah Wadsworth. On March 7, 1781, Washington again passed through Hartford on his way to Newport to confer with the French. Six days later, he stopped briefly in Hartford on his return to Newburgh, New York. But the most significant gathering was that of the Commander in Chief, Governor Trumbull, Wadsworth, Rochambeau, and General le Chevalier de Chasteleux at the home of Joseph Webb in Wethersfield, where the details of the Yorktown campaign were worked out. This time Washington was entertained at a formal reception, highlighted by the firing of 13 cannon.

When the French Army finally moved to join the American troops in Virginia, the main body of troops was kept out of Hartford proper. From June 22 to June 25, 1781, the French camped east of the river. The French officers were entertained in the village, and a French military hospital was opened in Second Meetinghouse. On June 26 the French camped at Farmington, and the following day they moved on to Southington.

Although the enlisted men did not get into town, Hartford people visited the French camps by the hundreds, attracted particularly by the military bands, especially as few Hartfordites had ever in their lives heard concerted instrumental music. Each evening there were dances, and Hartford's young ladies enjoyed a brief social life that might have made Hartford's founders turn over in their graves in the Ancient Burying Ground.

Word of the signing of the Treaty of Paris arrived in Hartford on April 24, 1783. There was a huge celebration, with feasting, fireworks, and military drills. And indeed, there was something of a repeat of the 1766 celebration of the repeal of the Stamp Act, as the fireworks display got out of hand and resulted in the almost total destruction of the State House.

A City of Steady Habits

~HARTFORD'S APPARENT
WARTIME PROSPERITY WAS AGAIN SUPERFICIAL.
MERCHANTS HAD CARRIED ON EXTENSIVE BUSINESS,
but much of their payment had been in rapidly
depreciating currency, and several of Hartford's businessmen found themselves totally ruined.

As soon as the war ended, Britain began "dumping"
goods upon the American market. The "dumpers" soon
appeared in even the smaller ports, and in the summer
of 1785 the schooner *Peggy* sold English goods in large
quantities while lying at anchor near the Public Landing.

The period between 1783 and 1789 was the poorest
for commerce in American history. In 1784, for example, Britain sent merchandise to America to the value of
£3,700,000 and received only £750,000 in return, with
the difference made up by a severe drain on American
specie. The American merchants were embarrassed by
their rash purchases, as the imports included much of
what might be regarded as luxury goods, and by 1785

the Boston merchants were again pledging not to make any further purchases until the economic situation improved.

Hartford's public leaders saw the root of the new country's economic woes in the weakness of the central government under the Articles of Confederation, and they were outspoken in favor of a stronger national government with power to levy import duties.

Hartford's townspeople, however, felt differently. On September 16, 1783, the Town Meeting went on record as opposing any "encroachment upon the sovereignty and jurisdiction of the states" and urged the Connecticut state government to exercise whatever powers were necessary to regulate commerce and to develop direct foreign trade to such an extent as to relieve Hartford's dependence upon Boston and New York.

It was also at this same time, and in this same mood, that arguments were advanced for the incorporation of Hartford as a city. Within the Hartford mercantile community there were even those who felt that Hartford, despite its temporary depression, showed greater economic potential than New London and New Haven, both still recovering from the losses they had suffered from British attacks during the war. Hartford was just then beginning to develop a flatboat trade on the Connecticut River, and this suggested almost unlimited riches in the transport and marketing of agricultural products from the north. Jeremiah Wadsworth was even suggesting that a canal be cut around Enfield Falls. Noah Webster, of later dictionary fame, was a constant contributor to the *Courant*, always urging incorporation as a means of improving Hartford's economy, insisting that the town government was incapable of regulating "the internal police" and of providing adequate wharves and streets.

Hartford's downtown was becoming increasingly urban, while the outlying sections had undergone little change during the past hundred years. Hartford's compact downtown, with its 250 houses, was occupied by about 1,500 people, or roughly 31 percent of the town's population. East-of-the-River had been set off as a separate ecclesiastical society (Third Church) in 1694, and a meetinghouse had been built in 1699. The "easterners" found their interests becoming increasingly incompatible with those living downtown, and on four occasions—in 1769, 1774, 1780 and 1782—they had petitioned the General Assembly for incorporation as a separate town. West Division (to become West Hartford in 1854) was set off as West Parish in 1711, but there was then no particular interest in a separate town for the "westerners."

Hartford's town government had become quite cumbersome. In 1664 there had been but eight town officers: four selectmen, two constables, and two surveyors. By the eve of the American Revolution, the number had increased to 76! Town Meeting still functioned as the legislative branch of the town government, and the meetings, averaging between four and five a year during the 1770s and early 1780s, were generally orderly. Nevertheless, it was felt by many that the Town Meeting did little more than rubber-stamp action that had already been taken by the selectmen.

That Hartford's town government was inefficient was particularly obvious in the performance of the constabulary. Police protection was virtually nonexistent, as none of the four constables had any training, much energy, or even serious interest in his work, which always was performed part-time. When someone needed services such as those that would now be handled by the police, he simply ignored the constables and did the best he could on his own.

Even old Governor Trumbull soon came to support the idea that several of Connecticut's larger towns should be incorporated as cities, arguing that under city

RIGHT: *The notice says "Watchmaker Only," but Thomas Hildrup made fine clocks as well, and he sold molasses, grain, tobacco, pickles, and assorted notions. In 1777 he assumed the duties of Deputy Postmaster, always operating the post office at his place of business. Since Hildrup moved 12 times in 18 years, many people must have wondered where to mail their letters! (CHS)*

ABOVE: *Thomas Hildrup's skill as an engraver is beautifully demonstrated on this watch case from about 1776. (CHS)*

THOMAS HILLDRUP,

WATCH MAKER ONLY,

At the shop for many years occupied by Dr. WILLIAM JEPSON, *a few rods North of the State-House,* HARTFORD,

PROPOSES, if properly encouraged, to open a Repository for buying and selling Watches, on commissions, they being in great demand, and not to be got in the usual way. Therefore, those persons that have any to dispose of, are requested to leave them as soon as possible---a regular book will be kept for the sales, that each party may be convinced of the justice done them. Also continues to repair, in a perfect and durable manner, and warrants them to perform well one year, casualties and very bad ones excepted. Gentlemen in the army, and others at a distance, forwarding their commands by post riders, &c. may depend on fidelity and dispatch. He desires such of his customers as have not an opportunity of applying personally, to be particular in directing their favours, as many have of late been carried elsewhere, to the deception of the parties. For the future, the work will have his name in types within the out side case. Constant attendance will be given from sun to sun, the year round. Every favour gratefully acknowledged, and punctually observed by the public's humble servant to command; THOMAS HILLDRUP.

Hartford, Nov. 15, 1776.

P.S. Four eight day CLOCKS, and a gold WATCH, for sale. Constant employ, and punctual payment to an assistant in the Watch business, who understands finishing.   nr8 3m

RIGHT: The Reverend Joel Hawes (1789-1867) attended Brown University and was graduated from Andover Seminary. Only one month out of school, he was invited to preach in Hartford's First (Center) Church, where he would serve from 1818 until his death. (CHS)

ABOVE: Looking-glass manufacturer Eli Gilman (1787-1842) was a partner in the firm Spencer, Smith & Company, which became Spencer & Gilman. After 1827 Gilman advertised under his name alone. (CHS)

government, land values would "increase in two years sufficient to defray the city-charges of twenty years." To the thrifty Yankees, this was enough. Enough for the downtowners, at least, for as the businessmen became increasingly convinced of the virtue of incorporation, the people at the periphery refused to accept the arguments and strongly opposed incorporation.

But there was a bit of shenaniganism in the process that led to ultimate incorporation, as East-of-the-River was assisted in its fifth appeal for incorporation and was able to hold its first Town Meeting on December 8, 1783, as East Hartford. With the rural vote thus reduced, incorporation received a favorable vote at the Hartford Town Meeting of January 6, 1784. On May 24, 1784, Hartford received a charter as "The Mayor, Aldermen, Common Council and Freemen of the City of Hartford."

The original territory of the City of Hartford was a mere 1,700 acres, roughly equivalent to the settled area of about 1640. It was bounded by the Connecticut River on the east, present Wyllys Street on the south, Washington Street on the west, and Belden Street on the north.

June 28, 1784, was set as election day, and the freemen met at the State House. As there was little understanding of the titles and functions of "city" officers, much of the day was spent in defining terms—to say nothing of politicking. June 29 was something of a repeat of the 28th, but on June 30, a full complement of city officials was selected.

Thomas Seymour was elected mayor, an office he was to hold for 28 years. And, as during the following decades there was to be similar longevity in office noted in the Board of Aldermen and the Common Council, Connecticut's sobriquet, "The Land of Steady Habits," might well be applied to Hartford during these years as "The City of Steady Habits."

The list of aldermen and councilmen reads like a "Who's Who" of Hartford of the time. Aldermen were Samuel Wyllys, Jonathan Bull, Jesse Root, and Samuel

Marsh. Members of the Common Council were John Chenevard, Barnabas Deane, Ralph Pomeroy, James Church, Chauncey Goodrich, Peter Colt, John Olcott, John Caldwell, Zebulon Seymour, Zachariah Pratt, Ashbel Steel, William Nichols, John Trumbull, Barzillai Hudson, William Bull, Caleb Bull, John Morgan, Israel Seymour, Daniel Olcott, and Daniel Hensdale. Jacob Talcott and James Wells were sheriffs, Hezekiah Merril was treasurer, and William Adams was clerk.

Missing from the list was the name of Jeremiah Wadsworth, the most ardent of the pro-city men and one who might properly have been called Hartford's "First Citizen." Wadsworth was then in Europe, having gone to France to collect the last of his French gold *louis d'or,* and he had directed that he be elected to no public office during his absence.

The expectations of those who had promoted incorporation were soon realized to an amazing degree. General Lafayette, who visited Hartford in October of 1784 amid much understandable fanfare, described it as a "rising city blessed with advantages which were the reward of virtuous efforts in the noblest cause." But the rhetoric of the occasion aside, Hartford did indeed prosper, and much of the prosperity may be credited to Jeremiah Wadsworth, who, from the time of his return from France, served as either alderman or councilman until his death in 1804.

The city fathers availed themselves of every opportunity to present Hartford as an inland commercial center, and inspectors were appointed to see that all goods sent out from Hartford were of the finest quality. New streets laid out on the flats along the river extended the commercial district. Prospect Street became the site of fashionable residences. A fire engine was purchased in 1785, and an informal company, "The Proprietors of the Hartford Aqueduct," attempted to set up a public water system, even progressing as far as to lay several hundred feet of wooden pipes. Although no conventional sewers were to be installed before 1843, regulations adopted late in the 18th century clearly suggest that public sanitation was a serious concern. Soap factories, tanneries, and slaughterhouses, some of them located quite near some of Hartford's most pretentious dwellings, were constantly being ordered to clean up or close up.

But Hartford's hoped-for trade with foreign ports was not realized. Most of Hartford's trade was simply river trade, although it was a profitable one, with the towns along the Connecticut River in Vermont and New Hampshire.

In 1783 Hartford became a major stop on a regular stage line between New York City and Boston. Postal service, too, was much improved by the Congress during the war, and for many years thereafter Thomas Hildrup, the Hartford jeweler, gave first-rate service as postmaster. The "ultimate" in intercity communication was the reasonably travelable New Haven and Hartford Turnpike, completed in 1799.

All these busy activities stimulated trade and even manufacture. A rum distillery, a large one for the time, was established on the bank of the Little River by Wadsworth and Barnabas Deane. A pottery was opened in 1787 by Archibald Welles, Jr., close by, giving name to Potter Street. William and George Bull opened a shop for the sale of the fuel-saving Franklin stove, and Frederick Bull greatly enlarged his shop for the sale of general hardware. Commerce Street was laid out between Front Street and the Connecticut River, and, as it attracted small shopkeepers who specialized in less-than-quality merchandise, the section was known for a while as "Cheapside." In this vicinity, Caleb Bull opened a retail store, and Aaron Bradley operated a blacksmith shop advertised as "at the sign of the Horseshoe, No. 3, Cheapside, Jones Street."

On Main Street and State Street (as King Street had been renamed) were

An 1810 ad for children's books with titles like The History of Nancy Truelove *and* Whittington and His Cat *was certain to attract customers to the Peter B. Gleason and Company bookstore. (CHS)*

various shops that reflected the new prosperity and perhaps something of a new urbanity. In 1775 one Mary Gabriel had appeared out of nowhere and advertised herself as a "mantua-maker and miliner from Paris." After that, retail shopping in Hartford was never quite the same. Postmaster Hildrup received stiff competition from James Tiley, a silversmith, goldsmith, and jeweler on State Street, and from Jacob Sargent, a watchmaker, who in 1795 opened shop "at the Sign of the Golden Watch." By about 1800 pewterware was being produced in several small Hartford shops, and by 1843 there were 23 jewelers and silversmiths operating in the city.

In 1788 Hartford fell just a bit short of taking a large step in the American industrial revolution, when Jeremiah Wadsworth organized the Hartford Woolen Company. Wadsworth was the largest subscriber to the capital stock of £1,250, and among the other 30 investors were Hartford merchants Peter Colt, John Caldwell, and Nehemiah Hubbard. A mill was erected along the Little River, and an Englishman was brought in to supervise the operation. Workmen with the requisite skills were almost impossible to find, but at its peak the mill was producing about 5,000 yards of broadcloth a year. President Washington wore a suit made of the material at his first inauguration, and members of the Connecticut Congressional delegation were similarly attired. Although the "manufactory," as it was called locally, sold its product as far away as New York City, success was not to come its way. The Connecticut General Assembly exempted the building from taxation and in 1794 awarded a bounty on the mill's production. Even a lottery in 1790, authorized for the purchase of additional machinery, could not sustain an industry whose managers were totally ignorant of the methods of industrial production, and in 1797 the plant was closed.

Wadsworth attributed the failure of the Hartford Woolen Company to the lack of adequate capital, and in 1791 he proposed a corporation of much larger proportion than the Woolen Company. Here he hoped to attract New York capital, and in his initial attempt he secured the promise of some $19,000. Unfortunately, the New Jersey Society for Establishing Useful Manufactures was being organized under the leadership of Alexander Hamilton, and the funds first promised to Wadsworth went to the New Jersey project instead.

But Wadsworth was eminently successful in other areas, particularly in banking, for here he had more experience than any other person in Connecticut. Wadsworth was one of the founders of the Bank of North America, president of the Bank of New York from 1785 to 1786, and one of the directors of the First Bank of the United States. Late in 1791 Wadsworth had his clerk, Peleg Sanford, sound out the Hartford business community as to interest in setting up a local bank and the possible extent of the participation of each. The response was favorable, and Wadsworth and a few close associates from the wartime years—Oliver Phelps, Barnabas Deane, and James Watson—began drawing up the plans. Every effort was made to make the bank a local affair and to keep out speculators. On May 14, 1792, capital of $100,000 was raised by shares of $40 each. The entire amount was subscribed immediately, most of it by men who had a connection with Wadsworth's wartime military supply business. Wadsworth was elected first president of the bank, but he declined, allowing John Caldwell to serve in his stead. The Hartford Bank opened for business on August 8, 1792.

Although the founders of the Hartford Bank were conservative men, it was the first bank in the United States to set aside the old system of keeping accounts in terms of pounds, shillings, and pence. Congress had declared the Spanish silver dollar to be the monetary unit for the country by the Currency Act of April 2, 1792, just as the Hartford Bank was being created. Thus, unhampered by previous records kept in

Ten Dollars Reward!

RAN away from the Subscriber, on the night of the 15th inftant, a Negro Boy, named *Cæfar*, 18 years old, nearly 6 feet high, ftout and well made, walks pretty erect, fpeaks fluently: He wore away a light colored failor jacket, a mixed green and black fwanfdown veft, a pair of blue overalls, a Holland fhirt, a pair of gray focks, a pair of thick fhoes, a brown homemade great coat, and a large old Hat; has a fmall fcar on his left cheek. He has lately been guilty of theft, and made his efcape through fear of punifhment. Whoever will return faid Negro, or fecure him fo that his mafter may get him again, fhall receive the above reward, and all reafonable charges.—All perfons are forbid harboring, trufting or employing faid Negro, on penalty of the Law.   SAMUEL M'CLELLAN.
Woodftock, Connecticut, May 16, 1803.

A runaway slave was not an uncommon occurrence. Although this young lad escaped in May 1803 from northeastern Connecticut, his master advertised for him in Hartford's Connecticut Courant, *offering a generous reward for his apprehension.* (CHS)

the old fashion, the Hartford Bank began business with all accounting in terms of dollars and cents, and on June 15, 1792, it began issuing its first bank notes in dollars.

It would be almost half a century later that Hartford would come to be known as "The Insurance City," but there was already, in the 1790s, some inkling of future preeminence. That there was simply "insurance" in Hartford at this time was nothing at all remarkable, for insuring began as soon as small vessels sailed from Hartford in the 1630s, and never did a sailing vessel leave a colonial port without insurance that the vessel and cargo would arrive at the destined port. Individuals acted as brokers in receiving promises from persons who would be willing to compensate the insured in the event of a disastrous voyage. During the 1790s this was still the conventional way of working maritime insurance. Likewise, similar arrangements were often made to compensate for loss of buildings and/or their contents. During the early 1790s, however, an informal—and unincorporated—group that called itself

After the 1720 State House was severely damaged in 1783, Jeremiah Wadsworth campaigned for a new building. Located at Meetinghouse Square, the new State House was completed in 1796 and built of brick with brownstone trimmings. From Hartford, Connecticut, 1889

FACING PAGE, BOTTOM: *In the 17th and 18th centuries each householder kept two or more leather buckets handy in case of fire. Family, neighbors, and passers-by would bring more buckets and form a line from a source of water to the person nearest the fire, who would then throw water on the flames. The State House had a shelf or so of fire buckets, each marked for identification with the State seal. (CHS)*

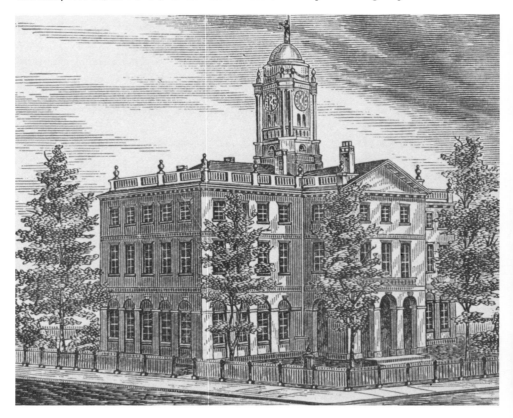

the Hartford Insurance Company became so formalized that it used printed policy forms, the earliest extant of which is dated February 8, 1794, for "insurance on the dwelling and its contents of William Imlay." Of particular interest are the seals of Peleg Sanford and Jeremiah Wadsworth as insurers. The later chartered company of that name did not come into existence until 1810, but it might be noted that those who participated in the organization of the later company were members of the earlier venture—as well as stockholders in the Hartford Bank.

Marine insurance, too, was formalized with the chartering of the Marine Insurance Company in 1803. By more than mere coincidence, John Caldwell, the first president of the Hartford Bank, was also the first president of Marine Insurance. This company was later absorbed by the Protection Insurance Company, which went out of business in 1854.

The Aetna (Fire) Insurance Company of Hartford was incorporated in 1819. Again, there was something of an overlapping of directorate with the Hartford Bank, but despite the fact that these early insurance companies were investors in the Hartford Bank, much of the capital consisted of personal notes of the stockholders who pledged the company to provide cash when it was needed to pay a claim. By 1881 the Aetna was the largest insurance company in the United States.

Hartfordites seem always to have had a penchant when it came to buildings, to tear down the old. Only one architectural vestige of this post-Revolutionary period of Hartford's history remains—what is known locally as the Old State House.

The 1720 State House had suffered severe damage in 1783, and repair had been both hasty and inadequate. Jeremiah Wadsworth, who quite properly regarded Hartford as "his" city, felt that the new state in the new nation deserved better of the new city, and he began a campaign to replace the old eyesore with a more

BELOW: Funds to build the State House of 1796 were raised by selling lottery tickets at five dollars apiece. Prizes ranged from $10 to $8,000 and the possibility of winning a prize was almost one in three. (CHS)

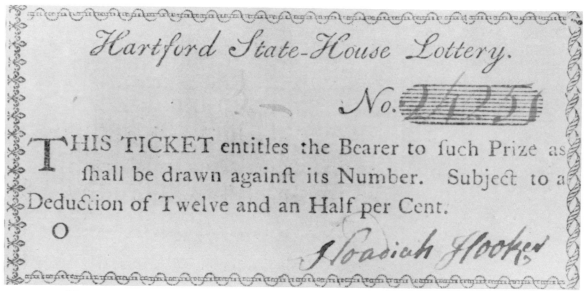

Hartford State-House Lottery.

No. 2425(?)

THIS TICKET entitles the Bearer to such Prize as shall be drawn against its Number. Subject to a Deduction of Twelve and an Half per Cent.

O

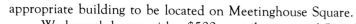

appropriate building to be located on Meetinghouse Square.

Wadsworth began with a $500 contribution, and 51 others contributed a total of $3,600. An appropriation by the General Assembly raised the available fund to $13,600, but even this was not sufficient to erect the building according to the plan of Boston architect Charles Bulfinch, and funds sufficient to the purpose had to be raised by a lottery. When the building was completed in 1796, the 1720 State House was moved to Church Street, near Christ Episcopal Church.

Few buildings in America have been subject to greater misunderstanding and historical misinterpretation than Hartford's Old State House has been. Since the restoration of the building in the 1970s, the zealous have made the claim that Hartford's Old State House is the oldest in the nation, but this is patently untrue. The Maryland State House at Annapolis was completed in 1779 and has been used as such ever since. Delaware's present State House in Dover has been in continuous use since 1792. In Rhode Island, Newport's "Old Colony House," built in 1739, was used as the State Capitol until 1900. Boston's "Old State House" was built in 1713 and served as Colony/State Capitol until 1795. Finally, in case the foregoing is not enough, the left wing of the *really* old "Old State House" in Newcastle, Delaware, built some time before 1664, was both Provincial and State Capitol until 1777, and for over a century thereafter was used as a city hall!

"In the Midst of Dissenters"

~AS THE TWO NATIONAL POLITICAL PARTIES—THE FEDERALISTS UNDER ALEXANDER HAMILTON AND THE REPUBLICANS UNDER Thomas Jefferson—lined up, there was little doubt that the Federalists would make the greater appeal in Hartford. Hamilton's policies of strong central government, sound national credit, easily circulating currency, and encouragement of industry naturally appealed to the Standing Order, and Jefferson's vaguely stated, quasi-agnostic religious attitudes guaranteed that he and his party could receive no support from the Congregationalists.

Hartford's civic leaders had long been on record as favoring a strong central government, and great was their rejoicing when on January 3, 1788, the convention to vote on ratification of the Federal Constitution of 1787 opened in the State House. The day was extremely cold, and the convention was adjourned to First Meetinghouse, which had recently installed a stove. The debate itself was not without its unpleasant moments, but it was the general public in the gallery that punctuated the proceedings with foot-tapping, foot-shuffling, whispering, coughing, and spitting. The vote on ratification was taken on January 9, with 128 delegates voting "for" and 40 delegates voting "against." Hartford's two delegates cast their votes for ratification.

President Washington undertook a ceremonial tour of the New England states in 1789 "to cement the bonds of the Union," as he put it. Washington at once made clear that the journey was being made at his own expense, and this news was especially pleasing to thrifty Hartfordites.

On October 19, Washington arrived in Hartford, where he was greeted by the Governor's Troop of Horse in full uniform and a large number of gentlemen on horseback. Washington spent the night at Bull's Tavern. The following day he visited the Woolen Manufactory, and the next morning he set out for Springfield. On the return trip, the President stayed once more with Mr. Bull, although this time there was no ceremony.

Washington made diary entries for each of the visits. Regarding the Woolen Manufactory, he noted that the product was "good," although not of finest quality. He also observed that Hartford was "more compactly built than Middletown," and he was surprised to learn that there was still no Episcopal Church.

Hartford's Federalists were fully supportive of the administrations of both Washington and John Adams. Jay's Treaty, negotiated in 1794 by Federalist John Jay, was immensely popular in Hartford, especially as the treaty opened the British West Indies to the smaller sailing craft that were engaged in exporting the Hartford region's agricultural surpluses.

When Britain and France became involved in the French Revolutionary and the Napoleonic wars, Hartford Federalists came out firmly on the side of the British. The Republicans, whose strength was largely in the South, chose the other side, and even Jefferson became blinded to the cruelties and bloodshed of the Reign of Terror, offering the excuse that a little bloodletting now and then is healthful to a nation.

During Jefferson's administration, the Hartford people, as did most New Englanders, turned even more against the second President from Virginia. Both the Embargo and the Non-Intercourse Act had a devastating effect upon New England's economy, as crops, for want of a market, were allowed to rot in the field, and ships decayed at dockside.

When Congress declared war against Britain in what Americans call the War of 1812, New Englanders were more sympathetic with Britain than they were with the American side. After all, the declaration of war had been along strict party lines. The Republicans, led by the "Warhawks," a group of young Western and Southern congressmen with territorial designs on both Canada and Florida, voted for the war, and the Federalists voted solidly against it.

New Englanders called this conflict "Mr. Madison's War," and they determined to let President Madison and his party fight it on their own. New England governors refused to permit the nationalization of the state militia, and New Englanders refused to invest in the government bonds sold to finance the war. The Hartford Bank would not purchase government securities, the Hartford Common Council passed an ordinance forbidding federal recruiting within the city, and the Courant took sadistic pleasure in reporting American military defeats.

The antiwar spirit reached a climax when prominent Massachusetts Federalists called a meeting at the Hartford State House for December 15, 1814, to discuss an antiwar resolution presented to the Massachusetts General Court by Harrison Gray

Otis. The convention consisted of 12 delegates from Massachusetts, 7 from Connecticut, 4 from Rhode Island, 3 from New Hampshire, and one (unofficial) from Vermont. Hartford had been chosen because of its pronounced Federalist tone, but there were already enough Republicans in the community to cause embarrassment. Pressure was put upon the clergy to see that none would offer an opening prayer, and, as the delegates went into their closed session, crowds gathered outside the State House to protest the proceedings. Someone lowered the American flag to half-staff, and a band of musicians paraded around State House Square playing funeral dirges. Even some Hartford Federalists felt that the holding of such a potentially treasonous convention was going too far.

The convention adopted a series of resolutions reflecting both New England sectional interests and Federalist partisan principles, and these were published following adjournment on January 5, 1815. There were resolutions against military conscription and the nationalization of state militia. There were also proposals to amend the Constitution so as to limit embargoes to 60 days, to require a two-thirds vote of both Houses of Congress to declare war, and to limit Presidential tenure to a single four-year term. No vote was taken on secession, but there is strong evidence that the delegates had resolved that if the convention's recommendations were not received favorably by Congress, New England would secede from the Union and make a separate peace with Britain.

Almost immediately, the serious matters discussed at the Hartford Convention became academic. On January 8 Andrew Jackson won the only American land victory in the Battle of New Orleans, and within two weeks of the convention's adjournment came news that the Treaty of Ghent had been signed on Christmas Eve of 1814. The terms of the treaty were *status quo ante bellum*, and all Americans could rejoice that although the United States had lost the war, the new republic had certainly won the peace.

Political Federalism was virtually defunct on the national scale, and from then on Federalist power in Connecticut would decline rapidly. The Hartford Convention has sometimes been called "Federalism's last gasp," but already there had been signs in Hartford that the Federalist Party had become a hollow shell.

One of these portents was the competition offered to the *Courant*. That noble old paper had seen its first rival in *The Freeman's Chronicle or the American Advertiser*, which, although it was to last only from September of 1783 until the following July, was to be followed immediately by the *American Mercury*, which was begun by Joel Barlow and Elisha Babcock and survived until 1835.

The *Mercury* began as a conservative paper, usually taking an editorial position not unlike that of the *Courant*. As the political parties took shape, however, the *Mercury* came out solidly in support of Jeffersonian Republicanism, taking a leading part in the agitation for a new state constitution.

As the *Mercury* moved into the Jeffersonian camp, the Federalists received new support from the *Connecticut Mirror*, founded in 1809 by Theodore Dwight. This paper was never a financial success, and in 1833 it merged with the *Mercury*, ironically, by that time staunchly Jacksonian Democrat!

The next step in the development of the newspapers came in 1817, when the Hartford *Times* was founded by John M. Niles, then a leading Hartford Republican, later a founder of the Democratic Party in Connecticut, and ultimately United States Senator. Niles made clear at the beginning that his paper would be anti-Federalist, but during the entire lifetime of the *Times*, it would always be "anti"—anti-Federalist, anti-Whig, and anti-Republican—until its demise in 1976.

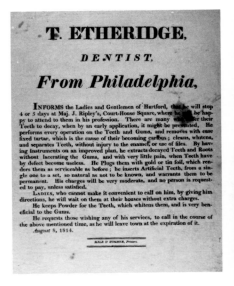

Philadelphia dentist T. Etheridge ran this 1814 advertisement in the Connecticut Courant informing "the Ladies and Gentlemen of Hartford that he will stop 4 or 5 days at Major J. Ripley's, Court-House Square, where he will be happy to attend to them in his profession." His services included plugging teeth "with gold or tin foil," or extracting them and making replacements "so natural as not to be known." (CHS)

HAVING received a confirmation of the diftreffing intelligence of the DEATH of the great, the highly beloved

WASHINGTON,

THE Inhabitants of the town of Hartford, defirous of teftifying their reverence and affection for the memory of " the man, firft in war, firft in peace, and firft in the hearts of his countrymen," propofe to attend Divine Service at the *North Meeting-Houfe,* on FRIDAY next. At half paft one o'clock in the afternoon, a proceffion will be formed at the State-Houfe, at which the Citizens of this, and the neighbouring towns, are requefted to attend. Each perfon who joins the proceffion, will wear a BLACK CRAPE on his left arm ; and the Committee reft fatisfied that no perfon will join the proceffion, without this badge of mourning. The propriety of wearing Crape on their left arms, on the melancholy occafion, is refpectfully fubmitted to the Citizens at large. The Proceffion will move precifely at two ; the people are therefore requefted to be punctual in their attendance. It is defired of the Citizens, THAT THE SHOPS AND STORES MAY BE SHUT THRO' THE WHOLE OF FRIDAY, that the Day may be devoted to this folemn Funeral occafion.

JOHN CALDWELL,
THOMAS Y. SEYMOUR,
ENOCH PERKINS,   } COMMITTEE.
THEODORE DWIGHT,
WILLIAM BROWN,

Hartford, Dec. 24, 1799.

But the journalistic opposition notwithstanding, and in spite of the not-too-successful attempts of the Republicans to gain at least an electoral foothold, during the first 15 years of the 19th century the Federalists continued to act as if their day would never end. All local offices were still held by Federalists, and all civil and civic honors went to those of the Establishment. Much of the Federalist power—and indeed the glory—was symbolized in the elaborate ritual of Election Day, the opening of the May session of the General Assembly.

Early in the morning, the Governor's Foot Guard, resplendent in scarlet-and-buff uniforms of the design of the Coldstream Guards, paraded in front of the State House. At 11 a.m. the governor led the short procession of Foot Guard, state officeholders, and about 100 clergy (Congregational, of course) to the First Church Meetinghouse. Four ministers participated: one offered the opening prayer, another preached the "election sermon" (a "State of the Church" message), a third gave the concluding prayer, and a fourth pronounced a benediction. Then the procession reformed and proceeded to the State House, where the Governor's Guards, as His Excellency passed, presented arms. Dinner followed, and at 2 p.m. the Assembly convened. The votes were counted, the results announced, and the victors installed. The ceremonies ended at about 6 p.m. with a salute from the Foot Guard. The next few days were filled with parliamentary debate and much social entertaining, and at each Hartford Federalist's open house the gustatory delight was "election cake," a

ABOVE LEFT: *When the news of George Washington's death reached Hartford, the following Friday was set aside for a solemn procession. Each citizen was asked to wear a mourning band of "black crepe" on the left arm, and shops were to remain closed "thro' the whole of Friday."* (CHS)

ABOVE: *George Goodwin & Sons got into the business of bookselling, printing, and publishing in 1815. The Connecticut Courant was probably their largest client. This paper label was a handsome example of the Goodwins' work.* (CHS)

uniquely Connecticut delicacy served by tradition only at functions incidental to Election Day. On the second day of the legislative session came the Election Ball, always held in one of the larger taverns.

America's first literary school—the Hartford Wits—found their common bond in their defense of the Standing Order. Most of the Wits were Yale graduates, none was a native of Hartford, and the members represented a wide range of professions. John Trumbull was a lawyer. Lemuel Hopkins was a physician. Richard Alsop of Middletown was part owner of a Hartford bookstore. Joel Barlow and Elisha Babcock were the publishers of the *American Mercury.* Theodore Dwight was a Hartford lawyer, editor of the *Mirror,* secretary of the Hartford Convention, and a brother of Timothy Dwight, president of Yale College. David Humphreys was a gentleman farmer from Derby. Jeremiah Wadsworth, although not himself a poet, was both friend and patron of the Wits, and it was Wadsworth who usually picked up the tab at the Wits' early informal meetings at the Bunch of Grapes or the Black Horse Tavern.

Although the Wits began writing even before the end of the Revolution, their works are characterized by an intense patriotic devotion to the new nation and, in their later writings, to the Federalist cause. John Trumbull's *M'Fingal,* written in 1775 and revised extensively in 1782, was an amusing satire on the Tories. Dwight's magnum opus was a 10,000-line mock epic entitled *The Conquest of Canaan.* Barlow published *The Vision of Columbus* in 1787 and revised and expanded it in 1807 as *The Columbiad,* in each edition shocking his readers with forecasts of such improbable events as the construction of a canal across the Isthmus of Panama and the elimination of the study of Greek and Latin in American schools. *The Anarchiad* (1786), a collaborative work in which most of the Wits had a hand, was a well-reasoned plea in verse for a stronger central government.

The verse of the Wits usually appeared first in the *Courant,* the *Mercury,* or the *Mirror* before it was published in book form, and, as there was then no copyright protection, there were frequent reprintings in other American papers. Collectively, the Wits were the most widely read Americans in their day, not solely because of their literary skills, which were considerable, but also because they were able to put into verse the intense nationalistic feeling of the American people.

But it was their political Federalism that spelled their doom as a literary movement. As Federalism declined, so did their literary output and their popularity. Joel Barlow continued to write, but he soon disassociated himself from the coterie and the Federalist Party and converted to the political views of the Jeffersonian Republicans.

The theater made its first appearance in Hartford during the days of the Hartford Wits. Before the Revolution, few in Hartford would have considered the theater as desirable, or even acceptable. But at Yale College, the academic nursery of the Wits, rudimentary forms of drama had appeared during their own undergraduate years, as Yalies were sneaking out in the evenings in defiance of college rules to participate in amateur dramatics at taverns in nearby Amity and Milford.

Having been brought up on such fare, it would seem reasonable that the Wits would have had some interest in serious theater in Hartford. Unfortunately, however, in 1773 the Connecticut General Assembly had passed "an Act for the Suppression of Mountebanks," sometimes called the "Circus Law," which was sufficiently broad to preclude professional (or traveling) performances of any kind.

It was something vaguely resembling a circus that first appeared in Hartford in defiance of the law. In June, 1787, Thomas Pool of New London put on an "equestrian show" in Hartford. The show consisted of feats of trick riding and a clown act, but Pool was not molested by the authorities.

South Church, the second meetinghouse of Hartford's Second Church, stands on Main Street at the corner of Buckingham. Built in 1827, the church has since been restored with white trim and red brick. (CHS)

Something approaching real theater came in the summer of 1788, when the *American Mercury* advertised:

By Permission.

Entertainment.

Mr. Smith respectfully informs the Ladies & Gentlemen of the Place, that on this, and Wednesday and Friday evenings next, at Mr. Frederick Bull's will be delivered a series of elegant

Dramatic Speaking,

ALSO a variety of Songs and Musical Dialogues, a copy of which may be seen at Mr. Bull's.

During the winter of 1788-1789, Bull's Tavern was the scene of both classical drama and parts of Royall Tyler's popular five-act comedy, *The Contrast.* In the early 1790s traveling companies presented several plays, including *She Stoops to Conquer,* and in 1795 an English company that had been dividing its time among Philadelphia, Boston, New York, and Providence offered to play regularly in Hartford if a proper building could be provided. Ephraim Root erected a small theater on what is now Temple Street, and in this enterprise he was assisted by 57 Hartford gentlemen including Jeremiah Wadsworth, John Morgan, Timothy Burr, Jesse Root, Barzillai Hudson, William Imlay, Peleg Sanford, Daniel Wadsworth, and Samuel Trumbull. These names, as well as others, represented Hartford's oldest families, but also to be noted is that several of them were Episcopalians, and that not one of the Wits participated. Of even greater interest is that one woman, Mrs. Francis Hodgkinson, an actress from New York, was "cut in" for a one-sixtieth share. Both this lady and her husband performed there occasionally, and Mr. Hodgkinson functioned for a while as manager.

Over the next few years there were visiting performances, usually sold out, by the Old American Company on tour and by the Hodgkinsons' resident company. The end of this worthy enterprise came in May, 1800, when the General Assembly passed "An Act to Prevent Theatrical Shows and Exhibitions," which provided for a fine of $50 for every performance in defiance of the law. Nor was the cause of music in Hartford advanced when in 1815 the Common Council passed an ordinance forbidding the playing of any wind or percussion instrument within the city limits between sunset and sunrise except by militiamen under command of their officers.

But the dramatic stage, even in its brief decades, could not hold its own against the "exhibition," and performances of this sort became increasingly frequent. In 1789 two "Arabian camels" were shown at Mr. Bull's, the exhibit being "highly praised" by President Ezra Stiles of Yale College. The next year a "Mr. Bennett" performed on the slack wire at the schoolhouse. And in August of 1795 the first real circus, Ricketts Equestrian Circus, "with riders, dancers, and a clown," came to Hartford. Mr. Franklin's Circus, with riders, clowns, and freaks, performed on South Green in 1799. By 1813 the circus had become such a popular form of entertainment in Hartford that Eleazer Potter made a large addition to the rear of his tavern "to be occupied as a circus." Potter was host to various traveling shows, and their popularity brought the operation to the attention of the General Assembly.

Meanwhile, two attempts were being made at permanent exhibitions. When the State House was completed in 1796, Joseph Steward rented a third-story room as painter's studio and exhibition room, or "Museum," as Steward always called it. Here he did portraits of local worthies from life, and of such persons as Benjamin Franklin from the popular steel engravings of the time. When the state government found need for the space, the museum was moved in 1808 to a location on Main Street opposite the Episcopal Church. In 1824 Steward's curiosities were taken to the fourth floor of the building on the corner of Main Street and Central Row, at which location they were soon forgotten and eventually disappeared—except for a few pictures that became the property of The Connecticut Historical Society.

On February 15, 1795, Reuben Moulthrop, the New Haven portrait painter, moved to "Mr. Jane's" the wax museum that he had been showing in New Haven for three years. Among Moulthrop's 15 figures were the King of France, President Stiles, and "The Drunken Sailor." Moulthrop's exhibition was enhanced, as the *Courant* announced, by "several beautiful airs by Master Salter (a boy of 9 years of age) on the Piano Forte, accompanied on the Violin by Mr. Salter—with sundry pieces on the Piano Forte, performances to be seen at any half hour each day"—admission 25 cents.

These changes in the pattern of life for early 19th-century Hartfordites were paralleled by profound changes in the city's religious life. Just as Federalist political power was on the decline, so, too, was the Congregationalist Establishment. First and Second churches had survived the Revolution—but barely. Membership was at a low ebb, and both meetinghouses had fallen into disrepair.

When Francisco de Miranda, the Venezuelan revolutionary hero, visited Hartford in August of 1784, he found First Church Meetinghouse to be "dirty and in bad taste," and the singing, as well as the manners and the attire of both the men and women, to be "quite inferior" to that of Wethersfield, where he had been just a week before. Second Church had been without a settled minister from 1777 until 1784, when Benjamin Boardman began a series of short pastorates. In the latter year, Second Church had a membership of only 27, or four fewer than it had at the time of its organization in 1670.

When the *Report of the Census of 1790* was published in 1792, one statistical figure shocked Congregationalist Hartford: the American population having any formal connection with organized religion was five percent! But if the national figure was cause for alarm, what about Hartford, where the percentage was even lower?

Ecclesiastical historians agree it was this disturbing data that set into motion the Second Great Awakening that had its origin in the Connecticut Valley of Connecticut and Massachusetts, when, in the mid-1790s, a group of Congregationalist ministers known as the Neo-Edwardsians attempted to rekindle the enthusiasm with which Jonathan Edwards had begun the First Great Awakening of 50 years before. The effects of this new Awakening would be felt in Hartford for years.

The successive pastors of Second Church conducted "revivals of religion" regularly, but with only modest success. Not so at First Church, for there Nathan Strong led large-scale revivals in 1798, 1800, 1808, 1813, and 1815; and Strong's successor, the Reverend Joel Hawes, continued the practice.

Both congregations built new meetinghouses, First Church in 1807 and Second Church in 1827, and both of these elegant structures are still in use. But even the new meetinghouse soon was not large enough to accommodate the congregation that had been gathered at First Church by the Second Great Awakening. In 1824 North Church was built on Main and Morgan streets for no other apparent reason. (This congregation would become Park Church in 1866.) Fourth Church was begun in 1832 by extreme revivalists who thought that First Church had not gone far enough in that direction. The Pearl Street Church, the Asylum Hill Church, the Windsor Street Church (officially known as the Pavillion Congregationalist Society), and the Wethersfield Avenue Church were all geographic accommodations to the town's later physical spread, but they were also convincing evidence that while post-Revolutionary Hartford Congregationalism was ailing, it was not beyond resuscitation.

This engraving is from a portrait of the Reverend Joel Hawes, minister of the First Church in Hartford from 1818 to 1864, and minister emeritus until he died three years later. (CHS)

RIGHT: *The fourth meetinghouse of Hartford's First Church (built on the site of the third) was painted cream color. It is pictured circa 1875. (CHS)*

ABOVE: *This engraving shows the North Church, built in 1824, which stood on Main Street at the corner of Morgan. (CHS)*

It was during the low period of the Congregational Establishment that other religious groups gained a foothold in the community. The Quakers had infiltrated quietly, and in 1788 they organized the Hartford Society of Friends. The Baptists were almost as unobtrusive, although they soon grew in considerable numbers. John Bolles, "the Father of the Baptist Church in Hartford," began holding services in his home before the first Baptist congregation of 16 members was formally organized in 1790. The first Baptist meetinghouse was located at Market and Temple streets in 1794, and according to tradition, the structure had originally belonged to a Methodist congregation upriver and had been washed downstream by a spring flood. In 1831 the congregation built a new house of worship on the site of the present Cheney Building on Main Street, only to move on to a still larger building at Main and Talcott streets. As early membership increased, a split-off group in 1834 built a meetinghouse—South Baptist Church—on the site of the present Federal Building. Both congregations were brought together in 1922 as Central Baptist Church, and the present structure at Main Street and Linden Place was begun in 1925.

During the late 1790s several Methodist preachers visited Hartford but found few hearers. On July 14, 1791, Francis Asbury preached in First Congregational Church and recorded in his diary that he could "scarcely find a breathing of living, holy spiritual religion here except amongst a few women in East Hartford."

Nevertheless, Methodist preachers continued to visit Hartford, although much of their thunder was stolen by the Congregationalist ministers as the Second Great Awakening got into full swing. In 1820, however, a small Methodist congregation was organized. The following year the *old* Old State House, which had been moved from the square to the rear of Christ Church, and which had already served as tenement house, school, and printing shop, was refurbished as the Methodist meetinghouse. Here the Methodists worshiped until a new church building was erected on Asylum Street in 1860. An offshoot of this church was South Park Church, which began in 1850. The 1720 State House, incidentally, was used, after the Methodists moved out, as the carriage factory of Force and Goodnow. Later it was moved to the rear of 185-187 Pearl Street, where it again housed a printing shop until 1910, when it was torn down to make room for the Telephone Company's new building.

ABOVE: *After studying diseases affecting the brain and nervous systems, Dr. Eli Todd (1768-1833) became aware of the need for an institution for the mentally disturbed. He was largely responsible for establishing Hartford's Retreat for the Insane, which opened in 1824. (CHS)*

ABOVE RIGHT: *From the corner of State Street we gaze down Main Street to the south. Church spires (from left to right) are: St. John's (Episcopal), South (Congregational), South (Baptist), and Center (Congregational). (CHS)*

During their early years in Hartford both Methodists and Baptists were frowned upon by the Congregationalists. The preachers of these denominations had little training in theology, and their sermons were offensive to orthodox Calvinists, who could not accept the idea of extemporaneous preaching—even though they themselves were insistent upon the use of extemporaneous prayers. The outdoor baptisms performed by the Baptists in the Little River were thought to be "publicly offensive." Gradually, however, the public came to feel that the members of these sects, although mostly from the more humble levels of society, were upright in their private lives and had as high a regard for the general well-being of society as had their critics. The Congregationalists also came to realize that the Methodists and Baptists differed little in doctrine and worship practices from themselves, and as the century progressed, the original differences came to be less and less important.

The Episcopalians, meanwhile, had been going their own not-so-silent way. Christ Church's membership grew rapidly, and there were converts from Hartford's oldest families. The parish rolls were soon graced with such old Hartford names as Adams, Bull, Burr, Goodwin, Imlay, and Wadsworth, and such new but equally important names as Bradley, Cutler, Morgan, Ogden, and Sigourney. Although Christ Church had had no settled rector until the arrival of the Reverend Menzies Raynor in 1801, the consecration of the parish's fourth rector, Thomas Church

Brownell, as Bishop of Connecticut in 1819, made Hartford the center of diocesan activity.

Hartford Episcopalians represented something of a crosscut of the local social spectrum, but most of Christ Church's leaders were responsible members of the business community, individuals of more-than-average formal education and with cultivated tastes somewhat beyond the commonality of the small city. Whatever may have been their cultural attainment, though, or even their social suavity, Hartford's Episcopalians were being excluded from the nascent banking and insurance operations. As they were recovering slowly from their complete discrediting in the eyes of the Establishment as Tories during the American Revolution, many of them felt that only with a college under their own control could they enter the ranks of first-class citizens.

In 1813 a number of well-to-do Hartford Episcopalians worked out a plan whereby both their own economic ends and the cause of higher education in Connecticut could be served, and the plan involved, of all things, a bank.

The Phoenix Bank was founded in Hartford in May, 1814, by Episcopal laymen. In their petition to the General Assembly for a charter, the promoters offered

to the State of Connecticut a "bonus" of $50,000 to be divided among Yale College, the Bishop's Fund, and "any purpose whatever, which to your Honours may seem best," the "purpose" being an Episcopal college.

The capital stock of the Phoenix Bank was to be $1,000,000, although it is said that the response was so great and so immediate that it could have been set at $7,000,000. The directors of the Hartford Bank even proposed raising the capitalization of their own institution to $1,000,000, but the suggestion came too late, and the Phoenix Bank opened on schedule. As shares were purchased, payments to a total of $50,000 were made to the State, and immediately the Yale Corporation and the trustees of the Bishop's Fund applied for financial grants. The Assembly promptly voted $20,000 to Yale. The Bishop's Fund received nothing, and the Episcopalians found that this elaborate scheme of legislative bribery had been futile.

The outcome was a violent newspaper controversy carried on through late 1815 and early 1816. The Episcopalians made clear that to deny the Bishop's Fund its share of the Phoenix Bank "bonus" was a flagrant disregard of the Episcopalian minority in favor of Congregationalist Yale. The Congregationalists vigorously defended the religious test, insisting that no Episcopalian should object, despite the fact that the test, actually a subscription to Congregationalist orthodoxy, kept Episcopalians from the Yale faculty.

This picture from the eastern shore looks toward Hartford from above the covered bridge, circa 1855. The sloop at right has a hinged mast so that it can be towed under the bridge. (CHS)

The ramifications of the bonus controversy were soon felt in Connecticut politics. Traditionally, the Episcopalians—representing a conservative element in Connecticut society—had supported the Federalist Party, and it was the Episcopal vote that had enabled the Federalists to remain dominant in the state long after Federalism had disappeared elsewhere. The failure of the Episcopalians to receive the Bishop's Bonus, however, turned them from their former Federalist support to a fusion of Republicans and Protestant sectarians known as the Tolerationist Party. By 1816 the party was well organized. The Republican minority provided the working organization, Episcopalians supplied the leadership, and Methodists and Baptists gave voting strength. So effective was the new alliance that in the September election the Tolerationists won 87 seats in the Assembly to the Federalists' 114.

The Tolerationist victory at the polls in 1816 frightened the Federalists, and the legislature adopted a conciliatory policy and passed "an Act for the Support of Literature and Religion," which appropriated the $14,500 due Connecticut from the federal government for Connecticut's minimal services during the War of 1812. Through the fund's disbursement among the religious interests and Yale College, the Congregational societies in the state received one-third; the trustees of the Bishop's Fund, one-seventh; the Baptists, one-eighth; the Methodists, one-twelfth; Yale, one-sixth; and the remainder was to stay in the treasury. Obviously, this was an attempt by the much reduced Federalist majority to salve the wound of the loss of the Phoenix Bank bonus. Yale was the only party to be satisfied. The Congregationalists thought that their share was too small, the Episcopalians regarded their $2,070 as poor compensation for the Phoenix loss, and the Baptists and Methodists regarded their small share as an insult. The whole bonus plan accentuated sectarian bickerings and hastened the ultimate Federalist downfall. In the state election of 1817, all religious elements outside the Congregational Establishment united forces, and the Tolerationists won both the governorship and a large majority in the Assembly. A year later the Council, too, passed into Tolerationist control.

By then, the chartering of an Episcopal college should have been an easy matter, especially as the new State Constitution of 1818 completed the internal revolution in the state and once and for all disestablished the Congregational churches.

A few days before Christmas 1822, Bishop Brownell met with 18 clergymen to draw up a petition to the General Assembly for a college charter, asking that it be located in either Hartford, Middletown, New Haven, or New London, and that final selection be left to the discretion of the trustees, with the act of incorporation to take effect as soon as $30,000 should be raised.

Bishop Brownell and his associates planned well. The suggestion that the college be named for Bishop Samuel Seabury was passed over, and the name "Washington" was chosen instead. Care was taken to include non-Episcopalians among the original incorporators, and among them was the Reverend Elisha Cushman, pastor of the Baptist Society in Hartford.

A charter was granted on May 16, 1823, an event hailed as a victory for Connecticut Episcopalians, the city of Hartford, and the friends of religious liberty throughout the country. Hartford dwellings and places of business were decorated with bunting, and in the evening cannons were fired and bonfires were lighted.

Washington College had been placed under a self-perpetuating board of trustees, and the charter made no mention whatsoever of the Episcopal Church. The charter forbade the "making of religious tenets of any person a condition of admission to any privilege in said college."

On Tuesday, July 8, 1823, at the first meeting of the trustees, a committee to

TOP: John Warner Barber's detailed panorama of Hartford was drawn in 1832 from the opposite bank of the Connecticut. Each steeple and tower is correctly in place, and considerable shipping activity is evident along the riverfront. (CHS)

ABOVE: The east lawn of the State House was set apart from the routine of the marketplace by a fence. (CHS)

procure funds for the institution was appointed. Subscription papers were made out in two forms: one (the particular subscription) for pledges to be made upon condition of the selection of a particular location for the college, and the other (the general subscription) for pledges to be made without regard to location. The committee was not confident that the entire $30,000 could be raised within the diocese, and it therefore appointed the Reverend Nathaniel Wheaton, rector of Hartford's Christ Church, to go to England to solicit donations.

In September, 1823, Wheaton sailed from New York, armed with a letter signed by Bishop Brownell and addressed "To the Bishops, Clergy, and Laity of the Church of England." The letter emphasized the difficult position of the Church in Connecticut, "Planted in the midst of Dissenters ... and opposed by many prejudices." Also mentioned was the common bond of religion uniting England and America: *"The best friends which Great Britain has in America, will be found among the members of the Episcopal Church; and ... every thing which conduces to the extension of this church, will be found to strengthen the bonds of relationship and amity which connect the two countries."*

The trustees, of course, had no idea that this letter would be circulated in Connecticut. Even if they had, there would have been little that could have been changed if the statement of the case were still to be clear to the English Church. Copies of the letter fell into unfriendly hands and were printed in the *Courant* of March 2, 1824. The inevitable consequence was a heated debate in the Hartford newspapers. With the Episcopalians seeking to strengthen "bonds of relationship," the Standing Order had full reason to believe that their earlier suspicions of Episcopal political loyalty had been justified. Likewise, the Congregationalists, who had enjoyed legal Establishment until only five years before, resented the Episcopalians' reference to themselves as members of *The* Church and to all others as Dissenters (both correct in English usage); and this could not help but revive the old fear of Prelacy.

Wheaton returned to Hartford in November, 1824, with a mere $946.67, with which, in accordance with his instructions, he purchased scientific apparatus and books for the college library.

By March, 1824, a "general subscription" of only $10,000 had been raised. Another $20,000 had to be secured, and the location of the college would depend upon the result of the "particular" subscription. Hartford's pledges in money amounted to $10,865. But what had not been anticipated was the response from the artisans, laborers, and shopkeepers of Hartford, many of them not members of the Episcopal Church. Goods and services, translated into monetary value for the subscription list, were pledged in excess of $4,000, and this must have convinced everyone that Washington College was to be truly a community enterprise. On April 20, 1824, Hartford Town Meeting voted $5,000 for the purchase of land for the college. This brought the Hartford pledge to almost $20,000. On May 6, 1824, the trustees voted that whereas the sum of $30,000 had been raised, the college would be established in Hartford. The trustees purchased a splendid tract at West and Buckingham streets about 100 rods west of the South Meetinghouse.

Classes were scheduled to begin on September 23, 1824, but the college buildings had scarcely been started by that date, and instruction for the first nine students began in the basement of the Baptist meetinghouse.

The two buildings were ready for occupancy at the opening of the fall term in mid-September, 1825. The brownstone structures were imposing. According to later description, they followed "the Ionic order of architecture, [were] well proportioned,

The Dexter *was one of a fleet of small upriver steamboats that shuttled between Hartford and Springfield. The boats were designed low, to slip under the fixed bridges along the way, and narrow, to fit into the canal at Windsor Locks. Courtesy, Connecticut Printers*

and well adapted to the purposes for which they were designed."

Washington College, more than anything else, brought Hartford's Episcopalians into full participation in community activities. Hartford was proud of her own institution of higher learning, and during the early years of the college's existence, Town and Gown relations were pleasant. The Washington Archers, a uniformed student marching group, were usually on hand to parade on national holidays, and on several occasions members of the faculty delivered the town's Fourth of July oration. When Hartford held her Centennial Celebration in 1835, the college took a prominent part. When The Connecticut Historical Society was organized in 1825, the entire faculty enrolled as charter members. What was certainly the most obvious example of Congregationalist forgiveness of the Episcopalians for their disturbance of the status quo was that First Church allowed the college to hold its commencement exercises in its meetinghouse until the completion of the present Christ Church. Episcopalianism had done much to make Hartford a brighter, livelier, and even more "intellectual" place, but nothing would be of more significance than the Episcopalians' effort to repeal the "Circus Law" that had kept Hartford in the aesthetic backwater.

The Hartford public had always enjoyed the circus-act type of entertainment that had been disguised as "educational exhibitions," but even here there had been occasional drivings-out-of-town. And quite early the townspeople had exhibited a fondness for music, although, again, most of what was offered was passed off as "devotional."

There were exceptions, of course, as, for example, when in 1805 George K. Jackson, an Englishman, presented a series of concerts featuring selections from Handel's oratorios in the several churches. There were also occasional instrumental performances of a secular nature given in conjunction with the "dancing assemblies" held during the 1820s in the public rooms of the Exchange Coffee House or Gilman's Saloon. The new City Hall, a beautiful Greek Revival structure erected in 1829 on Market Street, boasted a large public hall on its third floor, and here, on occasion, a musical performance would be given. The legitimate theater had been dead since the first attempts in the 1790s. By the 1830s, certainly a consequence of the Great Awakening's reviving the prohibition of "frivolities," musical entertainment had degenerated to the point where it consisted solely of "sacred concerts" given by visiting groups whose offerings were chiefly subjective, revivalist hymns.

Bishop Brownell could never reconcile himself with third-rate entertainment being performed illegally and a music-starved populace being deprived of anything better because of an antiquated law. In 1837 the bishop was joined by Judge William Hamersley in circulating a petition demanding the repeal of both the Circus Law and the Theater Law of 1800. When 1,000 signatures, most of them from Hartford, had been obtained, Brownell personally presented the petition to the General Assembly, declaring that Connecticut was the only state in the Union and the only part of the civilized world in which the entertainment covered by the existing laws was forbidden. The "Brownell Petition" stirred up a hornet's nest, and the Assembly was soon flooded with defenses of the existing laws as essential to the preservation of common decency.

The General Assembly turned down Brownell's request, and, as if to make a further point, it added billiards and ninepins to the list of forbidden pleasures. In 1852, however, the Assembly relented to the extent of allowing each town or city to decide for itself whether the theater should be permitted locally. In 1853 the Hartford Common Council announced its willingness to license theaters and circuses.

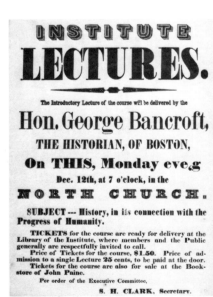

For more than 150 years Hartford has been on the "lecture circuit." The earliest city directories listed several public halls. Hartfordites could hear a prominent political figure or learn how people lived in distant lands. (CHS)

Bishop Brownell had lost his case before the General Assembly, but he, too, was able to make his point—in Hartford, at least. Although the Congregationalists would still maintain an official position against "frivolities," and the Methodist and Baptist preachers would thunder out sermons against "worldly pleasure," Hartford's attitude toward concerts and other forms of entertainment changed immediately, and almost beyond belief.

By the mid-1850s, Hartford social and aesthetic life had changed amazingly. During the social season, numerous dances were held by the "leading families." Among these the most fashionable were the Cotillion Parties—or "harmonical soirees"—held in Gilman's Saloon and the balls held by Blackford's Brass Band, the Hartford Quadrille Band, and the Hartford Brass Band. Music lovers enjoyed the annual visits of the Germania Society (a 40-piece symphonic orchestra) and Monsieur Paul Jullien's Ensemble (the principal competitor to the Germania Society).

FACING PAGE ABOVE: City Hall was used for an agricultural exhibition in October 1842. Admission was 12-1/2 cents. (CHS)

There were also concerts by Ole Bull, Adelina Patti (who appeared in Hartford in 1853 as an eight-year-old prodigy), Jenny Lind (whose one recital in Hartford was broken up by the booing victims of a ticket scalper), Louis Moreau Gottschalk, and the Pyne and Harrison English Opera Troupe. Those whose tastes had not matured beyond those of earlier decades enjoyed the appearances of the Baker Family, the "Ballad Concerts" of Mr. and Mrs. L. V. H. Crosby, the Welch Family, the Campbell Minstrels, and Davis' Ethiopian Serenaders.

The Young Mens Institute (later to become the Hartford Public Library) and the Hartford Arts Union sponsored lectures by such notables as Ralph Waldo Emerson, Oliver Wendell Holmes, and Wendell Phillips. Fanny Kemble gave Shakespearean readings, and Lola Montez, erstwhile mistress of King Ludwig I of Bavaria, lectured on "European Women." In the summer months there were almost nightly concerts by the city's bands, which had come into existence on the crest of the new enthusiasm for music. In the fall there were the Hartford County Fair (sponsored by the Hartford County Agricultural Society, organized in 1817) and the horse races at the Trotting Park in the South Meadows. Sometimes there were traveling panoramas: "The Burning of Moscow," "The City of Paris," and the ever-popular "Holy Land" and "Solomon's Temple." Not bad for a city that had once outlawed almost all performances!

Gleason's Pictorial Drawing Room Companion carried this engraving of Hartford's Main Street, circa 1845. The view looks south from the corner of State Street. The military group was probably a detachment of the Governor's Foot Guard. (CHS)

VII

The Great Age of Enterprise

~**A** FACTORY, BY DEFINI-
TION, IS A PLACE WHERE A NUMBER OF PEOPLE WORK
WITH MACHINERY IN THE PRODUCTION OF GOODS. IN A
way, the early water-powered gristmills along the Little
River would fit the description, but these small operations seldom involved more than the miller himself, a
journeyman or two, and perhaps an apprentice. The
Hartford Woolen Manufactory more precisely met the
definition, for here there were a score of workers who
used water-powered looms, and perhaps the short-lived
carding mill built on Main Street late in the 18th century and utilizing the treadmill power of dogs might also
qualify—if one cared to stretch the point a bit.

The craft-shop type of production had won Hartford
artisans a good reputation in such lines as furniture,
leather goods, and pewterware. Hartford silversmiths
were respected widely, and one of them, William
Rogers, in partnership with his brothers, Asa and
Simeon, opened a shop on State Street in 1825. Rogers

sold out in 1862 to Horace Wilcox of Meriden in the first of a long series of absorptions that would result in the International Silver Company.

In printing and publishing, too, Hartford had made a name. Hudson and Goodwin of the *Courant* took pride in having published the book version of Barlow's *Vision of Columbus* and Trumbull's *M'Fingal,* and they made a large profit from their 1780 edition of the *New England Primer* and Noah Webster's *Speller.* During the 1820s and 1830s Hartford was the textbook-publishing center of the United States, with more than 30 small firms engaged in the business.

Hartford's real publishing fame came in "subscription publishing," which was launched about 1820 by Silas Andrus. Here was a variation of the "Yankee Pedlar" operation, as agents would be sent out into the countryside with a blank-page, bound dummy of a yet-to-be-published book. Orders, accompanied by a small down payment, would be taken, and the number of copies to be printed would be determined by the number of advance subscriptions. Andrus was soon followed in this business by O.D. Cooke and Sons and Thomas Belknap.

Then came the series of quickly changing partnerships that finally became Case, Lockwood & Co., by the 1880s the largest printing house in the United States. Hartford was without question the major center for subscription publishing, and if one might wonder why Samuel L. Clemens (Mark Twain) moved to Hartford in 1871, the answer is simple: his publisher was there.

In 1819 William S. Marsh, one of Hartford's smaller printers, published John C. Pease and John M. Niles' A *Gazetteer of the States of Connecticut & Rhode Island,* a volume that has been regarded as a statistical gold mine ever since. In their description of Hartford, the compilers noted that blacksmiths and cabinetmakers were plentiful and that there were a cotton mill, 2 woolen mills, a linseed-oil mill, 6 tanneries, 5 potteries, a button-making shop, 2 tin shops, a Britannia-ware shop, a bell foundry, 15 shoe shops, 6 book binderies, 8 distilleries, a machine-card factory with a production worth $10,000 a year, a buggy-whip factory with a similar value of annual production, 2 hat factories (one employing 36 workmen), 2 looking-glass factories whose combined production amounted to $30,000 a year, and 4 coppersmiths, two of them "large scale" and the larger of the two employing some 20 men.

Hartford industry took a new turn in 1821 when the Alpheus & Truman Hanks Company, usually called the Hartford Iron Foundry, opened on Commerce Street. Production was at first limited to cast-iron plows, but a small machine shop was added in 1830. Samuel Woodruff joined the partnership in 1830, and H.B. Beach came in 1845. Eight years later the firm was reorganized as the Woodruff and Beach Iron Works. This company was the first in Hartford to become involved with steam technology, and during the 1840s and 1850s it was the largest producer of steam engines, boilers, and heavy machinery in New England. During the Civil War the plant turned out marine engines for use by the Union Navy. Despite the high reputation of the firm, Woodruff and Beach went out of business in 1871.

A similar operation was the Phoenix Iron Works, founded in 1834 by Levi Lincoln, the prolific Yankee inventor. The Phoenix first specialized in the ornamental ironwork that was an essential architectural element of the "Italian villa" style of the more pretentious Hartford residences in the decades preceding the Civil War. Phoenix later turned to the production of machinists' tools, including the widely used Lincoln milling machine, and thus was set another industrial trend that would make Hartford famous. The Phoenix Iron Works would become Taylor & Fenn.

These early industrial operations were scattered throughout the city. Those that produced chiefly for local sale and that did not depend upon water power were located on such retail streets as Main or State. Those that utilized water power were, of course, located along the Little River, and here, from that stream's confluence with the Connecticut westward for over a mile, most of the larger establishments were located. Such operations as tanning demanded proximity to flowing water, and it was in what is now Bushnell Park (the river has long since been put underground) that tanning, slaughtering, and brickmaking were carried on. And it was in the vicinity of these foul-smelling businesses that those who worked there for wages came to live in equally foul-smelling tenements.

By the 1830s Hartford's working class had already been set off, both socially and geographically, from the rest of the community. Hartford's more prosperous merchants and most of the rising industrial capitalists had homes on Morgan, Temple, Front, and Grove streets and on Lord's Hill beyond the present railroad station. Those who worked in the factories and larger shops lived in a slumlike narrow band that extended from the wharves on the Connecticut River, westward on the north side of the Little River, across Main Street at the present Wadsworth Atheneum and City Hall, and down Gold Street (then called Hotel Alley) to the warren of hovels that surrounded the tanneries.

Wages for these people were low. Skilled hands were paid $12 to $20 a month, and young men entered their lives of drudgery at between $6 and $8. For this, all worked a 12-hour day, 6 days a week—and there were no vacations.

This stage in Hartford's industrialization coincided with the rise of Jacksonian democracy, and the *Times,* staunchly Jacksonian, became the champion of the workingman, urging the "Workies" to unite in support of a 10-hour day and the Democratic Party. Perhaps because of the *Times'* encouragement, organizations made up of masters, journeymen, and apprentices were formed, but these were not labor unions in the modern sense, but, rather, self-improvement and charitable societies.

In 1836, however, something more like a modern labor union appeared as the "Journeymen Carpenters and Joiners Society." Whatever may have been the goals of the society, they were never put to the test, for in 1837 came the Great Panic, which resulted in severe unemployment. As workers were laid off, those who had been involved in any phase of the workingmen's movement were the first to be discharged. The effect of the Panic of 1837 was to set the labor movement back at least two decades.

But the efforts were not entirely in vain, as in 1855 the 10-hour day became law in Connecticut—except where both employer and employees should agree upon a longer day.

The railroad came to Hartford in 1839, and this new facility would have a profound effect upon both Hartford industry and Hartford society. The Hartford and New Haven Railroad had been chartered in 1833, and the capital of $1,500,000 had been raised in both New York and Connecticut. The early history of this line was a stormy one, for there was much opposition from both the stagecoach lines and the steamship companies. Nevertheless, Hartford soon became an important railroad center, as the line was extended to Springfield in 1844 and to New York City in 1849. During the 1850s a network of tracks connected Hartford with Manchester, Willimantic, Putnam, Norwich, and New London.

It was during the construction of the Hartford and New Haven Railroad that Hartford saw her first influx of non-English immigrants, the Irish. The first Irishmen had come to the Hartford area in the mid-1820s, when some 400 laborers from Galway and Cork worked on the series of canal locks built around the Enfield Falls on the Connecticut River about 15 miles north of Hartford. During the late 1820s and

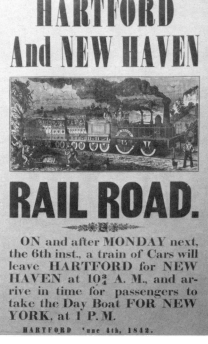

ABOVE: *From 1824 on, there was a regular overnight steamboat service between Hartford and New York. The Hartford and New Haven Railroad advertised a quicker route in 1842. (CHS)*

early 1830s, a contingent of Irish laborers had found employment in the construction of the Farmington Canal. As the completion of the canal coincided with the beginning of the railroad, most of the Irish workmen crossed Talcott Mountain to share in the backbreaking tasks of grading and laying tracks. As the Hartford and New Haven went into operation, it was usually possible for these men to stay on as members of the maintenance crews that worked out of Hartford.

The first of these new arrivals were single young men who shared rooms in the cheaper boardinghouses near the tanneries. Then came young married couples who took small quarters in the tenements. Perhaps no subsequent immigrant group was less welcome in Hartford than were these Irish. Most of them were illiterate, and none had any sort of vocational skill. Furthermore, these men had worked on the canal and the railroad for 75 cents a day and had adjusted their scale of living accordingly. Thus, they were unpopular with the resident workers, who saw a threat to their own jobs. But even the employers, who seemingly might have profited from their presence, gave no encouragement. In fact, for many years it was common to see the words "No Irish need apply" at the employment door of most Hartford factories. Nor did Hartford's black population welcome the Irishmen, for it was in the heavy lifting, loading, and digging sort of job that the newcomer was forced to compete with the black.

Only from the leaders of the Democratic Party did the Irishman receive a welcome, and even this was a qualified one. The Irishman was helped with his naturalization, for each new citizen meant a new Democratic vote, and although the politicians had little respect for the Irishman as an individual and would never have even dreamed of allowing him to run for public office, he was useful.

The arrival of the Irish saw the beginnings of the Roman Catholic Church in Hartford. As early as 1823 there had been occasional services according to the Roman liturgy in private houses and the State House, but it was not until 1828 that the Right Reverend Benedict J. Fenwick, Bishop of Boston, sent the Reverend R.D. Woodley to Hartford to organize a parish. Fenwick immediately purchased a lot on Wells Street, in the area where the Irish population had begun to congregate, but he soon learned that as the new Christ Episcopal Church was nearing completion, the Episcopalians' old structure could be purchased at a very reasonable price. Fenwick bought the building, moved it to a Talcott Street location several blocks away, and on June 17, 1830, consecrated it as the Church of the Most Holy Trinity. The Reverend James Fitton was installed as pastor.

Hartford Episcopalians had been particularly encouraging in the early efforts to further Roman Catholicism in the city, and it had been through the good offices of two Episcopal laymen, James Ward and Samuel Tudor, that Bishop John B. Cheverus had been permitted to say Mass in the State House. But an amusing incident occurred as the two bishops closed the deal on the old Christ Church building. Just before the papers were signed, Brownell said, "Well, Bishop Fenwick, as we have a fine new church building, we will let you have the old one," to which Fenwick replied, "Yes, and you have a fine new religion, and we will keep the old one." Touché!

The Roman Catholic Church prospered in Hartford, and its membership grew in proportion to the rapidly increasing Irish immigration. One of Father Fitton's first projects was to open a parochial school in the church basement. In 1839 a small burial ground was purchased at the western end of North Cemetery. Church-sponsored benevolent societies were organized to meet the economic and social needs of the Irish immigrants. By 1849 the membership had grown to such an extent that a second parish, St. Patrick's, was created, and in 1851 a beautiful Gothic St. Patrick's

ABOVE: Steamers did not attract overnight travelers only; often they were chartered for special holiday excursions and outings. In 1859 L. Boardman offered this trip to the mouth of the Connecticut River, connecting with "the cars" for New London or the boat to Long Island. (CHS)

Although he received little formal education, Samuel Colt became one of the most successful and flamboyant businessmen of his time. His accomplishments are many and include: the invention of the modern revolver, the creation of the massive Colt Patent Firearms Manufacturing Company, and the establishment of the Hartford Gas Company, but he is perhaps best known for his humane and fair treatment of his workers. From Clark, A History of Connecticut, 1914

Church was completed at the corner of Church and Ann streets. During the 1830s layman Alfred Tally published the *Catholic Press,* a weekly paper, in the basement of Holy Trinity.

The new immigration, the coming of the railroad, and a general acceptance by Hartford's business community of the idea of making Hartford an important manufacturing city infused a new spirit into the community. Population grew rapidly. From 6,901 inhabitants in 1820, the figure grew to 9,787 in 1830, to 12,793 in 1840, to 13,552 in 1850, and to 29,152 in 1860.

The railroad had done much to reduce freight costs, and Hartford's newer industries found it desirable to locate where they could use water power and also be near the railroad and use the new facility to carry raw materials and finished products. Hence, railroad spurs and sidings were extended westward along the Park River, by this time known popularly as the "Hog River" because of the pollution caused by the dumping of industrial wastes into the small stream. Also, each sizable factory attempted to provide living accommodations for the workingmen's families by building company-owned houses in proximity to the plant. These trends led to a territorial expansion of the city, as the city fathers annexed all contiguous, populated areas. In 1853 the city limits were extended both northward and southward, and in 1859 most of the Park (or Hog) River industrial sections were added. The southern line was extended to the Wethersfield town line in 1873, and additions of 1881 brought the city to its present geographical extent.

Among the largest of the new plants was the Jewell Belting Company (1845), later known as P. Jewell & Sons, which opened in the old tannery section. By the outbreak of the Civil War it was the leading industrial-belting producer in the world. Bidwell, Pitkin & Co. (1849), later Pitkin Brothers & Co., manufactured boilers, steam engines, feed-water heaters, and building-heating equipment. Sharps Rifle Manufacturing Co. (1850) purchased a 25-acre tract, then repaired the dirt road running along the river and renamed it Rifle Street (now Capitol Avenue). Sharps rifles soon earned a wide reputation. By 1860 nearly 450 men were employed, and the yearly output was 30,000 units. During the Civil War Sharps produced 140,000 rifles for the Union Army.

The largest pre-Civil War industrial operation was the Colt Patent Firearms Manufacturing Company. Although reared in Ware, Massachusetts, Samuel Colt was the son of Christopher Colt and the grandson of John Caldwell, both leaders in the Hartford business community at the turn of the 19th century. Colt (born in 1814) had little use for formal education, but by the time he was 21 he had invented the revolver, on which he secured patents in Great Britain, France, and the United States. In 1836 he opened a plant for the manufacture of revolvers in Paterson, New Jersey, with capital of $300,000 that he had raised among several New York investors. Despite government contracts for the new weapon, the company failed. Undaunted, Colt accepted more Army contracts and had the revolvers produced at the Whitney Arms Factory in Hamden, Connecticut, until 1847, when he began production in small rented quarters in Hartford, first on Pearl Street and later on Grove Street.

But Sam Colt had his eye on bigger things, and he soon began buying up land on South Meadows. On this tract Colt erected in 1855 what was probably the largest individually owned factory in the world. Along the bank of the Connecticut River, Colt constructed a huge flood dike, 15 feet high and 60 feet wide at its top, the largest flood-control project then undertaken east of the Mississippi.

Colt also built a workingmen's village of three-story buildings south and east of his huge H-shaped factory. In addition to providing comfortable homes at reasonable rentals, Colt opened a community house and library, offered an educational program, and encouraged his workers and their families to participate in sports. Colt had an extraordinary fondness for music, and this was reflected in his sponsoring Colt's Band, one of the better wind ensembles in the state and one that furnished music for the frequent summertime concerts and the many parades held in Hartford. For many years Colt's Band led the Connecticut contingent at the United States presidential inaugural parades and provided music for the commencements at Trinity College. The band was not a professional organization in the regular sense, and the members received no direct remuneration. They did, however, receive a full day's pay for any appearance in uniform. On Colt's frequent trips to Europe, he scouted for talent, looking for young men who could both play a musical instrument and work at a lathe.

Sam Colt's dike was soon grown over with willow trees, and the flamboyant industrialist came to have an odd reversion to thrifty-Yankee type. Deciding to put the willow shoots to practical use, Colt opened a factory for the production of willow furniture. When he learned that the world's best willow workers were to be found in a small village near Potsdam, Germany, Colt tried to induce a few of them to come to Hartford. None would come as individuals, but Colt offered good pay, and the entire village was induced to migrate, asking only that there be good German beer and some leisure time to enjoy music. To make the German willow worker feel completely at home, Colt built a small group of German-style homes, several of which still stand and are known as Potsdam Village.

Samuel Colt died in 1862, and the business, by this time incorporated, continued under a series of successful general managers and superintendents. His widow, Elizabeth H. Jarvis Colt, from her splendid Italian-villa-style Armsmear (now a home for widows and daughters of Episcopal clergy), presided as the *grande dame* of Hartford society until her death in 1905. In 1869 she built the Episcopal Church of the Good Shepherd, midway between the Armory and Armsmear, as a memorial to

The result of many years of hard work on the part of owner Samuel Colt, the Colt Patent Firearms Manufacturing Company grew from its meager rented headquarters on Pearl Street in 1847 to become the largest individually-owned factory in the world by 1855. From Asher & Adams, Pictorial Album of American Industry, 1876

her husband and their three children who died in infancy, and a few years later she built the Caldwell Colt Memorial Parish House of the Church of the Good Shepherd as a memorial to her son. Upon Mrs. Colt's death, the entire 140-acre tract to the southeast of Armsmear became the property of the City of Hartford as Colt Park.

Sam Colt was a capitalist, and nothing seems to have pleased him more than making money. He also was a showman, and one of his greatest pleasures was Colt's Band with its flashy military-style uniform. Colt was a social climber as well, and one of the highlights of his adventure-filled life was his presence at the coronation of Czar Alexander II. Certainly Colt was a civic-minded person, and although it might be said that having ample utilities was essential to his own industrial operations, he was one of the leading forces in setting up the Hartford Gas Company in 1849 and the Hartford Water Works in 1853. But in his own day he was best known for the humane way in which he treated his workers. Although Colt paid the highest dollar in wages and always wanted the most work for the dollar, he regarded each worker as an individual, and he never ceased trying to find ways to make his men happy and more productive.

The same could not be said for all Hartford employers of the time. Steam technology had been perfected to the point where any small plant able to supply water and fuel could be mechanized. Steam equipment was dangerous. Users of steam knew that it was dangerous, and they soon came to accept an occasional boiler explosion as one of the facts of industrial life. By the mid-1850s boiler accidents were occurring throughout the United States at the rate of one every four days, and factory owners simply regarded them as "acts of God."

On Tuesday, March 2, 1854, at 2:10 p.m., the steam boiler at the Fales and Gray Car Works on Potter Street exploded. Nine persons were killed outright, 12 died later, and more than 50 others were seriously injured.

A coroner's jury concluded that the cause of the Fales and Gray explosion was "an excessive accumulation of steam ... [and] that excessiveness of steam in said boiler was owing to the carelessness and inattention of the engineer." The jurors also offered a series of recommendations intended to prevent the recurrence of similar catastrophies: 1) regulations should be devised to prevent careless or irresponsible persons from being placed in charge of boilers; 2) regular safety inspections should be made by municipal or state authorities; 3) boilers should be placed *outside* the factories for which power is being provided; 4) employers using steam as power should pay close attention to the safety of workers; and 5) some measure should be adopted to prevent steam boilers from being rated for carrying more steam pressure than would be consistent with safety.

Each of the recommendations eventually came to be adopted by public agencies. Twelve days after the Fales and Gray explosion, the Hartford City Council appointed a committee to study steam-boiler safety, and in 1864 the Connecticut State Legislature passed a boiler-inspection law, under which all unsafe boilers would be "retired" until defects had been corrected.

Hartford's citizenry was appalled at the city's inadequate facilities for caring for a large number of injured people. Two months to the day after the explosion, a public meeting voted in favor of a public hospital, and before the end of the month the Hartford Hospital was organized. This institution soon became recognized as one of the best in Connecticut. In 1866 Hartford Hospital accepted its first intern, and in 1877 it introduced a two-year school of nursing. Readers may feel they were born a century too late when they learn that all medical and surgical services were free of charge until 1892.

ABOVE: *Francis Ashbury Pratt worked as a foreman at Colt Patent Firearms Manufacturing Company. Pratt was best known as an inventor and mechanic. Courtesy, Pratt & Whitney Co., Inc. From Cirker, Dictionary of American Portraits, Dover, 1967*

Another consequence of the Fales and Gray explosion was the organization in 1857 of the Polytechnic Club by a group of younger Hartford men associated with industries or institutions that used steam power. Elisha King Root was then superintendent of Colt's Armory, of which he later became president. Francis Ashbury Pratt was a foreman at Colt's, and Amos W. Whitney was employed in a similar capacity at the Phoenix Iron Works. These two would soon establish the Pratt and Whitney Machine Company. Edward M. Reed was superintendent of the Hartford and New Haven Railroad. Charles Brinkerhoff Richards, also of Colt's, was later to achieve international renown as an inventor of industrial machinery. Charles F. Howard was an Asylum Street merchant. Jared M. Ayres was a teacher in East Hartford. Jeremiah Merwin Allen was the steward at the American School for the Deaf, sometimes called "America's Pioneer Institution for the Handicapped," which had been founded in 1817.

Although the Polytechnic Club's stated purpose was that of "discussing matters of science in relation to everyday life," by the 1850s steam power had come to be such a part of American everyday life that it was the club's favorite topic of discussion. The members of the club reasoned that if the cause of a phenomenon were known, a remedy could be found. Steam boilers were material objects, the creation of human hands and entrusted to human hands for operation. Thus, good materials in construction, fine workmanship, careful operation, and periodic inspection to detect deterioration would virtually preclude boiler explosions.

When the Polytechnic Club learned that many of these principles had been arrived at independently in England, and that several companies had been created there for the purposes of inspecting and insuring boilers, they came to the conclusion that an inspection and insurance company on the English pattern would be both desirable and feasible. Unfortunately, the coming of the Civil War turned their attention to the immediate task of war production. In 1866, however, the Polytechnic men joined other Hartford businessmen in establishing the Hartford Steam Boiler Inspection and Insurance Company, an organization that was able to bring all the Polytechnic principles to reality.

These industrial developments did nothing really to help the labor situation in Hartford, and on the matter of the immigrants things went from bad to worse. Such large construction projects as Colt's Armory called for bringing in additional laborers, but once the factory buildings had been completed, there was no use for them inside. The wives and daughters of the Irishmen were able to find work as domestics, but the husbands were still unable to move upward on the wage ladder. Colt had brought in Englishmen and Germans, but these people had mechanical skills. There were even occasional physical clashes between the Irish and the other working people.

The immigrant question soon entered local politics. As the Whig Party declined, a new party, the American Party, sometimes called the "Native Americans" or "Know-Nothings," appeared on the scene. This organization was intensely patriotic, "nativist," and particularly opposed to Roman Catholicism. The party and its supporters were soon to be found in Hartford, and, although it could never be proved, when the Church of the Most Holy Trinity was burned in 1853, most Hartfordites agreed that the arson had been the work of the Know-Nothings.

In November, 1854, Thomas M. Day, a leading member of the American Party, purchased the *Courant*, and the paper's orientation immediately switched from Whig to Know-Nothing. Connecticut became ardently Know-Nothing and in 1855 elected William T. Minor of Stamford governor and William Field of Pomfret lieutenant governor. A year later Albert Day, a Hartford Know-Nothing, became lieute-

Amos W. Whitney co-founded the Pratt and Whitney Machine Company with Francis Ashbury Pratt in 1869. Whitney previously worked as a foreman at the Phoenix Iron Works and was known for his inventive skill in improving production methods. From Cirker, Dictionary of American Portraits, 1967

FACING PAGE, BOTTOM: *The Pratt & Whitney Company was incorporated in July 1869. Located on the north bank of the Park River, the factory was known for producing "intrinsically excellent tools of undeniable accuracy of working parts" such as the lathe pictured here. From Asher & Adams, Pictorial Album of American Industry, 1876*

nant governor. Connecticut Know-Nothings also sent William W. Welch of Norfolk and John Woodruff of New Haven to the United States House of Representatives. The party soon gained control of the Legislature, which, under Governor Minor's prodding, revised the state's constitution so as to make literacy a prerequisite for voting. Fortunately, the Know-Nothing Party was short-lived, for after the Presidential election of 1856 it disintegrated quickly. The newly founded Republican Party came forward as the political heir to the virtually defunct Whigs.

When the Civil War broke out in 1861, there was a complete reversal of attitude toward the Irish. The draft laws permitted the hiring of substitutes for those whose names had been drawn. "Substitute brokers" brought over thousands of young Irishmen, and the Hartford papers carried full-page advertisements of their availability. The Connecticut Legislature even repealed Connecticut's Prohibition law, arguing that the federal government needed the tax revenue from the sale of whiskey, but also feeling that it had made a deserved concession to the drinking preference of the Irish.

On Saturday, April 12, 1861, the Hartford telegraph office received news that the first guns of the Civil War had been fired against Fort Sumter. On the following day Hartford's churches were crowded, and each congregation, as a newspaper account read, "with heavy hearts but exultant patriotism ... sang 'My Country, 'Tis of Thee.' " In the afternoon a huge crowd gathered in State House Square, where the flag was raised and, with tears streaming down the cheeks of many, "My Country" was sung once more.

On April 15 President Lincoln, declaring that a "state of insurrection" existed, called for 75,000 three-month volunteers. Enlistments were prompt, and the Hartford Volunteer Rifles was one of the first companies to be accepted by the federal

BELOW LEFT: One of the initial enterprises in the education of the deaf began in 1816 as the Deaf and Dumb Asylum on Asylum Avenue. As enrollment grew, additional wings and porches were added. The enlarged institution is shown circa 1910. In 1920 the school moved to West Hartford and is now known as the American School for the Deaf. (CHS)

BOTTOM LEFT: Elaborate ads, complete with pictures and fancy type, helped 1861 Hartford businesses reach prospective buyers and customers. From Geer's City Directory, 1861

government. The Third Regiment was soon mustered into service in Hartford, and on May 10 and May 18 tearful crowds saw the men off to war at the Hartford Railroad Station.

Throughout the war years Hartford seemed most supportive of the war effort. Parades were held each time a new contingent of troops left for the South. Colt's and Sharps were working full steam. Irishmen volunteered for service in the Connecticut Irish Regiment (the Ninth), and scores enlisted in the two black regiments. Hartford insurance companies insured without premium all medical supplies, food, and blankets collected in Hartford and shipped to the Army by the Hartford and New Haven Steamboat Company. The *Courant,* now safely in Republican hands, and the Hartford *Evening Press* never missed an opportunity to praise the actions of President Lincoln and the Union Army. For a while it seemed that all of Hartford was working to preserve the Union. More than 4,000 Hartford men served in the Union Army and Navy, and almost 400 of them died in the service.

But that support was on the surface. Underneath, there was a pro-Southern spirit—"Copperheadism," as it was called—and it was the *Times* that kept the spirit alive. The *Times* had been pro-Democratic since the days of Andrew Jackson, and it had never deviated from that strict party line, even to the extent of openly defending the institution of slavery. On the Kansas and Nebraska question, the *Times* boldly sided with the slavocracy, and for the infamous Dred Scott Decision it had nothing but praise. Pro-Unionists were appalled that there was so much Anti-Union sentiment, and the Reverend Horace Bushnell, distressed by the active Copperhead spirit in Hartford, justified President Lincoln's suppression of habeas corpus as a legitimate perversion of the Constitution in the interest of preserving the Union.

In 1862 the Democrats, styling themselves "Peace Democrats," tried to unseat staunchly pro-Union Republican Governor William A. Buckingham of Norwich. The Democratic candidate was Thomas Hart Seymour of Hartford, Governor of Connecticut from 1850 to 1853, a veteran of the Mexican War, and U.S. Representative in Congress from 1843 until 1845. Seymour's platform was little short of treasonous, as he declared that should he be elected, federal conscription laws would not be enforced in Connecticut.

Buckingham won reelection, but Seymour was to make a second bid in 1864. That was a "Presidential year," and Lincoln's Democratic opponent was General George Brinton McClellan, the recently ousted Commander of the Army of the Potomac. McClellan had a rather strong following in Hartford. During the election campaign there were huge McClellan rallies, held in competition with the "Wide-Awake" parades of the Republicans.

News of Lee's surrender reached Hartford on April 9, 1865. A procession formed spontaneously, and the Hartford citizenry marched down Main Street headed by Christy's Minstrel Band, carriages, and fire steamers. That night almost every dwelling and commercial building in Hartford was illuminated.

In 1869 Gideon Welles returned to Connecticut after serving as Secretary of the Navy in the cabinets of Abraham Lincoln and Andrew Johnson. After an absence of eight years, he recorded in his diary:

> Hartford ... has greatly altered— I might say improved, for it has been beautified and adorned by many magnificent buildings, and the population has increased. ... A new and different people seem to move in the streets. Few, comparatively, are known to me.

These changes, and subsequent ones, will be the subject of the chapters that follow.

FACING PAGE, RIGHT:
Established in 1866 for the prevention of steam boiler explosions, the Hartford Steam Boiler Inspection & Insurance Company offered businesses protection against explosion through proper boiler inspection. From Geer's City Directory, 1867-1868

Passersby can't miss the little stove Mr. Phillips has placed on the sidewalk next to a hitching post in front of his store. Mr. Hills probably preferred to display his products indoors. (CHS)

Insurance City

~**B**OTH THE HARTFORD BANK AND THE PHOENIX BANK HAD BEEN EMINENTLY SUCCESSFUL, AS EACH SERVED A PARTICULAR CLIENtele: the Hartford's depositors and borrowers were largely Congregationalist and Federalist, and the Phoenix's were predominantly Episcopalian and Tolerationist. In 1824 the Connecticut River Company was chartered to improve navigation on the Connecticut River, and shortly thereafter the Connecticut River Banking Company was created as an adjunct to perform the normal functions of commercial banking. Because the primary company was regarded as performing an exceptional public service, the CRBC stock was to be exempted forever from taxation.

Also in 1824 the Connecticut Branch of the Second Bank of the United States was moved from Middletown to Hartford, and this brought an additional bank capitalization of $300,000 to the city. Although the Bank of the United States was the bank of deposit for the federal government, the Hartford Branch seems to have had little to do with the day-to-day financial affairs of the community. Nevertheless, it was the destruction of the bank upon the expiration on March 4, 1836, of the charter (which President Jackson refused to renew) that brought on the disastrous Panic of 1837. Furthermore, Jackson's infamous "Specie Circular," which required payment in gold or silver for all lands purchased from the federal domain in the West, prompted the Hartford banks to suspend specie payment. Fortunately, they survived the crisis.

Meanwhile, acting upon the assumption of the impending destruction of the Bank of the United States, a group of Hartford financiers had founded the Farmers' and Mechanics' Bank in 1833. It was this institution that after 1836 became the depository of federal funds for Connecticut. Obviously, the Farmers' and Mechanics' Bank was pro-Jackson. Another bank founded in the next year, the Exchange Bank, was definitely anti-Jackson, and in their petition for a charter of incorporation the Exchange promoters predicted, with amazing foresight, the Panic that would follow the coming destruction of the Bank of the United States.

The Phoenix Bank had paid a "bonus" to the State of Connecticut in return for its charter, but the matter of a bonus had been overlooked in the issuance of the charter of the Farmers' and Mechanics', thanks largely to Democratic Governor Henry W. Edwards and his legislative friends. For the Exchange Bank, however, a bonus *was* demanded, and a sizable bonus it was. On a capitalization of a mere $500,000, a payment of $15,000 was made to the State of Connecticut for the benefit of the Connecticut Silk Manufacturing Company, plus $8,000 for an iron railing around the Hartford State House.

The number of banks in Hartford and their obvious political preferences had little to do with the city's economic health, which was described frequently in the local press as "prostrated." The Whig victory in the election of 1840 brought encouragement, even to those of the Jacksonian persuasion, and the decade of the 1840s was one of growth and prosperity for banking in Hartford—so much so that a new series of banking institutions came into being as the country slowly recovered from the lingering effects of the Panic of 1837. The State Bank of Hartford was organized in 1848, and the City Bank followed three years later.

In 1852 the Connecticut State Legislature passed the Free Banking Act, which opened banking to virtually all those who chose to engage in it, and under this "easy incorporation" act were organized the Bank of Hartford County (later American National) in 1852, the Charter Oak Bank in 1853, and the Mercantile Bank in 1854. The act was repealed in 1855, but the multiplication of banks continued, and in 1857 both the Aetna and the Merchants' and Manufacturers' Bank (later the First National) were chartered.

These new ventures appeared at a most unfortunate time, for hardly had they begun operation when the nation's economy was struck by the Panic of 1857. The long period of expansion and speculation had reversed. Railroad stock, in which the banks had invested heavily, fell rapidly in value, and financial exchanges with the South and the West were seriously impeded. Money was scarce, and specie seemed to disappear.

The older Hartford banks weathered the Panic of 1857 fairly well, but the newer ones—the Bank of Hartford County, the Charter Oak, the Exchange, and the Mercantile—all went into temporary receivership, and the Bank of Hartford County was forced to reduce its capital.

The coming of the Civil War revitalized banking in Hartford, as each bank subscribed generously to the 20-year loans offered by the federal government. Also,

The Phoenix Mutual Life
Insurance Company was on
Pearl Street in 1897, on Elm
Street in 1921, and now it
occupies this striking structure
on American Row. Courtesy,
Phoenix Mutual Life
Insurance Company

under the National Currency Act of 1865 all Hartford banks except the State Bank and the Connecticut River Banking Company became "national" banks.

A new dimension was added to Hartford banking when the Hartford Trust Company was chartered in 1867. The following year, the Charter Oak Trust Company also came into existence, although, probably to avoid confusion, its name was soon changed to Security Trust. This institution would soon consolidate with the Fidelity Trust Company and eventually merge with others to become the Hartford National Bank and Trust Company, which by 1900 would be the largest banking institution in Connecticut. A similar process occurred as the Hartford Trust Company consolidated with the Connecticut Trust and Safe Deposit Company to become the Hartford-Connecticut Trust Company, which would come to serve the largest number of trust accounts in the state.

It is perhaps the savings bank that has, because of its "provident" function, been something of a link between banking and insurance operations. In 1819 Society for Savings was founded as the first mutual savings bank in the state. Its objectives were, as the bylaws read: "to aid the industrious, economical and worthy; to protect them from the extravagances of the profligate, the snares of the vicious and to bless them with competency, respectability and happiness."

Society for Savings was created by 41 public-spirited Hartford men, none of whom would have any intention of making the small, regular deposits at compound interest upon which the savings-bank idea was based. Hartford's working people quickly recognized the opportunity afforded them, and during the first six months of Society's operation, deposits, mostly in amounts of less than a dollar, amounted to $4,352.77. As the number of depositors increased, the money on deposit was lent on thousands of mortgages, and Society's resources helped start many a small business or even expand larger ones. At the time of Society for Savings' 150th anniversary in 1969, there were 248,687 accounts to the amount of $1,499,685,073. Later Hartford savings banks, all of them successful and serving a most useful function, were the State Bank for Savings, the Mechanics, and the Dime.

It is sometimes said that no Hartford bank has ever failed. The same, unfortunately, cannot be said of the city's insurance companies, but it might be noted that as Hartford's insurance people have been highly innovative, it was the unworkable innovation that on several occasions brought ruin to the investors.

Hartford's good name in fire insurance came largely from the several Hartford companies' handling of difficult problems in a most dramatic way. In December, 1834, fire swept the lower end of Manhattan Island and destroyed property valued at over $20,000,000. Most of the New York insurance companies immediately declared bankruptcy, and those that did not take this course made no immediate effort to compensate their insured. The Hartford Fire Insurance Company had relatively few accounts in New York City, but the company's losses amounted to over $60,000, a trifle compared with the total damages but still a large sum for a comparatively small Hartford company. Hartford Fire's president, Eliphalet Terry, took immediate action, and whether it was from a sense of Puritan conscience or Yankee cunning, Terry went to the Hartford Bank and offered his own sizable personal fortune in return for the bank's promise that it would honor all drafts he would make on behalf of Hartford Fire.

Upon his arrival in New York City, after a sleigh ride the entire way in sub-zero temperature, Terry announced that the Hartford would honor each and every claim made against the company. From a temporary office he wrote bank drafts to compensate the insured, and at the same time he wrote new policies for literally hundreds of

In 1899 the First National Bank constructed this building on the east end of the United States Hotel block. Ernest Flagg, who designed the chapel and the principal halls of the U.S. Naval Academy in Annapolis, was the architect. (CHS)

those who had been insured with companies that were unwilling or unable to pay. It was this incident, perhaps more than any other, that spread the good word of Hartford as the center for good insurance.

In 1845 fire again swept a portion of lower Manhattan. This time Thomas K. Brace, the president of Aetna, set up a table amid the smoldering ruins. The Hartford Steam Boiler Inspection and Insurance Company also followed this practice, as it invariably set up a table at the site of every insured building destroyed by boiler explosion, and the agents on the spot wrote policies for many times the amount paid out in damages.

When the Great Chicago Fire of 1871 virtually destroyed that metropolis, Hartford's insurance companies attempted to repeat the New York heroics. Aetna, Hartford, and Phoenix came through almost unscathed, but less fortunate were the Connecticut and the Merchants, and although the latter was rebuilt as the National, and the Connecticut met claims partially and then greatly reduced its capital, an early historian of Hartford insurance made the obviously exaggerated statement that suffering in Hartford was "second only to that of Chicago itself." After the Chicago fire, only four companies—Hartford, Aetna, National, and Phoenix—remained as licensed insurers.

But for those Hartford carriers that withstood the Chicago fire, it was their day of glory! Governor Marshall Jewell, a director and large stockholder of the Phoenix, happened to be in Detroit at the time. The Phoenix president, Henry Kellogg, sent the governor a telegram asking him to go to Chicago to assure the Phoenix's insured that all claims would be met. Jewell rushed to Chicago, where, standing on a packing crate among the still-smoldering ruins, he announced that Phoenix would pay in full all claims certified by the company's Chicago agent. It is said that the crowd was so heartened by the news that it "cheered, cried, and laughed by turns."

Still another trial of the Hartford fire-insurance business came with the San Francisco earthquake and fire of April 18, 1906, and again the companies came off remarkably well. As of January 1, 1901, there were six companies operating in the city—Aetna, Connecticut, Hartford, National, Orient, and Phoenix—to which soon were added the Automobile, Mechanics and Traders, Standard, Travelers Fire, World Fire and Marine, and the American office of the Rossia, the largest insurance company in Czarist Russia. The list could be extended by adding such smaller "mutual" companies as the Hartford County Fire Insurance Company, Connecticut Valley Mutual, and Hartford Tobacco Growers, all of which had headquarters in Hartford.

Despite Hartford's achieving preeminence in the fire-insurance line, life insurance was quite late in making its appearance. Although most Yankees had no scruples against insuring their material property against "acts of God," to insure one's life seemed to many Congregationalists to be a substitution of a human commercial agency for trust in Divine Providence. But while members of Hartford's Protestant clergy were denouncing life insurance as both impious and immoral, life-insurance companies were being set up in neighboring states, and Hartfordites began paying premiums on policies on their lives—premiums that added nothing to the Hartford economy.

Finally, in 1846, the Connecticut Legislature incorporated the Connecticut Mutual Life Insurance Company of Hartford. Other companies followed, and some of them had peculiar twists. In 1848 the Connecticut Health Insurance Company began business along lines suggested by its name, but as it had been organized without its founders' having any real understanding of projected risks and losses, it soon changed both its name and function to Hartford Life Insurance Company. This company experimented with a sort of "group insurance," whereby policies were issued for the insurance (as property) of black slaves. This phase of the business was protested angrily by Harriet Beecher Stowe and her Abolitionist friends, who staged a sit-down demonstration on the company's steps. The company stopped writing such policies, and whether from this or other concerns, it soon collapsed.

The Charter Oak Life Insurance Company (1850) met a similar fate because most of its small capital was in the form of stockholders' notes—few of which could be collected. Hardly more successful was the Continental Life Insurance Company, which, during its brief existence from 1862 until 1887, was the victim of bad management.

In 1851, at the peak of the Humanitarian Reform Movement, the American Temperance Life Insurance Company was founded to insure only those who would sign a pledge to abstain totally from alcohol. As there were just not enough non-drinkers in the area to work up an effective clientele, the company dropped its original name in favor of Phoenix Mutual Life Insurance Company and eliminated the pledge. In 1866 Connecticut General was formed to insure, at a markedly higher rate, the lives of those whom the regular life-insurance companies regarded as bad risks. The plan was abandoned after a two-year trial, and Connecticut General became a standard company.

Meanwhile, several of the fire-insurance companies had either added life insurance to their services or created subsidiary companies to pursue the business. Of these, Aetna first entered the line in 1850.

The Travelers Insurance Company began in 1863 almost as the result of a joke. James Goodwin Batterson, the Hartford architect and builder, while in England on an extended business trip, was amazed to learn that accident insurance was a popular form of protection in the British Isles. Thinking that such an insurance company

BELOW: In this view to the north along Main Street, a portion of the fence enclosing the State House grounds is visible in the right foreground. On the opposite side of the street is the Phoenix Bank. Jaywalking was discouraged by placing crosswalks of granite slabs; these slabs provided the only routes for pedestrians when the unpaved street was muddy. (CHS)

BELOW RIGHT: The design and decoration of the Exchange Bank, built in 1834 on State Street, suggests that it was a little bank with big ideas. Thirty years later this little bank became the National Exchange Bank. (CHS)

RIGHT: Phoenix Mutual Life Insurance Company, organized in 1851, advertised $11 million in assets with 30,000 policy holders. After the Chicago fire, the company held firm and paid all certified claims in full. From Asher & Adams, Pictorial Album of American Industry, 1876

could be created in Hartford, Batterson tried to interest his friends. All were skeptical. One day at noon, Batterson had been having a heated argument on the subject with James Bolton, president of the Hartford Bank. Hoping to test Batterson's sincerity on the matter of accident insurance, Bolton asked Batterson how much he would charge him for $5,000 in insurance against accidental death on his way home to noonday dinner and back to the bank. "Two cents," said Batterson, and Bolton handed him the desired sum. Bolton returned to his office safely, and Batterson retained the two cents.

Batterson made his point, a charter was received, and the Travelers Insurance Company began doing business as the first accident-coverage company in the United States. Despite the corporate name, Travelers began to write life insurance on a non-participating plan in 1865. Within a few years Travelers had entered virtually every type of insurance, becoming the first real multiple-line company in America. By 1980 the Travelers Group (the parent company and six subsidiaries) had an annual premium income of over $1,500,000,000 and ranked among the 25 largest corporations in the country.

During its earlier years the Travelers had many imitators. One of these was the Hartford Accident Company (1866), which in 1868 became a regular life-insurance company under the name of Hartford Life and Annuity Company, differing from the others only in that it made use of a "safety fund" whereby it carried its original insured according to the annuity plan until 1934.

Somewhere along the line, Hartford had become "The Insurance City." By 1981, 39 companies had their home offices in the Greater Hartford area. Combined, these companies had worldwide assets of $46,000,000,000. It was then estimated that each business day of the year saw $39,000,000 coming into the city and its immediate environs as premiums and that each year $13,000,000,000 was being paid out in claims.

BELOW: In 1931 the Aetna Life Insurance Company moved to Farmington Avenue. Since then, new buildings and extensions have created this "campus." Courtesy, Aetna Life Insurance Company

BELOW LEFT: The Travelers Insurance Company was located on Prospect Street in 1873. Travelers was the first accident insurance company in the U.S. (CHS)

BOTTOM: Incorporated in 1819, Aetna Insurance Company, "The leading American insurance company," insured against losses by fire or navigational hazards. The company added life insurance to its coverages in 1850. From Geer's City Directory, 1863-1864

CHAPTER

IX

The "New Yankees": Hartford's Minorities

~HARTFORD'S EARLIEST
BLACKS HAD ALL BEEN SLAVES WHO LIVED WITH THEIR
MASTERS, EITHER IN THEIR OWNER'S DWELLING OR IN A
small servants' building to the rear of the main house. As
Connecticut's "gradual emancipation" laws went into
effect, however, there was no longer any room for the
freed blacks at their former quarters.

Most of them, having little vocational skill and receiving little encouragement to acquire the means of obtaining a better life, found cheap rentals in scattered areas of
the city, usually a block or so on an east-side industrial
street or near the tanneries, sections known by such
names as "Hardscrabble," "New Guinea," and "Sinking
Fund." These were cheerless and unhealthy ghettos,
overcrowded and with a total lack of sanitary facilities
and pure water.

The relatively more prosperous blacks were concentrated, by the 1820s, in the Talcott Street section and on
South Green. In 1820 William Saunders opened a tailor

shop at 10 Talcott Street, a business that was to be carried on by his descendants until 1921. During the early 1820s Jeremiah Jacobs opened a cobbler's shop on South Green. Others followed, and by the 1850s there were scores of small, black-operated businesses in both of these sections. Many of them prospered, but there was considerable segregation. Hartford city directories, for example, had separate listings for blacks and whites. Black businessmen in the Talcott Street area, although they almost invariably lived at the same address as their place of business, had their residence listed among the blacks and their business listed among the whites.

The situation of the pre-Civil War blacks, as well as the attitude of those blacks who had some education and enjoyed modest financial success, may be illustrated by the case of Augustus Washington, a well-known Hartford daguerreotypist. Washington felt that there was considerable prejudice against his race in Hartford, and he found it incongruous that as a businessman he was obliged to pay taxes even though he was not allowed to vote. Washington's proposed solution to the problem was that all blacks should migrate to the new country of Liberia. Washington also observed, and probably correctly, that although blacks were treated with respect in their day-to-day business relations with whites, they were still precluded, as he put it, "from every avenue to wealth and respectability" and could neither secure employment in the government nor receive an education beyond the most rudimentary level. Washington ultimately moved to Liberia.

Traditionally, the blacks had attended white churches, where they had been seated either in the rear or in the balcony. In the early 1820s Hartford blacks began an interdenominational effort that resulted in the Talcott Street Church. One of the founders of this congregation was Jeremiah Asher, a Baptist, and when the formerly independent congregation became Congregationalist in 1833, Asher returned to the Baptist Church on Main Street, where he led a successful campaign against "Negro seating."

The Talcott Street Church's fourth minister, the Reverend James W.C. Pennington, was an escaped slave, who, thanks to Connecticut friends, received a good education and was assisted in making a trip to Europe. While in Germany, Pennington received an honorary doctorate from the University of Heidelberg. In 1850 Congress passed the Fugitive Slave Act, which ordered all United States marshals to assist in the return of runaway slaves. When Pennington's Maryland master took steps to recover his slave property, John Hooker of Hartford, a direct descendant of Thomas Hooker and a brother-in-law of Harriet Beecher Stowe, purchased Pennington from the owner for $150. Hooker held the bill of sale for two days before turning it over to Pennington, claiming that he wanted to know what it felt like to be the owner of a Doctor of Divinity.

Hartford schools, too, were segregated, but the impetus came from the blacks themselves. In the earlier years, such blacks as received any education at all were enrolled in the city's common schools. In 1830, however, the black community requested separate schools for children of their own race, and in 1833 two black schools were set up as part of the public school system. One school was at the Talcott Street Church, and the other was at the Zion Methodist Church, which had been organized on Elm Street a few years earlier. Neither of these schools offered instruction equal to that of the others within the system. The black schools were closed in 1868, and the entire public school system became integrated.

From the time of the American Revolution on, there had been considerable antislavery sentiment in Hartford. One of the earliest to speak out against slavery was Noah Webster, and it was perhaps Webster's widely circulated pronouncements that led to the organization in 1790 of the Connecticut Anti-Slavery Society. By the 1820s this society faded out, as the American Colonization Society, largely Southern in membership, grew in strength.

The American Colonization Society was not immediately concerned with the freeing of slaves, since its primary interest, an almost selfish one, was that of sending free blacks to Africa, particularly to Liberia. Although some blacks, such as Augustus Washington, were taken in by the idea, most preferred to remain in America and improve their lot here. Bishop Thomas Church Brownell, although not sympathetic with the spirit of the American Colonization Society, was concerned for the spiritual well-being of those blacks who chose to migrate. Under the bishop's direction, the African Mission School was begun at Christ Church in 1830 to train clergy for service in Liberia. The project received much publicity but little support, although three blacks who had completed the one-year program were ordained priests in the Episcopal Church. Two went to Liberia, and one served the first all-black Episcopal parish in New Haven.

In 1837 J.S. Bullock of Georgia came to Hartford to place his children in one of Hartford's private schools. In the Bullock household was a female slave, Nancy Jackson. When Bullock returned to Georgia, the children were left in Nancy's care. The black governess immediately sued for her freedom under Connecticut law, and the court decided in her favor.

As Abolitionism gained momentum in New England, Hartford blacks supported the movement with enthusiasm. August 1 became "Black Independence Day," as it celebrated the emancipation of the slaves in the British West Indies in 1827. Blacks and whites published antislavery newspapers. The *Christian Freeman* was published in Hartford for several years after 1835, and the *Charter Oak*, another Abolitionist paper, was begun in 1838. Within a year the *Charter Oak* boasted a circulation of 3,000. During the 1840s the Reverend James Pennington edited his own Abolitionist paper, the *Northern Star and Clarksonian*. William Saunders was the Hartford agent for William Lloyd Garrison's *Liberator*, although it had few subscribers in the city.

But Garrison himself was not especially popular in Hartford. On one of his few appearances in Hartford, actually at an anti-Bible rally (as the famous Abolitionist condemned the Bible because of its sanction of slavery), the meeting was broken up by the booing and jeering of Trinity College students.

Perhaps Hartford was not much given to rallies, choosing to work in a less spectacular way. As the Underground Railroad developed, Hartford became an important stop. A "Mr. Foster," who has never been identified and who may have been several persons using the name, was particularly active. It might be added, however, that those Hartford whites who were most active in the movement to free the slaves took a somewhat cynical attitude toward the freed. The Underground Railroad ran through Hartford, but the city was not the terminal. Runaway slaves were assisted on their way to Canada—not invited to remain in Hartford.

The question of slavery even entered local politics, when the Fugitive Slave Law was endorsed by a committee of Hartford Democrats. On the other hand, the Beechers, Hookers, Stowes, and others violated many a state and federal law in sending guns and ammunition to Kansas as the antislavery forces tried forcibly—even murderously—to keep slavery from the territory.

By the 1860s Hartford's blacks had developed a social life of their own. Although public lectures and entertainment were open to persons of all races, the blacks formed a social calendar around the two black churches and the Prince Hall

TOP: *The Reverend James Pennington was known internationally for his eloquent preaching and convincing commentaries, and for his part in the successful operation of the Underground Railroad by which escaped slaves made their way north to freedom. Courtesy, Connecticut Historical Commission*

ABOVE: *Pictured here is the Harriet Beecher Stowe house, on Forest Street, after its restoration in 1905. (CHS)*

Masonic Lodge. Balls were popular, and masquerades were especially so. In 1869 Hartford blacks organized a uniformed military company, the Cambridge Guard, along the lines of the Governor's Foot Guard.

After emancipation, Black Independence Day took on new meaning. In 1866 the celebration was advertised as a Grand Union Jubilee. Admission was 25 cents per person, the price including a picnic dinner with all the fixings. The day ended with a grand ball at Gilman's.

Perhaps the proudest day for Hartford blacks was the return of Connecticut's Twenty-Ninth Regiment at the end of the war. The regiment had been created in 1863, had fought in several battles, and was one of the first Union regiments to enter Richmond at the fall of the Confederate capital. The regiment's return to Hartford was a day of rejoicing, with a parade, a reception in City Hall, and a splendid banquet. On the following day, the regiment was given breakfast, paid, and dismissed. As one woman wrote: "Colored people for once can say that they have had the city."

The post-Civil War decades brought significant changes to Hartford's black community. In 1860 the reliable estimate was that only four percent of the city's blacks had come from the South. By 1870 Southern-born blacks constituted 25 percent of the black population, and by 1900 blacks who were descended from New England pre-Revolutionary families composed a very small proportion.

Having obtained the franchise, Hartford's blacks became loyal Republicans, making much of the fact that the Republican Party was "the Party of Lincoln." Although they never were encouraged, or even permitted, to run for public office, the Republican loyalty was to last for almost three-quarters of a century.

ABOVE: Pastors of the First (Center) and Second (South) Congregational churches officiated at the dedication of this little church in 1833, which at the time had just seven members. Over the years, membership in the Talcott Street Congregational Church grew and included many prominent blacks, including Deacon Holdridge Primus and, for several years, James Pennington as its minister. Courtesy, Connecticut Historical Commission

TOP: *An advertisement in*
Geer's Hartford City
Directory *in 1900 featured
"G. Grant Williams, General
Agent for High Class Negro
Literature." Mr. Williams
was officially accredited as an
agent for the magazine,* The
Young Colored American.
*Courtesy, Connecticut
Historical Commission*

ABOVE: *For a number of
years evening English classes
aided the integration of
immigrants into the Hartford
community.* (CHS)

Relations between Hartford Yankee whites and the blacks fell somewhere between "cool" and "cordial." With the Irish, however, it was another matter, because they competed with the blacks in the job market. During the mid-1830s there had been open clashes between Irish and blacks, and in July, 1834, there was what amounted to a three-day race riot.

This conflict was reflected in Hartford's political life, and the lineups that resulted in the post-Civil War decades became permanent. The Republicans had come through the war as the party of Union and respectability, while the Democrats were branded as the party of division and treason. Most Yankee Democrats switched their allegiance to the new party, and this left the Irish-Americans, who before the war had not been regarded as more than "voting fodder," in complete control, a position from which they were never to be dislodged. What few Yankee Democrats had remained were completely alienated by the party's nomination of William Jennings Bryan as the Presidential candidate in 1896. Thus, by the turn of the century, the Democratic Party had become, as one of the Hartford newspapers put it, "the party of the outs, the immigrants, the [Roman] Catholics, and the poor."

The Republicans, the Yankee party almost by default, made little effort to win the votes of most of the later immigrant groups—particularly the Poles and the Eastern European Jews. But there was a natural affinity between the Republican political leaders and the Italian-American voters. Although the alliance never went so far in Hartford as it did in New Haven—where the Democratic Party became the party of the Irish-Americans and the blacks, and the Republican Party became that of the Yankees and the Italian-Americans—it was a natural one. With the Irish control of the Democratic Party, there was little hope for Italian-American advancement with the Democrats. Also, as many of the recently arrived Italians were grocers, tailors, and shoemakers, as small businessmen they felt a kinship with the larger businessmen whose influence in Republican politics was impressive. A small business was a small business, but it was a business nevertheless.

The United States census of 1870 listed 10,644 of Hartford's population of 37,743 as "foreign born." Of these, 20 were listed as Austrian, one as Belgian, 396 as Canadian, 13 as Danish, 789 as English, 92 as French, 1,458 as German, 2 as Greek, 7,438 as Irish, 23 as Italian, 17 as Polish, 5 as Russian, 359 as Scottish, and 16 as Swedish. Ten years later (1880) the foreign born totaled 10,389 out of 42,551, with each immigrant proportion roughly that of 1870. Although to most Hartford Yankees these immigrants were still little more than "faces in a crowd," each group was making its cultural adjustment, albeit in the "halfway house" of the ethnic neighborhood. These ethnic enclaves would multiply and expand as the number of members of the respective groups increased.

The old slum by the tanneries had long since disappeared, for in the 1850s Hartford, prodded by the Reverend Horace Bushnell, had undertaken one of America's first projects in urban renewal in razing the shanties and creating Bushnell Park. The park project took almost two decades to complete, and the result was one of the most impressive municipal parks in America. But the park's greatest significance to this part of Hartford history is that it reshaped the ethnic contours of the city. South of the park, new and elegant townhouses were built along Elm Street, and newly rich manufacturers and merchants built imposing Italianate mansions on Washington Street. Blacks moved from the shanties to the "North End," which extended from Talcott Street northward along Main and Windsor streets. Irish families moved southward to the Barry Square area and the Franklin Avenue section, as developers opened one cross street after another and built three-story flats.

ABOVE: Charles Street was a cheerful minor artery of "Little Italy." Pictured here are some of the children of that community. (CHS)

BELOW: With cooperation from younger siblings, these two girls actively competed in a baby-washing contest at the Brown School Playground. (CHS)

Still-newer ethnic groups tended to concentrate in "colonies" of their own. The recently arrived Germans lived in the Park Street section. Poles located just south of the Park River between Main Street and Colt's. Lithuanians settled between Bushnell Park and Main Street. French Canadians, who began arriving at the turn of the century and by 1930 numbered 3,739 foreign born, located in the Park and Broad Street section. The Italians concentrated on the East Side along Front Street.

Each of these communities preserved some of the flavor of its old culture, and as most of the people were Roman Catholics, parish organization came to be along ethnic lines. Of these groups it was the Italians who preserved the greatest portion of their national heritage, so much so that the East Side was known as Little Italy. Here, in an area of some 10 or 12 city blocks, were Italian markets, small Italian restaurants (several ranked among the finest in town), and the shops of numerous barbers, tailors, and cobblers. Little Italy was the scene of many a colorful religious festival held by St. Anthony's Roman Catholic Church or the small Episcopal Church of St. Paul.

Hartford's Chinatown consisted, early in the 20th century, of about 20 Chinese business establishments on the south side of State Street between the Old State House and Front Street. Here were several small Chinese restaurants and Chinese import stores. The back rooms of some of these places functioned as opium dens.

Hartford's Jewish population was late in concentrating geographically. Jews were never strangers to Hartford following the unfortunate encounters with the law of "David the Jew" in 1659, for as early as 1661 several Jews were living in the home of John Marsh, and the town and city records suggest that a Jewish presence was constant from that point on. These were Sephardic Jews, originally from Spain or Portugal. Several were horse traders, while others were peddlers who worked out of Hartford selling small housewares in the back country.

These early Jews were quite inconspicuous. After all, the early Congregationalists have been described as "Old Testament" Christians, and the affinity between the two religions (especially the "thou shalt nots" and Sabbath observances) is obvious. The Connecticut Constitution of 1818, however, did not give freedom of religion to non-Christians, and it was not until 1843 that Jews were allowed to worship publicly. By that year there were enough Jews in Hartford to organize the first congregation (Reform), Beth Israel, with about 200 members. Beth Israel took over the former Baptist Church on Main Street, renamed the building Touro Hall, and used it as both a religious and social center until a handsome synagogue was built on Charter Oak Avenue in the 1870s. Beth Israel's first rabbi, Isaac Mayer, served as drama critic for the Hartford *Times*.

The German Jews were accepted easily into Hartford's city life, and by 1860 two members of this faith, Alexander Rothschild and Marcus Herlitscheck, were elected to the city council. German Jews soon became active in the legal and medical professions.

A second wave of Jewish immigration came late in the 19th century, when persecution was intensified in Russia, Poland, Lithuania, Hungary, and Rumania. These Eastern European Jews were largely Conservative, often less skilled vocationally than the earlier Germans (although some were expert furriers, cabinetmakers, and metalworkers), and much more inclined to live in ethnic areas. These newer arrivals formed neighborhoods along Main Street and Albany Avenue. By 1910 some 80 percent of Hartford's Jews were of Eastern European origin.

Immigration has had varied social effects upon American cities, but the immigrant has been blamed for creating conditions of which he had no part and in

TOP: *After almost 30 years of holding services at the old First Baptist Church on Main Street, the Congregation Beth Israel purchased land on Charter Oak Avenue and erected this synagogue in 1876. (CHS)*

ABOVE: *In one area of the marketplace, a rabbi dispatches a chicken in accordance with prescribed Jewish ritual. (CHS)*

which he was the victim rather than the cause. The immigrant, for example, did not make the slum; the slum already existed when the immigrant arrived, and, as he was usually poor at the time of his arrival, he was obliged to take whatever housing he could afford. Regarding Hartford, it may safely be said that the coming of the immigrant reduced the total area of slum districts rather than expanding it. Each of the ethnic neighborhoods had a pride that encouraged both landlords and renters to do their best to present the most favorable image of the groups.

By the 1890s one really decrepit slum remained, Gold Street, which bordered on the south side of the Ancient Burying Ground and what was left after the greater part of the poorest section of town had been taken over by Bushnell Park. Gold Street was then a dirty, narrow alley, the city's "red light district," and the habitat of the poorest of Hartford's poor.

Emily F.G. Holcombe, the wife of John M. Holcombe, president of Phoenix Mutual Life Insurance Company, decided that the Gold Street slum would have to go. Enlisting the support of the pastor of First Church, the Reverend George L. Walker, "The Gold Street Woman," as the crusader had come to be known, persuaded the city authorities that Gold Street would have to be rehabilitated. The worst of the buildings were torn down, and others were rebuilt. The street was widened, and the space between the street and First Church was planted in grass and shrubs. The passing of the last of Hartford's old slums was celebrated on April 21, 1899, when speeches were made by clergy and civic leaders, and Colt's Band led the assembled crowd in singing *Praise God, From Whom All Blessings Flow.*

Continued immigration to a city always has the effect of what sociologists call "cushioning." Each new group takes the low-paid, menial jobs at the bottom of the work force, and the arrival of each new group pushes the older group up a notch on the vocational scale. This was certainly true in Hartford, for by the end of the century, the Irish, who had been present for three-quarters of a century, had moved to a position of dominance in city politics, the police force, and the fire department and enjoyed considerable success in business and the professions.

Only once since the Civil War did Hartford's Irish become suspect. That was in the 1890s, when statewide Protestant clergy and laymen organized the American Protection Association. The APA began in New Britain in 1893, and within the year a local "chapter" appeared in Hartford. The APA was something of a throwback to the Know-Nothing movement of the 1850s, as it denounced the Irish Roman Catholics as being more loyal to Ireland and the Roman Catholic Church than they were to the United States. The Bridgeport *Independent Leader* was the APA propaganda outlet, but it found its opposition in Hartford's *Connecticut Catholic,* the predecessor of the *Catholic Transcript.* A significant piece of symbolism was effected by the new Bishop of Hartford, the Right Reverend Michael Tierney, who chose Washington's Birthday, 1894, as the day of his consecration in the new (1892) Cathedral of St. Joseph on Farmington Avenue. Although the bishop made his point in his sermon for the occasion that the Irish were just as good and loyal Americans as were the Yankees, the sermon brought an end to one of Hartford's most colorful traditions, the St. Patrick's Day Parade. Both the bishop and the *Connecticut Catholic* took the position that the parade had outlived its usefulness and that Ireland's patron saint should be honored with banquets and "intellectual exercises." Fortunately, the American Protection Association soon thereafter passed out of the picture, but so, too—unfortunately—did the St. Patrick's Day Parade.

Certainly it was the constant immigration that swelled Hartford's population, which by 1900 had reached 79,850, of whom 23,219 were foreign born. Ten years

ABOVE: *From the 1860s to the 1890s, horse cars offered Hartford folk reliable public transportation. From the Melvin Collection (CHS)*

BELOW: *It was easier to lay rails than to pave streets in 1862, when the Hartford and Wethersfield Horse Railway Company was organized. Its name pretty much described its route—along Main Street and Wethersfield Avenue, from Spring Grove Cemetery to the center of Wethersfield, which was a distance of about 4.5 miles. (CHS)*

later, when Hartford's population stood at 98,915, immigrants and the children of immigrants composed 67 percent, a proportion just below that of New Haven (69 percent), Bridgeport (72 percent), Meriden (72 percent), and Waterbury (74 percent).

The increase in population was reflected in the geographic spread of the city, and from the time of the Civil War it was no longer possible for the workers of a particular business or factory—Colt's excepted—to live within walking distance of the work place. Also, as wealth increased, those who prospered were no longer satisfied to live in the older residential sections of the city. The Nook Farm colony to the west and Washington Street to the south provided examples of locations that combined some of the advantages of country living with urban proximity. No longer was Hartford a "walking city," the term applied by urbanists to one with a radius of less than a mile.

All these shifts were dependent upon transportation, and it was the horsecar that had made them possible. Since 1863 the Horse Car line had operated between State House Square and the Wethersfield Green. Lines were soon extended in several directions. One followed Retreat Avenue to Vernon Street, and from there by Broad Street back to the center of the city. Another ran from Park Street to Central Row, then down State Street to the Connecticut River. A third line ran the length of Albany Avenue. In 1884 service was extended north on Main Street to Capen Street, and in 1885 a line was constructed across the bridge to East Hartford Center. By the mid-1880s the horsecar line represented the ultimate in intraurban transportation, although the unpaved streets of the time were described as a mixture of mud and manure. Riding in such conveyances was far from comfortable—bad odors in the summer and insufferable cold in the winter—but the possession of a horsecar line was one of the features that distinguished the city from the town.

The Capital of Connecticut

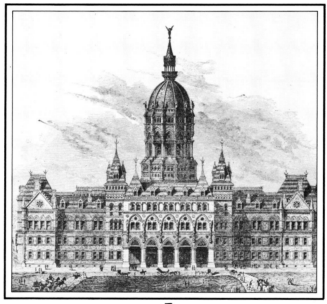

~IN 1870 HARTFORD BE-
CAME INVOLVED IN A CONTEST WITH NEW HAVEN AS
TO WHICH CITY SHOULD BECOME THE SOLE CAPITAL OF
Connecticut. The Charter of 1818 had retained the
arrangement whereby alternate legislative sessions were
held in New Haven and Hartford, but in the late 1860s
there was considerable agitation for a single capital,
especially since the state government had expanded its
functions through the creation of bureaus and commissions that were much in need of office space. Furthermore, the State Houses in Hartford and New Haven
were both in need of repair. Hartford seized the initia-
tive and offered the state $500,000 toward the erection
of a new capitol, and Hartford officials proceeded at
once to take steps to acquire the Trinity College campus
for its location.

A public meeting was held in Hartford on March 11,
1872, to sound out public opinion as to how high a price
might be offered. Although Hartford's municipal debt

then stood at $3,000,000, the sense of the meeting seemed to be in favor of purchase, even if the offer should reach $600,000. The Board of Aldermen consequently voted to purchase the Trinity Campus for $600,000, and on March 21, 1872, the college trustees accepted the offer.

Although the trustees were uncertain as to where the college would relocate, they sent President Abner Jackson to England to engage an architect for a complete, new campus and authorized him to commission a preliminary plan from any architect he might select.

Jackson engaged the services of London architect William Burges, and in September, 1873, he returned to Hartford with the most elaborate plan yet designed for an American college campus. Had the plan been completed, it would have been, as one Hartford paper boasted, "next to the Capitol at Washington, the most imposing edifice in the United States." In both spirit and detail, the Burges plan was executed in what would now be called "Victorian Gothic."

On October 12, 1872, the trustees decided in favor of a Vernon Street site and agreed to pay $225,000 for it. The trustees also voted to begin construction in April, 1874. To be completed in the first stage of development were a portion of the chapel sufficient to accommodate the current student body, the library, the dining hall, one block of lecture rooms, and two sections of dormitories. To superintend the actual building, the trustees engaged the eminent Hartford architect F.H. Kimball, who had recently been in charge of the construction of the Connecticut Mutual and the Charter Oak Life Insurance Company buildings.

On Commencement Day, July 1, 1875, Bishop John Williams turned the first sod, and excavation began immediately thereafter. During the winter of 1877-1878 the final touches were put on the new buildings, and on Friday, May 17, 1878, instruction was begun on the new campus. During the summer of 1878 the old buildings were demolished quickly.

The Trinity College part of the story had a happy ending, but the same could hardly be said of the new State Capitol. This was a story of bureaucratic bungling, naive aesthetic taste, and, of course, waste. In 1871 a commission was appointed by the legislature to solicit architectural plans and to make an appropriate selection. Five designs were submitted, but the committee could not agree, and the members resigned in 1873. A new commission was appointed, and this time 11 plans were offered. But again what made the selection process a particularly difficult one was the matter of basic architectural style.

The state capitols that had been erected from the Jeffersonian era on had all been executed in the Classical Revival style, whether Greek or Roman or a combination of the two. By the 1870s, however, "Gothic Revival" had become the vogue, as evidenced by the plans for Trinity College then being drawn by Burges, and "Gothic," or some variation thereof, was a popular choice for dwellings and such buildings as city halls or public libraries. The trouble was that state capitols had never been built in "Gothic." It just wasn't done. But the commission would have it no other way. A "Gothic" capitol it would be, and the design selected was that of Richard Upjohn, an architect who had wide experience in academic and ecclesiastical buildings but who never in his life had designed a state capitol, or, for that matter, any sort of government structure.

The original plan was for a Gothic, somewhat churchlike building with a steeple, but capitols did not have steeples, and there was immediate public opposition to the idea. Upjohn next proposed a clock tower, but again public pressure convinced both the architect and the commission that all capitols have domes—not clock

Architect Richard M. Upjohn originally designed a Gothic-style state capitol with a steeple. But because of public pressure in favor of the traditional dome, the design was altered and the resulting building, completed in 1880, is a Gothic building set off by a gold leaf Roman dome. (CHS)

towers—so, a dome it would be, regardless of the incongruity of a gold-leaf Roman dome on a Gothic, quasi-ecclesiastical edifice. Although the result was garishly handsome, Frank Lloyd Wright, the renowned American architect, described it as the most ridiculous building he ever had seen.

But the problems were not only with the design, for at all stages of construction there were also technical difficulties. When the masons had halfway completed the tower over the Grand Court, everything gave way, and the partially completed dome tower came down in a great mass of rubble. Work had to start all over again. Other less spectacular disasters slowed down the speed of construction and greatly increased the cost. The original estimate for the entire building was $900,000. When it was finally finished in 1880, the total amount spent was just short of $3,000,000.

Whatever its aesthetic deficiencies may have been, the new Capitol stood as the symbol of Hartford as The Capital City. Hartford's city fathers, as well as the citizenry, acquired a new civic pride, and one of its first manifestations was the largest gathering yet held in Hartford, and this even before the new Capitol had been completely finished.

September 17, 1879, the anniversary of the Civil War Battle of Antietam, had been designated by the Connecticut Legislature as Battle Flag Day. The principal event of the celebration was a mammoth parade in which the Civil War battle flags were carried from the old Hartford Arsenal to the State Capitol, where they were placed in permanent display cases. Following the parade there were addresses by visiting dignitaries, and then followed a sumptuous dinner, at which, in tents pitched in Bushnell Park, thousands of veterans and their friends consumed literally tons of food. At 7 p.m. began a "grand illumination," and it was estimated that of the 100,000 persons who witnessed the parade, some 30,000 remained in Bushnell Park for the evening display.

The "illumination" was the brainchild of Morgan G. Bulkeley, the president of Aetna Insurance, and there were those who attributed Bulkeley's election in 1880 as mayor of Hartford to the success of this event. From the Willimantic Linen Company's plant were brought the six arc lights that were placed strategically about the

LEFT: *Small college that it was in 1873, Trinity found the Burges design overly ambitious, and only a part of his planned complex was actually built. Courtesy, Trinity College*

BELOW LEFT: *The* City of Hartford *was renamed* Capitol City *after the steamboat line was reorganized in 1882.* Capitol City (*under one name or the other*) *provided comfortable accommodations and dependable service from 1852 to 1886.* (CHS)

State Capitol. Power was provided by a small engine borrowed from the Colt factory. On the roof of the Plimpton Building on Jewel Street was placed a 3,000-candlepower searchlight, equipped with colored-glass lenses that could transform the beam into green, red, blue, or purple, and so mounted that its light could be directed at random about Bushnell Park and the lower part of the city.

From 7 o'clock until 10, the amazed and delighted spectators, seated upon blankets on the park's grassy slopes, watched the searchlight play on the Ford Street Bridge, the Capitol, the decorated arches, the fountain, and at random about the park. "Now and then," as the *Courant* reported, "the light would strike some unexpected spot, and there would be a slight scream and a lively scramble as some affectionate couple who had been seated near together on the river bank would find themselves in daylight and beat a retreat."

The following day the lights were returned to Willimantic and the engine to the Colt factory. For most of those who had witnessed the electrical display, the evening of September 17 had been one of entertainment, splendid entertainment, but nothing more. For those interested in the economic potentiality of electricity, however, a new age had begun. Hartford would soon demand public electrical service. The city was ready for the new Electrical Age.

Hartford at that time was thriving as an important banking, industrial, insurance, and wholesale-distribution center. During the year 1880, more than 500 steam vessels and 270 barges had dumped thousands of tons of coal, lumber, salt, iron, fertilizer, dyewoods, potatoes, cement, lime, and other commodities on the river docks of Hartford, certainly a significant volume for a minor, inland river port.

Geographically, the city was still confined to a radius of two miles from the Old State House, which had just then become Hartford's City Hall. The commercial area extended some eight city blocks from the Connecticut River westward to the railroad depot at the foot of Asylum Hill, and from Sheldon Street on the south to Belden Street to the north. Residential areas had sprawled in each direction along the main traffic arteries toward Wethersfield, New Britain, Farmington, and Windsor.

BELOW: *The handsome and new Hartford public high school as it appeared in the 1880s.* (CHS)

Transportation was well provided for. Regular steam-packet lines ran between Hartford and New York, and connecting lines provided accommodation to Boston, New London, or Providence. Railroads also offered service to Boston, New York, Providence, and Springfield. For intraurban travel, there were horsecar routes serving the outlying sections. Public hacks served short-term travel needs, and 21 livery stables offered horse-drawn vehicles for hire. Visitors were accommodated at the 21 hotels, which ranged from the palatial Allyn House to flophouses, and there were 144 saloons.

Police protection was insured by a force of 45 patrolmen, and the fire department employed almost 100 men. Sanitary engineering was a science then in its infancy, and the inadequacies of the sewerage system were a constant vexation to householders. The water system was much more satisfactory; from six reservoirs, a daily average of 6,000,000 gallons flowed through 70 miles of underground pipes to 4,962 homes, business houses, and industrial concerns.

Hartford streets were, for the time, well lighted. Since 1821, when a few feeble oil lamps had first been installed at public expense, the City had accepted responsibility for providing street illumination, and since the incorporation of the Hartford City Gas Light Company in 1849, the number of gaslights had risen steadily until 1880, when more than 1,000 jets gave off their yellow glow along 80 miles of city streets.

There was a splendid school system, culminating in Hartford Public High, and there were several proprietary academic operations that offered training in the "commercial branches." There were also the Theological Institute of Connecticut—chartered in 1854 and soon to become the Hartford Theological Seminary—and Trinity College. Fifty-two churches and synagogues ministered to those of almost every religious persuasion. Local and world news was provided in 11 weekly or daily papers. Magazines directed toward religious, vocational, and educational interest were also published in Hartford, and the city was, with its 24 printing houses, enjoying the last glow of her golden day as an important publishing center. Telegraph service had been available since the early 1850s, and the first telephones had been installed in 1878.

Several of the city's industries were nationally known. Colt's Patent Fire Arms Manufacturing Company, the Weed Sewing Machine Company, Hill's Archimedean Lawn Mower Company, and the National Stove Company were among the major manufacturing plants. Altogether there were 800 factories of all sizes and descriptions—foundries, breweries, tanneries, machine-tool works, and woodworking shops, to name but a few—and in 1880 they paid wages of $8,457,000 to 20,951 employees.

Hartford had entered the Electrical Age with Battle Flag Day, and it was assumed that electricity would soon be available commercially. The question was who would provide it.

Hartford investors soon became eager participants in starting the American Electric Company, formed in New Britain late in 1880, but this company was involved in producing electrical systems, not in supplying electrical service from a central power station. Consequently, a power struggle began for investor support and legislative favor between the older-type utilities and the promoters of yet-unborn companies to be created for the specific purpose of supplying electrical service.

Hartford's oldest utility was the Hartford City Gas Light Company, and, as it was assumed that much of the city's electricity consumption would be in street lighting, the gas company regarded itself as the logical producer of electricity. The company had supplied street illumination as well for more than 30 years, and it had pro-

TOP: In 1889 Sage, Allen and Company began at the corner of Main and Pratt streets. Later, the company moved into larger quarters on the other side of Main. Today, it is one of Hartford's finest department stores, with branches in several Connecticut towns and shopping malls. (CHS)

ABOVE: The new Union Station in 1889 with its elevated tracks alleviated the hazardous traffic situation at the foot of the Asylum Street hill. (CHS)

vided much of Hartford's indoor illumination as well. In 1880 it also had some 800 cooking stoves connected to its lines. In March 1881 the gas company petitioned the Connecticut Legislature for a charter amendment to permit it to produce and distribute electricity within its gas-franchise territory.

Hartford's second utility company was a newcomer. The Hartford Steam Heating Company had been chartered on March 25, 1879, to furnish steam through underground pipes for heating and power. Pipes were laid through the principal business streets during the summer of 1880, and the system was put into operation that fall. Leakage of steam accounted for both bad service and costly operation, and by the spring of 1881 there was reason to believe that the $500,000 business venture had been a failure. The steam company nevertheless felt that its Pearl Street plant could be utilized in the generation of electricity, and in the spring of 1881 it, too, petitioned for a charter amendment to permit the sale of electricity as a sideline.

There were those in Hartford who felt that the best interests of the city would be served by an electric company operating independently of both the City Gas Light Company and the Steam Heating Company. One of them was Mayor Bulkeley, who began making plans for an independent company. Bulkeley persuaded both of the utility companies to abandon their plans, and on April 12, 1881, the Hartford Electric Light Company was incorporated by act of the Connecticut State Legislature. In June of 1881 American Electric installed a lighting system in the Allyn House. Shortly thereafter, the American Theater on Market Street installed a single outside arc light. The theater's newspaper advertisements always read, "Look for the Electric Light"—a light that provided enough illumination for the theater's pit band to read music in the short sidewalk concert that preceded each evening performance.

Bulkeley's position as mayor of Hartford raised the question of conflict of interest, and the Hartford Electric Light Company got off to a late start. Nevertheless, when the company's subscription books were opened on January 12, 1882, there were sales of 200 shares, at $100 each, totaling $20,000, hardly a working capital for even the most miniscule corporate undertaking. Only 20 percent of this amount was to be put up immediately, and even this was not paid in cash but was represented by real estate or secured notes. On February 6, 1882, the directors held their first session and elected A. C. Dunham as president and Sylvester C. Dunham as secretary.

In late May, 1882, an agreement was made whereby the Light Company would have steam supplied by the Steam Heating Company's boilers. By the evening of Saturday, April 7, 1883, all was ready, and at sundown lights were turned on at the depot, at Rathbun's Pharmacy, Marwick's Drug Store, Goerz Brothers' Saloon, Conrad's Bakery, and Mansuy's Carriage Shop at 17 Elm Street. On Pearl Street, a single streetlamp was exhibited in front of the company's plant. It was not an imposing exhibition, but the Hartford Electric Light Company was at least in business.

The Hartford newspapers commented most favorably on the inauguration of service, and Hartford businessmen, too, evidenced their support of the new enterprise, as in rapid succession lights were installed in Brown-Thomson's "One Price Clothing Store," Cadden's Clothiers, Heublein's Saloon, and Smith, White & Co.'s furnishings store. In less than a month four dynamos were in operation, and 100 lights had been subscribed.

On January 14, 1884, the Common Council voted to accept the Hartford Electric Light Company's proposal for street lighting and to give the experiment a six-month trial. On the night of May 2, 1884, 26 streetlights were put into service, as the Courant reported, "to the satisfaction of all who witnessed the display." And certainly the achievement was a proud one for the city, for the Courant further added that

ABOVE: Hartford has always given visitors a wide range of hotels from which to choose. The Heublein Hotel was one of the better ones; its dignified comfort is apparent in this picture of the lobby. (CHS)

BELOW: The Thorne typesetting and distributing machine revolutionized the print industry with its quick and efficient rotary operation. Hartford publishers such as the Evening Post, Forum, and Current Literature took advantage of this progressive device to aid them with their publications. From Hartford, Connecticut, 1889

After the Civil War, Weed Sewing Machine Company rented unused sections of the struggling Sharps Rifle Company. Branching out from its usual sewing machine production, Weed in 1878 took a contract to produce bicycles. From Hartford, Connecticut, 1889

These two photographs were taken 25 years apart. One was in 1888, a day or so after the blizzard, and the other was in the 1910s. Both look east on Asylum Street from the corner of Trumbull. Some new construction and facade changes in the block are evident in the second view. (CHS)

Hartford was at last "on a par with its sister cities." Hartford's first 26 arc lights installed on the city's streets had displaced 163 gas lamps. Even at this early date it was agreed that the brighter lights would help reduce crime and that the savings on police-department budgets could pay for the additional cost.

Late in 1884 the Schuyler Electric Light Company moved its office and factory from New York City to Hartford. Schuyler was one of the smaller incandescent-system manufacturers, but its location in Hartford more or less established the city as a minor center of electrical-equipment manufacture. The Waterhouse Electric and Manufacturing Company was organized in January, 1886, by Hartford industrialists who had connections with such well-established firms as Colt's, Pratt and Whitney, and Billings and Spencer. Five of the directors were described by *Electrical World* as "mechanical experts." The Waterhouse plant was set up in Colt's Armory. Two other small electrical manufacturers soon were to operate in Hartford—the Mather Electric Light Company and Eddy Electric.

On May 24, 1887, David Henney secured a charter for the Hartford Light and Power Company, but only after vigorous opposition by the gas company, Hartford Electric Light, and the Hartford business community. The Hartford Light and Power Company never was really able to get its house in order, and throughout its decade of existence it suffered one embarrassment after another. In one instance, however, the Hartford Light and Power Company was able to pull off a spectacular coup—that of supplying electric power for the Hartford and Wethersfield Horse Railroad. Early in 1888 Elizur J. Goodrich, president of the Horse Railroad Company, announced that a contract had been drawn up to purchase cars and that an arrangement had been made with Hartford Light and Power to provide electricity.

On September 21, 1888, the first electrified car made the run from the car barns at 109 Wethersfield Avenue in Hartford to Main and Church streets in Wethersfield. The run was made in 20 minutes and the return in 18. With horses, the round trip had always taken a full hour. Electrification of the horsecar line spread rapidly, and by 1892 the last of the horses had been retired.

The Hartford Electric Light Company took over the Pearl Street Station of the Light and Power Company in March, 1896, and the two systems were completely

integrated without interruptions of service for the customers of either company.

These developments, small as they may seem when considered individually, were symptomatic of a general acceptance of electricity. By 1890 electricity had become very much a part of Hartford's way of life, as the city streets were by then entirely lighted by electricity, several hundred homes were lighted by incandescent lamps, most of the downtown stores had been equipped for either arc or incandescent lighting, electricity was propelling streetcars, and in a few industrial plants electricity as a source of power at least had gained a foothold.

Electricity had become, by the 1880s, one of the appurtenances of urban living, and by the 1890s the same could have been said of the electric car. In the first decade of the 20th century, it would be the automobile, and here Hartford would write a small and curious chapter in the history of American technology. The story is simple, short, and sad.

Following the American Civil War, Sharps Rifle Company fell upon hard times, and as production declined sections of the plant were rented out to the Weed Sewing Machine Company and other manufacturing concerns. In 1870 Sharps was sold to P. T. Barnum, the famous showman, and production operations were moved to Bridgeport. The Weed Company then took over the entire Sharps building. Weed, as Sharps had done before, leased portions of the plant to other concerns, but Weed itself took contracts with numerous manufacturers for the production of machinery having nothing to do with the sewing machine. One such contract was with Albert Pope of Boston for the production of bicycles, the "Columbia," the first such contraption to be produced in America. George H. Day of Hartford, reputedly a "mechanical genius," was placed in charge of Pope's bicycle department.

Pope, meanwhile, was experimenting with machinery far more complex than the bicycle and, assisted by Day, he completed several prototype horseless carriages. In 1890 Pope purchased the Weed Company and changed its name to the Pope Manufacturing Company. Day became vice president and treasurer of the company. Hiram Percy Maxim was hired as his chief engineer, and in 1895, Pope, Day, and Maxim produced their first gasoline-engine automobile, the Pope-Hartford. Historians of technology agree that this production marked the beginning of the auto-

In the 1880s, Billings and Spencer Company, organized by Charles E. Billings, manufactured many steel tool items which were used in other manufacturers' products. From Hartford, Connecticut, 1889

These two photographs of Main Street were taken just two seasons apart. Looking south from Mulberry Street, it was business as usual in the fall of 1887. In March of 1888 the Great Blizzard struck. Rails were out of sight for a week, but public transportation was resumed when the wheels were taken off the horsecars and replaced with sleigh runners. (CHS)

mobile industry in the United States. Had the Pope Company limited its production to internal-combustion-engine cars, Hartford, rather than Detroit, might have become the automotive capital.

Pope's preference, however, was for the electric automobile, and in 1897 the company began producing the Columbia Electric. In 1899 the editor of an English technical journal declared Hartford to be "the greatest center of activity in the automobile industry today." Pope's choice was a bad one. The electric automobile was then simply not practical. Furthermore, the Pope Company became involved in a lawsuit with Henry Ford, and Ford won his case. By 1912 the Pope Company was defunct.

Oddly, considering that Hartford was so much involved in automobile production, the "newfangled machine" was slow in being accepted by residents of the city. As streetcar service was excellent and railway service was of the highest standard, many Hartfordites preferred to use public transportation rather than purchase an automobile.

The Pope-Hartford was a handsome automobile, but it was expensive, and for those who preferred to "buy Hartford," it was a choice between a Pope-Hartford and no car at all. Then, too, there was the influence of the Hartford Electric Light Company, which shared Thomas A. Edison's belief that the electric automobile would triumph over that fueled by gasoline. It was in this confidence that a small fleet of electric cars was built up to completely replace the horse-drawn vehicles that had served for 20 years as the standard equipment for Hartford Electric Light.

In 1909 the Light Company took the Hartford sales agency for the General Vehicle Company, a Long Island City, New York, manufacturer of electric trucks. But the "G. V.," despite considerable advertising on the part of the company, did not become popular. Although Hartford Electric Light was able to provide complete repair and battery service for battery-driven vehicles, there were, during the first year, only three electric trucks, other than those owned by the company, under the vehicle department's care. And somewhat ironically, at about the same time that the Hartford Electric Light Company began its full-scale battery-charging service, the company began replacing its own electric cars with gasoline-driven Fords. In 1912, in fact, the Elmer Automobile Company, the Hartford Ford agency, featured a picture of the Hartford Electric Light Company's fleet of Fords in one of its advertisements. Although the company kept a nominal "G. V." agency through World War I, few trucks were sold, and in 1922 Hartford Electric Light began to liquidate this phase of its operations.

Horses long remained a part of everyday life in Hartford. As late as 1910 several pieces of Hartford's fire-fighting equipment were horse drawn, and trash collection was completely by horse and wagon. Even at that late date there were several livery stables with horses for hire, and there were still 20 blacksmiths plying their trade in the city.

A *pioneer in the manufacture of bicycles in America, Albert Augustus Pope contracted Weed Sewing Machine Company to build the "Columbia," the first American-made bicycle, in May 1878. An advocate of electric automobiles, Pope turned from bicycles to manufacturing "Columbia Electric" automobiles in 1897. From Cirker,* Dictionary of American Portraits, *Dover, 1967*

Albert Pope's greatest contribution to Hartford was his gift to the city of the 75-acre Pope Park in 1895. This large expanse was close to the Pope factory, and it served as the recreation grounds for the thousands of working-class families who occupied that part of the city southwest of the State Capitol.

Significantly, Pope Park was created while the Reverend Francis Goodwin was chairman of the Hartford Park Commission. Goodwin operated with the slogan of "More Parks for Hartford," and his plan was to have Hartford circled by parks much like the Fenway System then being laid out around Boston. At the same time that Pope Park was being developed, Goodwin persuaded Charles N. Pond to donate his large estate in the northwestern part of the city as Elizabeth Park, in memory of Pond's wife. Goodwin also persuaded Henry Keney to donate Keney Park in the North End. It was appropriate that Goodwin Park in Hartford's extreme southern end, and which completed the city's major park system, should have been named for the indefatigable commissioner.

The impetus toward parks and open spaces was paralleled by the construction of handsome new business buildings—particularly newer headquarters of the Hartford banks and insurance companies. These structures were of neoclassical design and invariably were built of granite or marble. All of this was something of a reflection of the "City Beautiful" movement that stemmed from the neoclassical architecture of the World Columbian Exposition of Chicago in 1893, and whose influences were felt in virtually every municipality in the country. In 1907 Hartford followed the example of other cities in creating a City Plan Commission for the purpose of making long-range studies regarding land use and urban beautification.

But the City Beautiful idea, while obviously responsible for a transformation of "public" Hartford, did not bring beauty to all the city's residents. The United States Bureau of Labor reported in 1905 that of the cities it had studied in regard to housing conditions, Hartford was the worst of those of its size. The bureau noted particularly that most working-class homes were without bathtubs and that the tenement occupants took their weekly baths in the commercial bathhouses located in the poorer sections of the city.

XI

Modern Times

~**W**ARS OFTEN MARK
TURNING POINTS IN HISTORY—WHETHER THE HISTORY
IS OF THE WORLD, A NATION, OR A CITY. SUCH, CER-
tainly, was the case in Hartford, for it was with the First
World War that the modern city emerged.

On the eve of the outbreak of World War I, Hartford
was enjoying a considerable economic prosperity, and
the business community, led by an energetic Board of
Trade, was most optimistic. The 1911 *Annual Report* of
the Board noted that new industries were coming to
Hartford, and that the Grand List, which then stood at
$91,037,095, represented an almost 10 percent rise
from the previous year. In typical booster fashion, the
Board estimated Hartford's population at 113,944, even
though the census of 1910 had reported only 98,915.
Hartford was then listed as Number 62 among American
manufacturing cities, and even among Connecticut cities
in that survey Hartford ranked below Bridgeport's Number 33, New Haven's 46, and Waterbury's 48.

When Austria-Hungary declared war on Serbia on July 28, 1914, most Americans expected little more than a "Third Balkan War." Nor in November of 1916 were the Connecticut voters influenced by Woodrow Wilson's campaign slogan, "He kept us out of war." The state went Republican by a clean sweep, and the Democratic *Times* declared that "Hartford regards the European war as terrible, and is glad it has no part in it."

On February 20, 1917, the Connecticut Legislature authorized an inventory of men and materials available in case of war. The industrial summary revealed that 34 Connecticut firms employing over 40,000 workers were already operating under contracts with the federal government. Among these were such Hartford companies as Colt's, Veeder-Root, Maxim Silencer, and Hartford Machine Screw. And it certainly must have been well known that the Colt plant was busily supplying the Allies with orders that were being handled through Canada.

When the United States declared war on Germany on April 6, 1917, the declaration came as no surprise, for already Governor Marcus H. Holcomb had, at the request of the Secretary of War, Newton D. Baker, appointed a State Council of Defense. Through its various subcommittees, the Council soon became the State's principal agency in coordinating the war effort.

The publicity committee undertook the formidable task of making Connecticut's people aware of wartime needs, and during the war years it sponsored hundreds of war rallies that were intended to stimulate enthusiasm for the war effort.

Food supply became an immediate and serious concern. A Junior Food Army and a Connecticut Canning Corps enlisted large numbers of children and adults, and in May, 1917, the Connecticut Assembly passed an act permitting high-school students over 14 to volunteer for farm work. Home gardens flourished, and vacant lots and institutional grounds were parceled out for cultivation by anyone who applied.

Hartford, with a relatively small population of German extraction, had no serious problem with the antialien attitudes prevalent in the larger ethnic melting pots. The committee on education, however, did carry on its program of "Americanization" under a subcommittee on "American Loyalty" and distributed its pamphlets (with such titles as *What We Are Fighting For*) to grade-school children of Hartford's immigrant families.

Of the Connecticut "Big Five"—Remington Arms and Ammunition, Remington Union Metallic, Winchester, Marlin-Rockwell, and Colt's—Colt's was probably the farthest on the way toward full-time war production when war was declared. From a prewar labor force of 800, Colt's employment soon rose to over 8,000. And, as the company found that it was unable to produce revolvers, machine guns, and automatic rifles in sufficient quantities to satisfy the demands of the United States government, it surrendered its patent rights for the duration of the war on a royalty basis. Although Colt's was the Hartford area's principal war-materiel producer, numerous small plants about the city were engaged in producing goods for United States troops and those of America's Allies.

Most of the plants producing war goods went on round-the-clock, seven-day schedules. Householders were requested to conserve electricity. Hartford soon became accustomed to "lightless nights" after the city ordered that all street lighting be discontinued, and streets were in total darkness. The adoption of daylight-saving time, too, helped conserve electricity by shifting the peak load.

Despite their wartime profits, Hartford's industries suffered from the increased cost of bituminous coal. In 1916 coal could be purchased for $3.60 a ton, but by the summer of 1917 the price had risen to $7 a ton and always there was the problem of

In 1917 the domestic science curriculum at Hartford Public High School was coordinated with the war efforts. These girls were part of the program known as the "Girls Army." (CHS)

FACING PAGE: With several quicksand faults in the Hartford area, subway construction would have been difficult and costly. Instead, trolleys provided most of the public transportation in Hartford from 1890 until they were completely replaced by buses in the 1940s. (CHS)

securing any coal at all. When war was declared, there was just enough coal on hand to last the factories and the utility companies for two months, and at no time before the end of hostilities were they able to stockpile beyond that point.

There were troubles in the labor force, too. At the Light Company, for example, 80 men, or one-fifth of the total, went into the Armed Forces. Each man who was drafted or who volunteered was assured that he would be returned, upon his discharge from service, to the same position he had held at the time of his induction. Although in retrospect the arrangement seems to have been the only conceivable one, it was far from universal. Virtually all companies held the jobs for those who were drafted, but there was usually no such arrangement for those who volunteered.

One Hartford company to be particularly hard hit by the draft and by encouraged volunteering was the Hartford Steam Boiler Inspection and Insurance Company. As had been the case in the Spanish-American War, Hartford Steam Boiler, because of the particular skills of the engineering and inspection staffs, found that more than 10 percent of its employees went into the National Service. Many of the inspectors served in the Navy, usually in charge of the engineering staff of transport vessels or fighting ships.

Such plants as Colt's Patent Fire Arms and Pratt and Whitney Tool were thought to be vulnerable to sabotage by the Germans, and guarding the plants became a necessity. Arrangements were made through the Hartford Police Department whereby supernumeraries would be on duty at all times.

In the summer of 1916 Congress passed the National Defense Act, which permitted the colleges to provide Reserve Officer Training. The program was begun at Trinity on a volunteer basis on March 22, 1917, but early in 1918 the R.O.T.C. was replaced by the Student Army Training Corps, an ill-conceived program whereby the government literally turned the campuses into Army camps. None of the colleges benefited academically from this move, for it indiscriminately filled the colleges with many young men who were totally incapable of profiting from even the much diluted form of higher education that was being carried on for the Army. Since long hours of drill left little time for study, there was a reduction in the number of academic courses. The spring of 1918 marked the high tide of the war spirit at Trinity. At an "Open Air Patriotic Service," held on Sunday, June 18, 1918, the day before commencement, Ex-President Theodore Roosevelt urged the Trinity community to the greatest heights of patriotic endeavor.

News of the signing of the Armistice of November 11, 1918, came as something of an anticlimax, as for several weeks the Hartford newspapers had been suggesting that peace was near. On November 8 a rumor spread that the war had ended, and workers in factories and offices rushed into the streets, bringing traffic to a halt. The rumor proved to be false, and the Hartford citizenry was dejected. Four days later, however, news of the real Armistice reached Hartford. This time, a spontaneous parade of some 10,000 marchers went through the city, providing their own "music" with tin horns and pans. A more sedate parade was held on April 30, 1919, when Johnny was welcomed home officially by a crowd estimated at 200,000.

With the end of hostilities, the American economy and American industry tried to return to what President Warren G. Harding was to call "normalcy." However, the city's insurance companies, particularly those specializing in machinery coverage, found that the resumption of peacetime production brought many problems. Industries engaged in war production had worked their plants around the clock and around the calendar, and by the end of the war much of their machinery was fatigued and obsolete. And a serious blow to those insurance companies involved with boilers, machinery, and industrial plants was the passage in October, 1919, of the Volstead Act, which prohibited the manufacture of any beverage of more than one-half of one percent alcohol.

The life-insurance companies, too, had their problems. When the war began, the companies offered to assist the United States government in carrying the war-risk policies that had been promised all who entered military service. Although the offer was not accepted, the Hartford insurance companies made a contribution (and a costly one at that) of their own by continuing at no additional premium all policies in force, even though the policyholders had been sent overseas.

The influenza epidemic of 1918 resulted in some 500,000 deaths in the United States alone, and the many death claims paid by the companies placed a heavy strain upon Hartford's insurance industry. Each company met all of its claims, although several companies recovered a portion of the loss by reducing the amount paid to stockholders in dividends.

Hartford insurance had survived the war quite well, but the manufacturing companies were less fortunate. War contracts had ended, and there was the difficult transition to peacetime production. Even those industries that were able to make the change were still beset with the problem of obtaining sufficient coal to operate their machinery. On November 1, 1919, the miners went on strike, demanding a 60 percent pay boost, a six-hour day, and a five-day week. The strike was short, and the union settled for a 14 percent pay increase, but hardly had the coal strike ended when a railroad strike was called.

On November 2 the United States Fuel Administrator ordered 40 carloads of coal destined for Hartford to be held in railroad yards. The Hartford consignees feared that there might be a total cutoff of the supply. Such was not the case, but the long-range consequence was a rise in the price of coal to an unbelievable $17.50 a ton.

BELOW LEFT: The opening of the new armory marked the closing of the old. The cavalry was mustered for the occasion, and the First Regiment Armory on Elm Street was torn down shortly thereafter. (CHS)

BELOW: Teams clear snow from a pond for skaters in Riverside Park. It was a tedious process, and if a horse broke through the ice, the city closed the pond to skating. (CHS)

Labor felt that it had not shared in the wartime industrial prosperity, and local labor leaders, despite the huge layoffs at Hartford's factories, urged those workers who still had jobs to strike. Underwood Typewriter Company suffered a long work stoppage. Dissatisfied with Samuel Gompers' nonpartisan political stance, the Hartford Central Labor Union and 26 other labor unions formed the American Labor Party to run candidates for local and state offices in the election of 1919.

Inflation rose at about the same rate as unemployment. Between July, 1914, and November, 1919, according to figures provided by the National Industrial Conference, all household budget items had increased 82.2 percent. When a group of Hartford women organized the Hartford Housewives League, a spokeswoman for the group noted that the spirit of wartime sacrifice had turned to sullen anger.

Before radio or television reported the weather, this kiosk near the Old State House displayed barometers, thermometers, and updated weather forecasts. (CHS)

The anger in some quarters was far from silent, for the postwar period saw a small but extremely vocal group emerge in support of Russian Bolshevism, and there were all varieties of Communist sympathizers ranging from moderate Socialists to the International Workers of the World. The pastor of Hartford's small Greek Orthodox Church estimated that half of his congregation had been converted to Communism.

On March 2, 1919, about 2,000 persons gathered in the Grand Theatre to hear speakers from the I.W.W. condemn American capitalism and praise the Bolsheviks. Shortly thereafter, the Hartford Board of Aldermen voted unanimously to forbid either the Communists or the I.W.W. to conduct public meetings, display the Red flag, or distribute Communist literature. Violation carried a fine of $100 and imprisonment for six months.

Federal agents made numerous arrests, and the *Courant* reported that of all Connecticut cities, Hartford was probably the center of "Red" activity. Continued raids on alleged Communist gathering places filled the Hartford jail to the bursting point. Most of those incarcerated were aliens, either Russians or Lithuanians. Some of them were guilty only by association, as most of those individuals who went to visit imprisoned friends or relatives were themselves incarcerated. "Dangerous" aliens were kept behind bars for months without a hearing, and several complained that they had been denied needed medical attention. Under the direction of United States Attorney General A. Mitchell Palmer, many of the radicals were deported, some were sentenced to long prison terms, and a few were found innocent of their charges and freed. By the spring of 1920, Hartford's phase of the "Red Scare" had come to an end.

As these terrifying events were unfolding in Hartford, the business community was undertaking one of the most expansive programs in the city's history—the industrial and commercial development of the South Meadows. Actually, it had already begun in July, 1917, when the Hartford Electric Light Company purchased about 95 acres of land in the Meadows, with the intention of building a new powerhouse on the site.

Those familiar with Hartford's geography must have wondered whether the company was serious. South Meadows was then a large, low-lying tract, subject to flooding with each spring freshet, and totally unoccupied. South Meadows extended from the dike at the edge of the Colt's development southward to Wethersfield Cove. It was the Light Company's announcement that brought to public attention the hitherto-unused meadowland just two miles south of Hartford's business center, the city's only remaining area for extensive industrial development.

The City Council persuaded the United States Army Corps of Engineers to make a survey. Late in June, 1919, the Army Engineers announced that the Connecticut River along South Meadows would be widened and deepened, that the dredgings from the river would be used in the construction of a dike, and that some 1,000 acres of land would be reclaimed.

This was sufficient assurance for Hartford Electric Light, and on August 13, 1919, the company announced that a power plant would be constructed as soon as

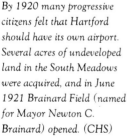

By 1920 many progressive citizens felt that Hartford should have its own airport. Several acres of undeveloped land in the South Meadows were acquired, and in June 1921 Brainard Field (named for Mayor Newton C. Brainard) opened. (CHS)

the land could be prepared. Soon the Standard Oil Company announced its intention of developing a huge oil depot on an adjoining tract.

On December 13, 1919, a writer for the Hartford *Times* rhapsodized over the future of the South Meadows. Somewhat prophetically, he visualized "two miles of busy waterfront alive with the movement of barge and boat and crane and car and noisy with the sound of whistle and bell and shouts of men, a riverside lined with docks and warehouses, areas studded with factories ... an industrial center laid out with fair streets and parkways, [and] somewhere in it a flying field with facilities for aircraft carrying passengers or mail or aerial express." The South Meadows project soon received the enthusiastic support of the Chamber of Commerce, and the estimated $300,000 to be spent in land reclamation was generally regarded as a sound municipal investment.

Without waiting for the construction of a dike, the Light Company began work. A railroad siding was built as soon as the spring flood of 1920 had subsided, and during the summer thousands of tons of fill—mostly coal ashes—were brought in from the Dutch Point Power Plant and by the Edward Balf Company, which had the municipal ash-collection contract. Actual construction was begun in the fall.

The building of the South Meadows plant came at a most opportune time. As was true in all cities that had been engaged in war production, unemployment had remained a problem. The policy agreed upon by Hartford manufacturers was one of dismissing women employees not supporting families and hiring discharged veterans in their stead. But this replacement was not an even exchange, for most of the Hartford factories had either closed or gone on short shifts. With 1,000 men on the construction force, the South Meadows project certainly was welcomed.

The power plant was not the only major construction then under way on the South Meadows. The new airfield—soon to be named Brainard Field in honor of Mayor Newton Case Brainard—was being laid out, and this busy activity attracted the curious, especially on Sunday afternoons. Light Company officials were much concerned that the not-altogether-welcome visitors might be injured, and guards were stationed at the approach to their tract. On May 2, 1921, the guards refused to allow several members of the Hartford Aviation Association to use the road that crossed the Light Company's property. Hartford's corporation counsel sharply

Hartford police wore civilian clothes on the job until 1860. By 1920, when this full-dress review was photographed, uniforms were an established part of the force. (CHS)

In this 1918 photo of the east side of Main Street we see the Wadsworth Atheneum, its Morgan Memorial wing, and, beyond that, Hartford's Municipal Building. (CHS)

reminded the company that the deed under which the land had been acquired clearly specified that the road should be kept open forever to all who wished to use it. With this, the unpleasant incident was closed. The airport was dedicated on June 12, 1921, the second municipal airport in the United States. The dedication of the new Light Company plant was on December 19, 1921.

South Meadows developed slowly but steadily, as one business after another located there. Oil-storage tanks came to stand next to warehouses, and wholesaling businesses, particularly those dealing in foodstuffs, located near the Regional Market, a public facility that opened in 1952. With the development of Bradley International Airport in nearby Windsor Locks following World War II, the size of Brainard Field was greatly reduced by the laying out of new streets, a move that limited the airport's usefulness to small planes. A considerable portion of the "lower" Meadows was later taken up by the city's sewage-treatment plant.

In 1925 the Pratt & Whitney Company brought Hartford into the Air Age when its small plant began to produce small, air-cooled Wasp airplane engines for both the Navy and commercial use. Soon the company began turning out the 525-horsepower Hornet engines. Within 10 years the work force at P & W rose from 25 to 2,000, and the company moved its main production to East Hartford. This small beginning resulted in United Aircraft, which soon included Hamilton Standard Propeller and Sikorsky Aircraft, all part of the corporation now known as United Technologies, the largest employer in New England.

The Hartford Foundation for Public Giving also was established in 1925. The agency grew into the largest dispenser and coordinator of public philanthropy in Connecticut. The forming of the foundation was the culmination of the history of philanthropy in Hartford, a city long noted for its giving and its givers.

The history of private philanthropy in Hartford began in 1809, when the Hartford Female Beneficent Society was organized, as its charter declared redundantly, to

The principal building of the United States Arsenal on North Main Street, built in 1805, was this barracks and drill hall. "Eyebrows" over the windows and other details make it a more pleasant sight than what might have been stark simplicity. (CHS)

afford "relief to needy indigent females." In 1822 what is now the Institute of Living was incorporated as the Hartford Retreat for the Insane. In 1842 Daniel Wadsworth endowed the Wadsworth Atheneum, the first art museum in New England. In 1852 the Hartford Young Men's Christian Association was organized, just a year after the first YMCA had been founded in Boston. Fifteen years later the WCA (later the YWCA) was inaugurated. Hartford Hospital was started in 1854, and other hospitals followed. In 1898 the Congregation of the Sisters of Saint Francis opened Saint Francis Hospital, and in 1923 the Hartford Jewish community organized the city's third general hospital—Mount Sinai.

Hartford also saw the creation of the more obviously "social service" agencies. The Woman's Aid Society was organized in 1878, as the purpose was stated euphemistically at the time, "for the reformation of fallen women," although in later years its attention was directed toward the assistance of unwed mothers. In 1884 the Open Hearth Mission began care for homeless men, operating on the philosophy that none should be fed, clothed, or sheltered without at least a token payment. The Open Hearth's transient guests sawed cordwood in exchange for some minimum of human comfort.

With the establishment in the early 1890s of what were to become the Family Service Society and the Children's Services, charities in Hartford assumed their modern character. These organizations, together with the Visiting Nurse Association (1901), the Charter Oak Council of the Boy Scouts of America (1914), and the Greater Hartford Girl Scouts (1920), saw the city operating with the full complement of social agencies assumed in a community of Hartford's size and collective economic means.

These were the major charities, but over the years associations were organized by both Christians and Jews for the relief of members of the several sects within each faith. And there were also the Widows' Society (1847); the Hartford Orphan

Asylum, begun in the 1860s as an adjunct of the Female Beneficent Society and later to become the Child and Family Services of Connecticut; the Watkinson Asylum and Farm School for Orphan Boys; and the Union for Home Work, organized in 1872 by Mrs. Samuel Colt to farm out sewing work to indigent widows in their homes. The Union would, by several mergers and reorganizations, ultimately become Hartford Neighborhood Centers.

Through the years the contributions to the various agencies were generous, and periodically there were small-scale fund drives. Trustees and their friends remembered the institutions in their wills—sometimes with what were regarded at the time as large sums. Although each incorporated charity hoped to build up a productive endowment through bequests, it was the "dead hand" of the testator that threatened to tie up well-intended sums of money whose original purpose no longer existed.

Early in the 1920s trust officers of two Hartford banks—Maynard T. Hazen of the United States Security Trust Company and Clark T. Durant of the Hartford-Connecticut Trust Company—had faced problems arising from wills. As they shared their thoughts with Arthur Pomeroy Day, the Hartford attorney reputed to have drawn up more wills than any other member of the city's legal profession, they decided to set up a public foundation that would enable banks and trust companies to hold donated funds in perpetuity and to appropriate the income from these funds to community betterment. In 1925 Hazen and Durant persuaded the Connecticut General Assembly to pass an act authorizing the creation of the Hartford Foundation for Public Giving.

The foundation received considerable publicity in the local press, but the community-trust idea was slow in finding acceptance in Hartford, as bankers and attorneys never attempted to apply any pressure in favor of the foundation, for fear that an imperfect understanding of the foundation on the part of the client would suggest conflict of interest.

Several Hartford residents made modest bequests to the foundation, and in 1936 the first distribution was made. Between that date and 1980, however, the Hartford Foundation for Public Giving accumulated assets of $45,175,052 and made distributions of over $25,000,000 to social-service agencies, education, and the arts.

The decade of the 1920s—sometimes called the Roaring Twenties, the Prohibition Years, or the Jazz Age—meant bootlegging, the Charleston, and the ukelele. There was something of a moral change, many would have said a moral decline, as women smoked cigarettes, bobbed their hair, rolled their stockings, and shortened their skirts. Schoolteachers were reprimanded by their principals for wearing skirts that reached only to the knee, and office employees were discharged for cutting their hair. Cocktails became popular, as hosts and hostesses attempted to stretch their illicit and expensive whiskey. All of this was attributed to the letdown that followed what was then referred to as the "Great War." But it also reflected what most people regarded as a new national prosperity, as well as a new materialism, or a greater concern for the new creature comforts that reflected a higher material standard of living.

Charles Lindbergh, shortly after his transoceanic flight in 1927, received a rousing welcome in Hartford and other cities. He is seen here standing in an open touring car as it proceeds slowly along Main Street. (CHS)

This overview of a part of Hartford's West End was photographed in the 1920s showing the then incomplete campus of the Hartford Theological Seminary. The seminary has now moved to smaller quarters nearby, and the University of Connecticut Law School is about to occupy these buildings. (CHS)

These were carefree years, and as the decade was drawing to a close few individuals cared to admit that business conditions in Hartford were not all that might have been desired or that there were portents that all was not well with the national economy. By early 1929 the coal and textile industries were in difficult circumstances, and oil producers were suffering from a cutthroat price war that had resulted from a glut of petroleum products. Farmers were trying to sell unmarketable produce, and there were many farm failures and mortgage foreclosures, which, in turn, bankrupted lending institutions from Maine to California. By September even the great building boom, which had contributed so much to the postwar prosperity, had collapsed, and construction slumped to 25 percent below the level of the preceding year.

These conditions were reflected ominously in Hartford. Factories went on short schedule, and hundreds of workers lost their jobs. Hartford newspapers reported an unusually large number of business failures and personal bankruptcies, but the heaviest blow to the local economy fell when the Hartford Rubber Works moved to Detroit. By September 19, the prices of corporate shares on the New York Stock Exchange stood at an all-time high, and the profits of millions of Americans were measured—on paper, at least—in the billions. In early October stocks took a sharp downward slide, and by the middle of the month the leading industrial issues were losing from 5 to 90 points in a single day. Then came "Black Thursday," October 24, 1929, when stock plummeted by 50 to 100 points. Millions of stockholders wanted to sell, but none wanted to buy. The great crash had come, and the Depression had begun.

Connecticut was a highly industrialized state, and all of these effects were soon to be felt. The Manufacturers Association of Hartford reported in 1931 that 81 factories that then employed 36,250 persons had kept 8,873 employees on their payroll in excess of their production demands in an effort to spread the work. A year later the Connecticut Department of Commerce reported the doleful news that more than 1,000 Connecticut firms had gone into bankruptcy, and that these companies had liabilities of more than twice their assets. By the fall of 1932, eighteen Connecticut banks had failed, and by 1934, sixteen more were in the process of liquidation.

The actual employment statistics were equally depressing. A factory-employment index prepared by Metropolitan Life Insurance Company revealed that industrial employment for 1932 was 54 percent below that of 1929, and a Connecticut Commerce Department report indicated a 40 percent decrease in payrolls from 1929 to 1932.

Hartford suffered during the Depression, but there were elements in the city's economy that softened the blow. It is an axiom in the industry that insurance lags behind other businesses in both entering and leaving depression periods. Thus, with a large proportion of Hartford's gainfully employed population on the payrolls of the city's many insurance-company home offices, there was a relative security during the earlier Depression years. Also, several major building programs were undertaken during this period, and these projects kept a large number of construction workers on the payroll of local contractors. During the 1930s Trinity College erected a new dormitory, a chemistry laboratory, a million-dollar chapel, a field house, and a dining hall. In 1931 Hartford Steam Boiler Inspection and Insurance Company began construction of a new office building with the twofold purpose of availing itself of the low cost of building materials and relieving unemployment in the community. Bushnell Memorial Hall also was built between October 1928 and January 1930.

Following the stock-market crash, political and business leaders attempted to keep up morale. In December, 1929, the mayors of Connecticut's principal cities joined in expressing an optimistic outlook for 1930, and Hartford's city fathers took pride in a nationwide survey that placed Hartford among the 25 best-lighted cities in the United States.

But times of economic distress are hardly times for civic boasting, and the City authorities decided to trim sail. There could be no appreciable increase in City taxes, as the property holders had made clear their opposition to any such measures. In fact, in September, 1931, thirty-five Hartford manufacturing firms petitioned the City for a reduction in taxes, and they held out the threat of moving their plants from Hartford if their demands were ignored.

Budget cuts were the order of the day, and one of the first municipal services to suffer was lighting. In March, 1932, the City ordered the elimination of every third streetlamp, 19 of the 80 traffic signals, and the entire floodlighting at Brainard Field. Dispensing with the Christmas lighting—a saving of a mere $240—in the downtown shopping district was too grim a thought for the merchants, and the Chamber of Commerce undertook to raise the money among the Hartford retailers. The money was raised, albeit with considerable difficulty, and the lights were put up as usual.

Perhaps the plight of the unemployed was best symbolized by the "hunger march" in the spring of 1932, when on several occasions hundreds of the unemployed—although certainly not all of them from Hartford—surrounded the State Capitol and presented petitions demanding a state appropriation of $12,000,-000 in direct relief to the unemployed.

Hartford's business community generally was agreed that the problem of unemployment was a local matter that should be solved on the local level and, if at all possible, by private charities. In October of 1931 the Hartford Community Chest had set a campaign goal of $1,090,063, of which $250,000 was to provide work for the unemployed.

Gallup and Alfred, at the corner of Asylum and Haynes streets, sold records along with Victrolas on which to play them. A three-dimensional replica of the Victor trademark, "His Master's Voice," sits by one of the Victrolas. (CHS)

But this attitude was not to prevail. Franklin Delano Roosevelt was elected President in 1932 by such a spectacular majority that the result was interpreted by many as a repudiation of the Hoover administration's ineffectual measures to end the Depression. And with the new Democratic President came a predominantly Democratic Congress, willing and eager to enact bold legislation in the interest of recovery from the Depression and reform of the social and economic systems from which many of the new legislators believed the Depression had been bred.

The new President had little difficulty in convincing his Congress that recovery could best be achieved by a policy of raising the prices of commodities, services, and labor, while at the same time strictly regulating American industry and expanding the federal program of public works. On June 16, 1933, Congress created the National Recovery Administration (NRA), an agency whose function would be to prepare and supervise a series of codes of fair competition and employment for each of the nation's major industries. The act set aside the long-standing antitrust laws, as the codes were directed toward intraindustry cooperation rather than the competition encouraged by the Sherman and Clayton acts. A general code prohibited the employment of persons under 16 years of age, set the maximum work week at 40 hours, and established a minimum wage of 40 cents an hour.

In all, 557 separate industrial codes were adopted. All were thrown together hastily, and it was apparent from the beginning that the larger corporations had dictated the terms. However, Section 7 of the National Industrial Recovery Act (NIRA), the clause that specifically granted labor the right to organize, was later to cause many a regret to those corporation executives who had encouraged it.

The evening of Tuesday, September 19, 1933, was designated by the National Recovery Administration as NRA Night, and across the entire nation there were parades. In Hartford 20,000 persons, virtually all of the city's gainfully employed, marched. There were 100 floats, 500 decorated trucks, and 30 bands. All Hartford people who were fortunate enough to have work joined in singing *Marching Along Together* and *Happy Days Are Here Again*. Unfortunately, happy days were not really here.

Although the NIRA at first had been hailed by organized labor, Hartford's union leaders soon became extremely critical of the act, branding it the foe of the workingman. Small businesses, too, ignored the codes and joined the opposition. Even big industry, under whose sponsorship the act had been introduced, had cooled, and by the spring of 1935 the NIRA had few friends. All were relieved when the United States Supreme Court, on May 27, 1935, declared the act unconstitutional.

The NIRA was but one of many pieces of New Deal legislation under which the Hartford manufacturers were to chafe. The Social Security Act of August 14, 1935, caused some confusion, for several of the companies had just instituted their own generous contributory retirement plans. The Guffey-Snyder Bituminous Coal Stabilization Act of August 30, 1934, contained price-fixing features that threatened to keep the price of fuel at a high level. The act was declared unconstitutional, however, in May, 1936.

Hartford benefited immeasurably from the programs of the Works Progress Administration (WPA), later the Works Projects Administration, which was created on May 6, 1935. In Hartford, streets were repaired, parks were improved, and public buildings were refurbished. There also were projects of a more ephemeral nature, and these were criticized as "leaf-raking" jobs or "busy work."

Although the primary intent of the WPA was to provide work for manual

Theodore Roosevelt waves to the crowd from an electric car motoring down Pearl Street. His police escort consists of six policemen mounted on Columbia bicycles. (CHS)

laborers, other projects involved artists, actors, and musicians, and here Hartford was to benefit. Hartford had an unusually large number of musicians who were out of work. With the popularity of motion pictures, the theaters had dispensed with their pit orchestras, and radio, in an effort to cut costs, had reduced the number of musicians used in the broadcasting studios. To take up the slack, the WPA created the Hartford Symphony Orchestra. Similar orchestras had been set up across the country, but this was one of the few to survive the elimination of the WPA. Local support was able to keep the symphony going, and it was to become one of the better orchestras in a city of Hartford's size, giving its own regular concert series and later serving both the Connecticut Opera Association and the Hartford Ballet Company.

One of the few bright spots of these Depression years was the celebration during the summer of 1935 of the tercentenary of Connecticut's settlement. In Hartford the theme of the celebration was "Progress." The festivities—which included pageants, concerts, art shows, and dramatic performances—ran from April through October and culminated in a huge parade on Columbus Day.

When spring came, however, the Tercentenary Celebration was only a memory, as Mother Nature dealt Hartford a most unkind blow. January and February of 1936 were cold and snowy months throughout New England, and snow piled up in almost unprecedented quantities. During the second week in March temperatures rose rapidly, and as the mountains of snow in New Hampshire and Vermont melted, the Connecticut River began to rise.

By Thursday, March 19, Hartford's previous high record of 29.8 feet, set by the May flood of 1854, had been passed. The Connecticut River Bridge was closed, and families in the low-lying East Side were evacuated quickly. Hundreds of persons were removed, some from second-story windows, by Coast Guardsmen who navigated their whaleboats through the "canals" that once had been Front Street and its adjacent lanes and alleys. Bushnell Park became a huge lake. All highways out of Hartford were impassable, and thousands of displaced persons huddled in buildings on higher ground, while City authorities doled out what food and blankets were available. By Friday the high-water mark of 35 feet above normal river level had been reached. Bellboys in hip boots splashed through two feet of water in the Bond Hotel's lobby, handling the luggage of guests who had been brought by boat from the railroad station two blocks away. By Saturday the flood stood at 37.5 feet.

The flood of 1936 was the most destructive in Hartford's history. The cost was five lives and $35,000,000 in property damage, and it was particularly unfortunate that the flood had come at a time when Hartford was just beginning to shake off the effects of the Depression.

In 1938 Nature struck again, with the most severe hurricane in the city's history. On September 21 at 4 p.m., the hurricane struck with full force, leaving the city a shambles: streets blocked by fallen trees and utility poles, crushed automobiles, stranded trolley cars, and debris from hundreds of destroyed or damaged buildings. The Connecticut River rose rapidly, and an army of City employees, WPA workers, and college students and other volunteers began to strengthen the dikes. Fifty-pound bags of sand were piled one atop another by the soon-weary workers. By 5:30 p.m. on Friday, September 23, the river attained a height of 35.1 feet above normal, held at that crest until 10 p.m., and then slowly began to fall. Again, there was the heroic evacuation of the East Side, where many small shopkeepers, still making payments on loans taken out following the disaster of 1936, were threatened with bankruptcy. Fortunately, most of these businesses were able to receive aid through the Federal Disaster Loan Corporation.

Concentric circles are caused by a bandstand's reflection in the floodwaters covering a corner of Bushnell Park. The Traveler's (Insurance Company) Tower and its reflection are also apparent. (CHS)

ABOVE: At the crest of the flood, Front and Commerce streets became navigable waterways. High water reached several blocks inland from the Connecticut River. (CHS)

ABOVE LEFT: Here we see the extent of the March 1936 flood. Colt's Armory is awash; the arches of the Bulkeley Bridge are barely seen; and most of the railroad freight yards have disappeared. Parts of East Hartford (on the right) are completely submerged. Saxe Studio photo (CHS)

This was the last such disaster to hit Hartford, for even before the flood and hurricane had struck, elaborate provisions were being made to erect a system of dikes from North Meadows, past the low-lying East Side, and down the river to the Wethersfield line. This project, the last one carried out under the WPA, was not completed until 1941, but it enclosed South Meadows plants and Brainard Field, which had been outside the older and obviously ineffectual barriers. Thus, the danger of flood has been virtually eliminated.

Hartford would recover from floods and hurricanes, as she would from the Depression, but it would not be through the WPA or other federal agencies. Rather, it would be World War II that would revitalize the city's economy and make Hartford once again a major center of military production.

On Sunday, December 7, 1941, the day that President Roosevelt said would live in infamy, the Japanese Air Force attacked the United States Naval Base at Pearl Harbor, Hawaii. On December 8 Congress declared war against Japan, and on December 11 the Axis powers declared war on the United States.

But long before the declaration of war, the United States had been preparing feverishly for the conflict. Lend-lease and the unprecedented defense appropriations of 1940-1941 had transformed a Depression-ridden nation into an "arsenal of democracy," as President Roosevelt called it. Within a year more than 6,000,000 workers were added to America's payrolls, and unemployment virtually was eliminated.

In Hartford the rate of defense production was somewhat in advance of that of the nation as a whole, as such plants as Colt's, Billings and Spencer, and Pratt and Whitney Tool turned out vast quantities of metal and plastics on contracts with British, French, and United States governments. The most talked-of defense industry in the Hartford area was, of course, United Aircraft. At its Pratt & Whitney plant, United Aircraft was producing airplane engines in prodigious quantities, and the marvel was that the plant, which just a few years before had employed about a score of men, was now utilizing thousands, and that the facilities for production were growing as rapidly as construction workers could build.

With Hartford's rapid industrial expansion came an unprecedented influx of people. Workers with varying degrees of mechanical skills came from other parts of New England, from the industrial centers of the Midwest, and from the rural South. Housing became a serious problem, and even the large-scale program of government-sponsored, low-cost apartment construction soon proved to be inadequate. A reliable estimate of the time was that during 1941 alone there were 18,000 newcomers to the city. Hartford's central position in a highly industrialized state prompted the Army and Navy Munitions Board to place the city on the list of 14 "most vital strategic industrial areas in the country," and it was this presumably vulnerable position that caused Hartford to take careful measures for civilian defense.

As part of its effort to conserve food and scarce, war-needed materials, the federal government instituted a program of strict rationing. Hartfordites, however, were notorious for their refusal to observe gasoline rationing, and in 1943 the *Courant* noted that gas sales were more than twice the amount allowed by law. During the war years many women who never had worked before found employment in the factories.

During 1944 economic conditions in Hartford remained relatively stable, despite a slight decrease in industrial employment during the fall, when optimism concerning a possible end to the war prompted some departures by migrant workers. But the summer of 1944 was one of disaster for the Hartford community. On July 6 a tragic fire in the Ringling Brothers Circus tent took the lives of 168 persons, many of them children, and injured 500 more.

While such local news was monopolizing space in the Hartford papers, faraway events were bringing the war closer to its end. On August 15, 1945, the Japanese surrendered, and the most devastating war in history was over.

Then the victors came home. The Hartford insurance companies and banks had kept all jobs open for the men and women who had served, but even these found housing scarce. Many a returned veteran with a war bride, or recently married to the girl who had waited for him, was obliged to live with relatives. Even when rented quarters could be found, rents were extremely high and going ever higher.

The unskilled had little chance in the job market, but the federal "G.I. Bill of Rights" provided for college education or on-the-job training, which held veterans out of the work force and allowed them to raise their vocational ambitions. The G.I. Bill enabled Trinity College to return quickly to a normal collegiate life. It actually helped Hillyer College (founded in 1879) to emerge as a full-fledged institution of higher learning and to set it on its way toward merging, in 1957, with the Hartford Art School and the Hartt School of Music to form the University of Hartford. Also to profit from the postwar boom in higher education were St. Joseph College (conducted since 1932 by the Congregation of the Sisters of Mercy) and Hartford College for Women (begun in 1933 as a "depression branch" of Mount Holyoke). Rensselaer Polytechnic Institute set up the Hartford branch that would become the Hartford Graduate Center.

One of many presidents to visit Hartford, Woodrow Wilson greets citizens with a tip of his hat. (CHS)

Probably the worst threat to American economic well-being in the post-World War II years was inflation. President Harry S. Truman was aware of both the economic dangers and the popular feeling against wartime controls, and within a matter of months, price controls on nearly all commodities and services were ended. Congress also lowered the federal income tax slightly. Although prices remained at the wartime high levels, serious inflation, except in rents, did not particularly trouble the Hartford consumer until the outbreak of the Korean conflict in June, 1950.

World War II hardly had ended when a grassroots movement for municipal reform began among Hartford's citizenry—particularly the college-trained business and professional people—who had become dissatisfied with Hartford's city government, with its antiquated ward representation and the resulting favoritism and political patronage. To effect the reform, the Citizens Charter Commission was formed by members of both the Democratic and Republican parties. The commission's goal was to achieve a city government under a nine-member council to be elected from candidates who would run at large and without party designation. Although the idea was opposed by the old-line politicians, it received unexpected popular support, and in December, 1946, a completely new type of municipal government went into effect. The *Times,* abandoning its long-standing partisanship, proudly declared that "the citizens are at last on the top."

Also effective during the decades of the 1940s and 1950s was the Greater Hartford Chamber of Commerce, a particularly farsighted group that then represented the younger (or middle) management levels of Hartford's retailing, banking, manufacturing, and insurance concerns. And it was indeed the Chamber, under the leadership of its president, Arthur J. Lumsden, that would provide the impetus for the large-scale urban renewal projects launched in the late 1950s.

Meanwhile, the country once again had become involved in war. On June 25, 1950, the North Korean Army crossed the 38th Parallel, and on that same day President Truman ordered General Douglas MacArthur and the American military forces stationed in South Korea to lead a formidable counteroffensive. The Korean War meant the tightening again of government controls, the reimposition of the draft, the beginning of a most alarming spiraling of inflation, and a drain upon the city's labor force that was just enough to cause uneasiness in Hartford's personnel offices. Once again Hartford's war industries boomed, and once again interest turned to civil defense, as air-raid shelters were improvised in public buildings, factories, and even homes.

Also to be noted was a significant population shift. Between 1950 and 1960 approximately 56,000 people moved into Hartford, while during this same decade 95,000 others moved out. This reshuffling represented a loss of almost 10 percent of the city's population. Most of these outward moves were to such nearby communities as Bloomfield, East Hartford, Windsor, and Wethersfield, each of which experienced a population growth proportionately larger than Hartford's loss.

Hartford's racial makeup was also changing. In 1950 Hartford listed 13,000 blacks; the census of 1960 counted 25,000. Hartford, like Connecticut's other large cities, rapidly was becoming the home of the blacks and the home of the poor. In 1960 Hartford had one-third of all families living in the 29-town Greater Hartford Metropolitan Region, but it also had more than 50 percent of those families with incomes of less than $5,000, and just under 20 percent of those earning more than $10,000. Furthermore, the lowest-income families were concentrated in the largely black North End, while the more affluent families were to be found in the western portion of the city near the West Hartford line.

Dwight Eisenhower gives a victory sign on one of his trips through Hartford. (CHS)

Equally as important as the absolute decline in the population of the City of Hartford from 177,397 in 1950 to 162,178 in 1960 was the amazing growth of the Greater Hartford Metropolitan Region. In 1950 the nine surrounding towns—West Hartford, East Hartford, Bloomfield, Windsor, Windsor Locks, Wethersfield, Enfield, Avon, and Simsbury—were inhabited by a total of 133,145 persons, while 10 years later the suburban population stood at 224,286. Here Hartford's long-range problems were to be seen plainly. Cities in the American South and West almost invariably had annexed all contiguous, populated territory, and such cities showed steady population growth with each new federal census. Hartford did not have this seeming advantage, as each suburban community stood firmly by its refusal to be annexed to the city.

And yet, all of the surrounding towns were appendages to the city. Most of the residents of the towns worked in the city, did their major shopping downtown, and relied upon Hartford's cultural institutions for both entertainment and edification. Municipal boundaries remained, but Greater Hartford had by 1960 become a total community of almost 400,000. By 1970 the United States Bureau of the Census would place Greater Hartford in the Hartford-New Britain-Bristol Standard Metropolitan Statistical Area as number 33 in the country, with a population of 1,035,195.

In this process of population redistribution, Hartford had become, as the urban specialists described it, "ghettoized." The economic and social conditions of Hartford's blacks were aggravated further in the spring of 1958, when the City of Hartford announced plans for one of the largest programs of urban redevelopment ever undertaken by an American municipality. The plan was to level most of the supposedly substandard buildings that lay between Market Street and the Connecticut River—an area some four city blocks in width and a dozen or so in length—and to erect three high-rise office structures, a large hotel, headquarters for the city's major radio and television stations, extensive underground parking facilities, and a modern shopping mall.

The development, named Constitution Plaza, was completed in 1962 with financial backing by Travelers Insurance Company, and it won nationwide acclaim for its architectural design and its overall concept as a downtown business and financial center. Unfortunately, the Plaza project was far from successful, for although the office buildings soon were rented to near capacity, the shopping mall, from the beginning, consisted chiefly of empty storefronts.

Constitution Plaza replaced the old Italian East Side, and the city fathers, lured by the prospect of federal slum-clearance money, soon began the destruction of the southern portion of the black North End, the Polish Sheldon Street area, and a considerable portion of the Colt village.

Constitution Plaza did not contain a single dwelling unit, and its former population scattered to all parts of the city and to the suburbs. Many of the Italian families and businesses came to concentrate in the Franklin Avenue area. There, much of Little Italy was preserved, even to the extent of reintroducing the Italian Festa held each year since 1978. A similar exodus was noted in the case of the Sheldon Street area Polish-Americans. These geographic moves often represented upward social mobility, as the immigrants and children of immigrants were absorbed, through education, hard work, and personal ambition, into the area's middle class.

For the blacks, however, there was little choice, for as the Windsor Street area was leveled, black families simply pushed farther northward, moving eventually into the Blue Hills sector, which formerly had been predominantly Jewish. And all the

The Old State House, shown in this picture with the Hartford National Bank building behind it, has been meticulously restored. Courtesy, Old State House Association

while, a steady influx of Puerto Ricans to the North End led to further uneasiness as blacks gave the newcomers something less than a hearty welcome.

Traditionally, Hartford's blacks had been passive in their attitude. Early in 1963, however, the attitude was changed, when a small but articulate group of white college students and seminarians organized the North End Community Action Project (NECAP). These activists, affiliated with the Northern Student Movement, moved into the ghetto, tutored black children, encouraged voter registration, picketed the homes of slumlords, led a "kneel-in" at a local restaurant, and even headed a sit-in at City Hall.

They were encouraged, and sometimes actively courted, by a revived National Association for the Advancement of Colored People (NAACP), the International Ministerial Alliance (IMA), and the Congress on Racial Equality (CORE), the local chapter of which was organized by the Reverend Richard Battles, pastor of the Mount Olive Baptist Church and a friend of the Reverend Dr. Martin Luther King, Jr. When the more radical Black Muslims appeared on the scene, the older black groups were mildly distrustful. Battles, however, found all activists kindred souls and, according to the *Times* of November 26, 1963, one said, as he pointed to his breast, "All of us Negroes have a little bit of Black Muslim down here."

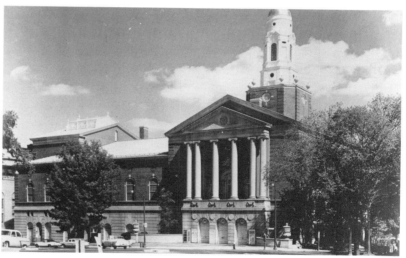

The Horace Bushnell Memorial Hall, which seats 2,500, has presented lectures, symphony concerts, and other events since the 1930s. Courtesy, Horace Bushnell Memorial Hall

Although a proposed NECAP school boycott was called off, the Hartford Board of Education quickly got the message and resolved to improve the educational opportunity of black children. As 95 percent of Hartford's blacks lived in the North End, the city was operating virtually two separate school systems—one for the whites and another for the blacks. The Board of Education was genuinely determined to rectify the situation and turned to the Harvard University Graduate School of Education to devise a plan for school integration.

The Harvard Plan called for building several new middle schools on the fringe between white and black sections and, as Hartford's white population was declining so rapidly, busing black children to predominantly white suburban schools. The plan met with fierce resistance, as the white population of the city objected to the middle-school proposal, and the suburbs offered little assistance. Consequently, the Board of Education began a $42-million school-building program that totally ignored the Harvard recommendations and kept the schools as segregated as they had been before. In 1966, however, Project Concern, a pilot program of the federal government, began busing blacks from Hartford schools to West Hartford, Farmington, Manchester,

South Windsor, and Simsbury. Local resistance, both in the city and in the towns, precluded total success.

Hartford's blacks had become active in programs to improve their condition, but there was little to show for the effort. In 1967, for instance, Hartford had 5,816 families, mostly black, on its welfare rolls at an annual cost of more than a million dollars. Urban housing, where blacks could rent, was in short supply. Puerto Ricans, who were arriving daily, were just as "ghettoized" as the blacks. Events in Hartford soon would take a turn for the worse, as they became tied up with the turmoil that in the late 1960s beset college campuses as well as the ghettos of virtually all American cities.

Although the assassination of Dr. King in April of 1968 provided the immediate spark, discontent and unrest in Hartford had been festering for a long time, stemming in large part from the unpopular Vietnam War and the painfully slow progress being made in the Civil Rights movement. Cities across the nation already had had serious race riots with extensive loss of life and property. Hartford's turn came in the summer of 1968, when residents of the North End set fires to buildings, obstructed the flow of vehicular traffic, and assaulted police officers and fire fighters. During the oppressively hot and humid 1968 Labor Day weekend, residents of Hartford's North Main Street area rioted and burned down the Ropkins Branch of the Hartford Public Library. Although the building was close to a fire station, the rioters prevented the fire fighters from laying their hoses, and the structure was completely destroyed.

Much credit for successfully dealing with this critical situation was given to the Hartford Foundation for Public Giving, which immediately pledged a considerable portion of its allocations to the needs of those minority groups whose disadvantaged situation was being demonstrated so openly. The foundation always had allocated funds with the residents of the North End in mind, and a major contribution of $20,000 had just been made in 1964 toward establishing a Hartford branch of the National Urban League. The difference in 1969 was the approach. Crash programs were financed in part by the foundation to try to buy time until sounder, long-range programs could take over, and to attempt to correct basic conditions rather than just alleviate their symptoms.

The foundation was the first to admit that there were errors of judgment, but such is invariably the case in a crash program of any sort, and the heroic efforts were not without the seemingly inevitable disappointments. Nevertheless, the foundation was able to report in the *Yearbook* for 1970:

> The democratic way is slow and fumbling, but eventually tolerance and faith in the basic decency of most Americans, black and white, will win out, and a better society will emerge.

There can be little doubt that the foundation-sponsored programs went a long way toward pouring oil upon troubled waters.

During this period of urban unrest, which extended well into the early 1970s, Arthur J. Lumsden of the Greater Hartford Chamber of Commerce led top corporate leaders in creating the Greater Hartford Corporation and the Greater Hartford Process, one of the most extensive programs in the nation to deal with urban problems. As part of that effort, the Greater Hartford Community Development Corporation (DEVCO) was created to initiate housing rehabilitation in the North End and to acquire land to build a "new town" in Coventry. Because of understandable opposition from the residents of that quiet, rural town some 15 miles from Hartford, the "new town" idea was abandoned.

Hartford's greatest failure in the 20th century was to provide adequate housing for low-income families, but there certainly were persistent efforts from all sides to make Hartford more pleasant for those who chose, or who were obliged, to live there. One of those most concerned for the improvement of the quality of life in the city was Elizabeth L. Knox, who, after having served for 12 years on the Hartford City Council, died in 1966 and in her will endowed the Knox Foundation with the specific intent of beautifying the city. As Miss Knox expressed the idea, the "spiritual" slums, as well as the physical, must be removed if the city is to become truly beautiful. The Knox Foundation, particularly in the mid-1970s, was especially helpful in providing outdoor entertainment and recreation for those who had long since come to be called Hartford's "disadvantaged."

Hartford never became the place of beauty visualized by Miss Knox, but there were genuine efforts to make it so, and several of them have stories of their own. None is more interesting or, indeed, more circuitous than that of the spectacular piece of sculpture by Alexander Calder that is a bright spot of downtown Hartford. The story goes back to 1906, when Ella Burr McManus left $50,000 to build a memorial to her father, Alfred E. Burr, an early publisher of the Hartford *Times*. Mrs. McManus' will stated that the memorial "must be artistic in design and humane in purpose, preferably a drinking fountain for both human beings and animals." By the time Mrs. McManus' fund was available, horses were fast disappearing from the streets of Hartford, and so, after much study as to the appropriate use of the bequest, the trustees decided to use the legacy to construct a public library. Architects drew plans that, being clearly "artistic in design," were fully in keeping with one of the provisions of the will. But the probate judge, ruling that a library is not "humane in purpose," rejected the proposal.

However, the story was to have a happy ending, although neither human beings nor animals were to benefit in quite the way Mrs. McManus had intended. By 1960 the reinvested income had swelled the fund to more than $1,000,000, and the trustees again came forth with a proposal to meet, in part at least, the terms of the will. This time they were able to persuade the probate court that a huge mall with a fountain and a piece of sculpture would be both appropriate and acceptable. In September, 1966, an agreement was signed between the Trustees of the Ella Burr McManus Fund, the Wadsworth Atheneum, and the City of Hartford. The mall was constructed on Main Street on land between the Atheneum and the Municipal Building and directly opposite the office of the Hartford *Times*. In addition to carefully laid walkways and plantings of trees and shrubs, the mall featured a fountain and Calder's massive steel sculpture titled *Stegosaurus*. The project finally was completed in 1973.

Stegosaurus provoked much comment. Councilwoman Margaret Tedone was displeased: "From the Council offices," she remarked, "it looks like a great big piece of metal dropped there, like debris, from a plane crash!"

Nor did Mayor George Athanson approve: "One day I see this THING going up. I don't mind being Calderized, but I don't want to be Stegosaurusized! Why was a two-ton dinosaur known for its miniscule brain chosen?"

James Elliot, former director of the Wadsworth Atheneum, defended the selection by explaining the sculpture's artistic merits: "In spite of its lumbering, primordial quality, it is beautifully realized in semiabstract form [and] ... a spectacular addition to the downtown cityscape."

Even more controversial was the *Stone Field Sculpture* of Carl Andre, located in

What once were private homes have been remodeled to accommodate professional or commercial tenants. The University Club (shown here) preserves some of the quiet charm of the 19th century on Lewis Street. Courtesy, University Club of Hartford

the minipark just south of First Congregational Church. There, on August 22, 1977, 36 large boulders were placed in six parallel rows, ranging from one to 11 rocks and forming a huge triangle that covers most of the grassy plot. Immediately, the *Stone Field Sculpture* raised the question of whether it was a work of art or a spoof. Most observers seemed to be unfavorably impressed, despite the claim that Andre was the leading name in a new "minimalist" school of sculpture, and they were shocked to discover that Andre's fee was $87,000. It was little comfort to learn that the Hartford Foundation for Public Giving and the National Endowment for the Arts had shared the cost of the artist's fee—plus $6,500 for an "expert" to choose the sculpture.

Hartford's old theaters, several of which had once been famous for their splendid presentations by traveling companies, had given way to motion pictures, but legitimate theater returned to Hartford in 1964 with the creation of the Hartford Stage Company, a professional, nonprofit repertory theater that began operations in makeshift rented quarters in downtown Hartford. The company performed to full houses nightly, and in 1977 it dedicated its new multimillion-dollar, 350-seat theater on the corner of Main and Trumbull streets.

In June, 1971, the first Greater Hartford Civic and Arts Festival was held on Constitution Plaza. Here music, drama, dance, painting, and sculpture were brought together for a week-long gala. Throughout this aesthetic sampling there were concerts by the Hartford Symphony, school bands and choruses, rock groups, and Gospel singers. There also were performances by the Hartford Ballet Company, the Mark Twain Masquers, and the Hartt Opera Theatre. More than 50,000 persons attended the first festival. For several years following, the festival was repeated, and each year the number of participating organizations increased. Attendance at the 1974 festival was more than 150,000.

But the program of greatest long-range potential toward encouragement of the

BELOW: Mark Twain is one of Hartford's most famous citizens. He lived in several states before settling in Connecticut in the 1870s. (CHS)

BELOW RIGHT: Some years before Mark Twain lived in Hartford, he was a river pilot on the Mississippi. Apparently he instructed architect Edward Tuckerman Potter to create some resemblance of a Mississippi riverboat in the design of the Twain home. Courtesy, Kingswood-Oxford School

arts in the Greater Hartford area was set up in 1971, when the Greater Hartford Chamber of Commerce created the Greater Hartford Arts Council, a fund-raising organization intended to make a united appeal on behalf of all the arts to Hartford-area business and industrial corporations. The Greater Hartford Arts Council's first campaign (1972) raised $303,000 from 85 companies; the 1973 campaign raised $364,000 from a greatly broadened base of 155 companies; and the 1974 campaign raised $507,000 from more than 200 corporations.

Somewhat related to the arts is the Hartford Architecture Conservancy, organized in 1973 with the intent of preserving what was left of Hartford's older buildings that had either historical or aesthetic interest. Although many quite correctly regarded the idea as one of locking the stable after the horse had been stolen, the conservancy has done noble work in preserving numerous remaining examples of Italianate and Victorian architecture. Operating on the concept of recycling and working with a small revolving fund, the conservancy frequently has stayed the wrecking ball and secured purchasers who have made the once-condemned buildings both beautiful and serviceable. Several buildings on lower South Main Street, "The Linden" in particular, and an entire block of Congress Street were restored with the blessing of the conservancy. An especially pleasing restoration was that of the Cheney Building at 942 Main Street, built in 1876 and designed by the distinguished architect H.H. Richardson. The structure was refurbished during the late 1970s for retail shops, offices, and luxury apartments.

Every city, and indeed every community, has a focus. In earliest Hartford this focus was, of course, the meetinghouse. In the 19th century it was probably the city hall, especially as Hartford's particular City Hall was—in addition to being the seat of municipal government and a police station—a market house and an auditorium for public gatherings.

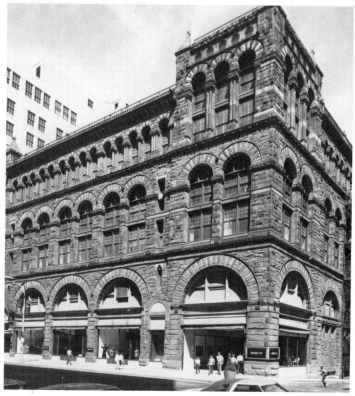

In time, however, and as public and private transportation dispersed the population to the outlying areas that were to become Greater Hartford, even this focus declined in importance. Furthermore, as Hartford's offices dismissed their workers at four-thirty, and as Hartford's stores no longer remained open in the evening, that hour saw an exodus of thousands of white-collar workers and an almost complete absence of humanity on the downtown streets. One former Hartfordite, who made a considerable name for himself in the entertainment world, described nighttime Hartford of the 1960s as a "cemetery with electric lights." His unflattering description was painfully close to being accurate.

By the late 1960s every self-respecting city in America had come to assume that a civic center was one of the necessities of urban life. Impetus for a Hartford Civic Center came from the Greater Hartford Chamber of Commerce, which soon persuaded the City Council to give official support and the Aetna Life & Casualty Company to provide the necessary financial backing.

The Civic Center provided an interesting example of an urban project undertaken with both public and private funding. In 1970 a Hartford referendum approved a bond issue of $30,500,000 to build the Coliseum, and at the same time, Aetna Life & Casualty invested $35,000,000 in the shopping-mall portion of the complex. Shortly thereafter Aetna Life & Casualty was joined by International Telephone and Telegraph Company in erecting the adjacent Sheraton Hotel.

The Civic Center opened on January 5, 1975, and to a considerable degree it lived up to expectations as the catalyst for revitalizing downtown Hartford. Literally dozens of new restaurants opened in the immediate vicinity, and on the nights the New England Whalers were playing a home hockey game or a rock-and-roll band was performing, the central city became alive once more, for a few hours at least.

On January 7, 1978, five hours after a capacity crowd of about 9,000 people had gone home from a sports event, the Coliseum roof collapsed. But despite widespread fears that the destruction of the Coliseum would end the urban renaissance that the Civic Center had engendered, within two years the structure was completely rebuilt and even enlarged. The Civic Center's most glorious moment came on October 28, 1981, when the Connecticut Opera Association, assisted by the Hartford Symphony, staged the most spectacular indoor performance ever attempted

ABOVE LEFT: The profitable lifetime of an office building is said to be 55 years. The American Industrial building is the tall brick structure on the right. Built in 1921, it was demolished two years short of that life expectancy. (CHS)

ABOVE CENTER: There was no place for it in a new development planned for the area, and one Sunday morning in 1974 the American Industrial building fell in less than 30 seconds. (CHS)

ABOVE: Explosive charges toppled the structure into vacant space to the north.

FACING PAGE: In this 1973 view of Hartford's changing skyline, the Traveler's Tower continues to top all other high-rises, including One Financial Plaza which was still under construction. The modern buildings seem to dwarf the white steeple of Center Church. (CHS)

TOP: *In the early 1970s construction was begun on a civic center that would enclose a shopping mall connected to a sports coliseum. The feature of this arena was its "space frame" roof—a three-dimensional web of small structural members put together on the ground and then jacked up to rest on four corner posts. Courtesy, The Hartford Courant*

ABOVE: *On the morning of January 7, 1978, the roof of the Veterans Colosseum collapsed. Fortunately no one was in the building. Months of investigation did not uncover the cause. The Veterans Colosseum has since reopened with an increased seating capacity and with a traditional truss construction of its roof. Courtesy, The Hartford Courant*

of Verdi's *Aida*, with a cast of more than 1,000 musicians, singers, and dancers and almost 100 elephants, camels, and horses.

In the 35 years following World War II, Hartford had experienced profound change, and even the city's type and function had undergone noticeable change. Many of the factories that once lined the Park River had been razed or stood as empty reminders of Hartford's earlier industrial preeminence. Most of the core city's industrial operation had been relocated in industrial parks in the suburbs and beyond, and this had encouraged a migration of skilled industrial workers to the outlying areas. The central city remained the base of retailing, insurance, banking, and state government, but even here there were exceptions. Shopping centers were developed in virtually all suburban communities, Connecticut General Insurance Company moved to Bloomfield, and state-government agencies built huge office buildings in Wethersfield.

The Greater Hartford Chamber of Commerce was determined to halt the exodus of at least the insurance companies to the suburbs, and in this effort the Chamber was eminently successful. Since Connecticut General's move, no other company followed suit, and virtually all Hartford insurance companies made additions to their existing facilities. Other corporations also chose to build new headquarters in Hartford's downtown. Among these the most notable was the structure called One Financial Plaza, known locally as the "Gold Building" for its gold-glass exterior. This was built in 1974 as the headquarters of United Technologies Corporation, and it is the largest rental office building between New York City and Boston.

The completion of the Gold Building marked the beginning of a new spurt of major office-building construction in Hartford. Even as this book was going to press, there were six large structures in various stages of completion: City Place, bounded by Pearl, Trumbull, Asylum, and Haynes streets; One Corporate Center at Church and Main; Hartford Steam Boiler on Columbus Boulevard; Hartford Federal Twin Towers at State and Main; One Commercial Plaza at Trumbull and Church; and Phoenix-Helmsly at Columbus Boulevard and State Street. Other plans were still on the drawing board, and several of these were for apartments or condominiums.

By an interesting coincidence, *Connecticut Magazine* devoted almost half of its April, 1982, issue to an "inside special" titled "Hartford: Our Surprising Capital." The lead article, "Hartford Coming Alive," carried the subhead, "This born-again metropolis has got its business boom. Now it is trying to become more livable." And so indeed it was, with the Hartford Convention Bureau working to bring thousands of visitors to the city annually, the Downtown Council seeking eagerly to create "people places," City Manager Woodrow Wilson Gaitor enjoying the reputation of having made Hartford a cleaner city than it ever had been before, and Thirman Milner, the city's first black mayor, calling for a "new era" with a municipal government representing all the people but having a special concern for the city's 70 percent minority population. Plans were also in the making for the October, 1982, celebration of the 350th anniversary of the founding of First Congregational Church and for the 350th anniversary, in 1985, of the beginning of the City of Hartford in Connecticut.

History, of course, concerns itself with the past, and on the foregoing pages we have followed Hartford's progress from a small frontier village to a revitalized, medium-size city. Throughout Hartford's history, there have been good times and there have been bad, but that, it seems, is the stuff history is made of. If the future is anything of a projection of the past, Connecticut's Capital City appears to be destined to a happy and healthy life for at least another three and one-half centuries.

The Old State House, now surrounded by modern skyscrapers, has been restored as a civic monument. Photo, Dominic Ruggiero; courtesy, Connecticut Department of Economic Development

The five Kellogg brothers did lithography that added to Hartford's renown in the mid-19th century. They covered a wide range of subjects, including war, romance, the Bible and, of course, Hartford. Shown here: (right) "Don't Wish You May Get It;" and (below) a view of William Henry Harrison's campaign headquarters on the corner of Asylum and Trumbull streets, a site which the Brownstone Restaurant now occupies. (CHS)

These portraits of Samuel Burr and his wife, Rebecca Stillman Burr, were painted in 1792. At that time Mr. Burr owned the largest store in Hartford, located on Burr Street which is now the north end of Main Street. (CHS)

The Putnam Phalanx, named for General Israel Putnam of Revolutionary War fame, was organized in 1858 as a "marching club." It has taken part in most Hartford parades since that date. These gentlemen were officers of the Phalanx in the 1860s. (CHS)

The library (facing page) and the billiard room (below) in Mark Twain's home are now furnished either with pieces owned by the Clemens family or with items appropriate to the years they lived in Hartford. The opulence of the interior complements the riverboat theme of the exterior. Courtesy, Mark Twain Memorial

RIGHT: Referred to as "America's Pioneer Institution for the Handicapped," the American School for the Deaf was founded in 1817. It is pictured here on a Staffordshire china platter from the same era. (CHS)

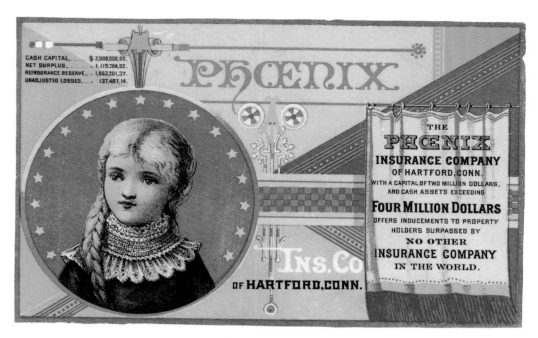

Hartford has long been known as an "insurance capital" and as a seat of heavy industry. Large manufacturers appreciated Hartford's easy access to transportation and raw materials. Those advantages attracted many small factories too. On two of the postcard ads pictured here are companies not as well known as giants like Colt or Pratt and Whitney. Imperial Egg Food "beats the world," and Williams Root Beer Extract was "the perfect temperance drink." Also pictured is an ad for Phoenix Insurance Company, one of Hartford's oldest.

Charles N. Pond donated his large estate including this house to the Hartford Parks Commission. The estate, in northwestern Hartford, became Elizabeth Park, named in memory of Pond's wife.

The third building from the right was once the office of Phoenix Insurance Company. When it was built it was the tallest office building on this section of Main Street. In this view we can see the effects of modern growth—the old Phoenix Insurance building is now dwarfed by its neighbors.

MAIN STREET LOOKING SOUTH, HARTFORD, CONN.

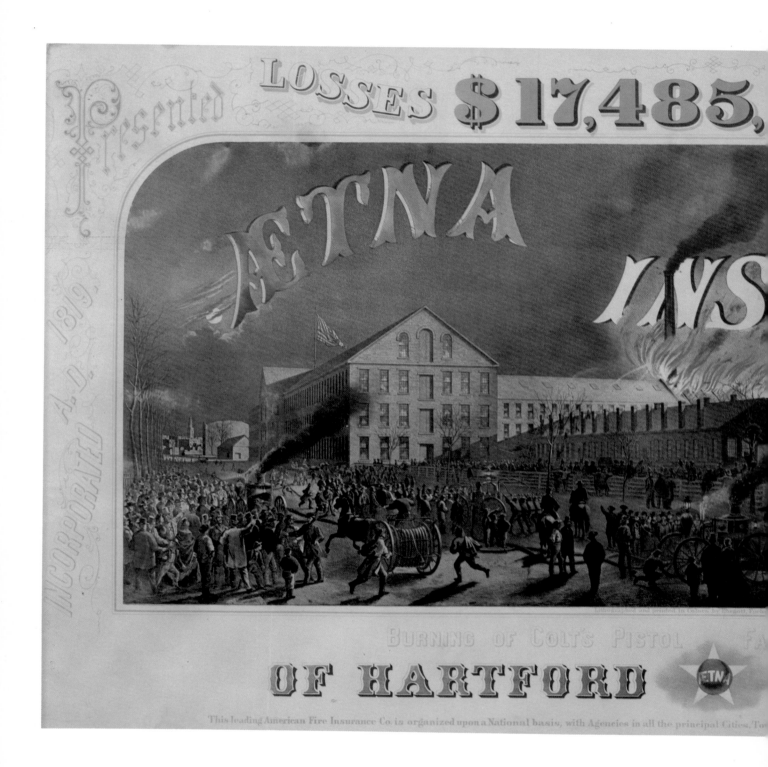

Aetna and other Hartford insurance companies gained many customers because of their exemplary record. When other insurers declared bankruptcy to avoid compensating their customers after disasters, Hartford companies honored all claims. In this ad depicting the 1864 destruction of Colt's Armory, Aetna proudly proclaims the more than $17 million paid to their customers. (CHS)

Before the United States Postal Service was organized, local postmasters issued their own stamps. These came from the Hartford Post Office. (CHS)

Captain Joseph Wadsworth supposedly hid the Connecticut charter in an oak tree when the English-appointed Governor of New England came to rescind Connecticut's self-rule. The Charter Oak then became a popular subject for artists and storytellers. It was nearly 1,000 years old when E.W. Clay painted this watercolor of it in 1834. (CHS)

In 1855 Samuel Colt built his armory on Hartford's South Meadow. At the time it was the world's largest, individually-owned factory. He also established a private ferry for those employees who lived in East Hartford directly across the river from his armory. (CHS)

The late afternoon sun highlights a portion of the west facade of the State Capitol. In 1870 the State of Connecticut chose Hartford over New Haven as the permanent site of state offices. After many construction mishaps, cost overruns, and much bureaucratic mismanagement, the capitol building opened 10 years later. (CHS)

ABOVE: The Connecticut Historical Society houses a wealth of information chronicling Connecticut's past. Pictured here is the former residence of Curtis Veeder, which CHS purchased as its headquarters 30 years ago. Since then CHS has added book stacks, museum galleries, and an auditorium. (CHS)

LEFT: From 1874 to 1891 Samuel Clemens, better known as Mark Twain, resided in this rambling mansion. Today the restored mansion, located in Hartford's West end, is open to the public. Photo by Dominic Ruggiero; courtesy, Greater Hartford Convention and Visitor's Bureau

LEFT: *This view from the Connecticut River of downtown Hartford is dominated by the Traveler's Tower, One Financial Plaza (the "Gold Building"), and the Phoenix Mutual Life Insurance Building. Thanks to the Reverend Francis Goodwin, chairman of the Hartford Parks Commission at the turn of the century, residents can sail and enjoy parklands only a short distance from the downtown area. Photo by Dominic Ruggiero; courtesy, Connecticut Department of Economic Development*

LEFT: *The Connecticut Theological Institute, founded in 1834, was originally located in East Windsor Hill. It changed its name to the Hartford Theological Seminary and moved into the city 31 years later. Before the seminary occupied this gleaming white building on Sherman Street, it had addresses on Prospect, Broad, and Elizabeth streets. (CHS)*

Alexander Calder's massive steel sculpture, Stegosaurus, dominates Burr Mall. It created some controversy when it was first erected, but it still stands between Wadsworth Atheneum and City Hall. Photo by Jim Rigby; courtesy, Greater Hartford Convention and Visitors Bureau

CHAPTER
XII

Partners in Progress

~ WHEN THOMAS HOOKER AND HIS FOLLOWERS CAME TO WHAT IS NOW HARTFORD IN 1636, THEY BROUGHT WITH THEM DEEPLY HELD Puritan convictions. However, they had not left their homes in Massachusetts because of religious dissension. They moved west in search of better opportunities for themselves and their children.

Until the early 19th century Hartford could hardly be called much more than a provincial, agricultural town. As the alternate capital for the colony and state of Connecticut, its major economic activity consisted of trade via the Connecticut River. Most of the warehouses, shops, and services depended on that trade. The embargo and ensuing War of 1812 temporarily slowed down even that activity.

Once the conflict was over Hartford began to change economically. This was due in large part to what has always been the city's major resource — people. Its leading citizens were ready to give support to new industries in those pre-Civil War years. Others, residents and those from other towns, brought ideas which they believed could become successful enterprises.

Some of these fledgling industries failed because of the turmoil of a free economy. But, as the following pages indicate, many succeeded beyond the greatest expectations of their founders. Hartford's banks provided much of the needed capital, the railroad's arrival in 1839 opened up new markets, and workmen, often from the surrounding countryside, proved to be easily trainable in a variety of crafts and skills. Hartford had a solid base upon which to build its future.

The city's early industries produced furniture, silverware, and leather goods, and included recognized printing and publishing firms. Other manufacturers developed steam engines, boilers, heavy machinery, and firearms. All of them benefited from water power as a convenient source of energy. Insurance companies expanded in size and number throughout the century, making Hartford well-known, at least by name, all over the world. Not only have they provided employment for countless thousands, but their contributions to the community have helped to enrich the quality of life for Hartford.

A characteristic of 19th-century America was the arrival of people from Ireland, Germany, Italy, Poland, Russia, and many other countries. With their coming Hartford became more metropolitan and new businesses and services reflected the importance of these people to the economic and cultural life of the city.

By the beginning of the 20th century Hartford had become a major American industrial and financial center. Gas, electricity, water, as well as the new automobile and the soon-to-be "aeroplane," were indicative of how far the city had come. Its relationship to surrounding towns was growing closer as corporations formed and branched out to the suburbs.

Hartford's industrial expertise was of vital importance to the nation's defense efforts during the wars of this century. Aircraft engines, specialized component parts, and wiring, among many other products, were manufactured in the area. While important in and of themselves, these defense industries developed new areas of technology. Today Hartford companies are leaders in the communications, computer, and electronics fields and high technology has become a major part of the area's economy. Banking and insurance expansion is making the city a national center of finance.

Hartford can boast of a rich cultural and educational environment, modern communications outlets, and excellent health facilities which offer residents of the capital region the best facets of modern life. Thomas Hooker and his followers would find little to relate to today in the community they founded, but they could take satisfaction in knowing that their early struggles had helped to produce an attractive, modern American city which respects and takes pride in the accomplishments of the past.

American School For The Deaf

In 1807 Dr. Mason Fitch Cogswell was a respected Hartford physician. He lived next door to a French Huguenot family, the Gallaudets, whose son, Thomas Hopkins Gallaudet, was to become a leader in the education of the deaf. Cogswell's daughter, Alice, had lost her hearing from a childhood disease when she was two years old. Gallaudet, a Yale graduate, was able to make significant progress in teaching the child, causing Cogswell and other prominent citizens of Hartford to send the young man to Europe to learn the methods for instructing deaf children.

Arriving in Paris in 1815 Gallaudet visited the Paris School for the Deaf, the world's first such institution. He was instructed by the Abbé Sicard, its director. Sicard's deaf assistant, Laurent Clerc, returned with Gallaudet to Hartford and became instrumental in developing the Hartford school, the first special-education facility in America.

The Connecticut General Assembly granted incorporation for the American Asylum for the Education and Instruction of Deaf and Dumb Persons in 1816 and

The present campus of the American School for the Deaf.

A snack break for two youngsters at the American School for the Deaf.

donated $5,000 toward the institution. This action represented the first legislative aid to the education of the handicapped in the Western Hemisphere. The school opened in 1817 on Main Street with seven pupils including Alice Cogswell.

Word of the effort being made at Hartford spread, and in 1819 Congress appropriated 23,000 acres of public domain in the territory of Alabama for the school's use. As a result of the sale of this land, a site was purchased where the present Hartford Group is located on Asylum Hill, so named because the school was situated there between 1821 and 1921.

Much of the success of this institution was due to the work of Gallaudet, who taught there for 13 years, and Clerc, who dedicated the remainder of his life to its cause. Clerc emphasized the use of sign language and, through numerous contacts,

brought the work of the school to the public's attention. One of the dormitories on the present campus is named in his honor, but the school is his greatest monument.

The present campus, occupied in 1921, is at 139 North Main Street, West Hartford. Approximately 200 faculty and staff provide instruction and services for 300 full-time students. A comprehensive, special-education program is provided ranging from pre-primary to high school ages. The campus includes complete facilities for all activities including dormitory life, vocational education, athletics, and recreation.

Modern technology has been enlisted to promote better programs and methods. The use of satellite teleconferences, for instance, between Hartford and Europe, particularly the original Paris school, will let experts discuss and exchange ideas and programs. The American School for the Deaf, as a pioneer in education for the hearing impaired, is an institution of which Hartford can be truly proud.

Avon Old Farms Hotel

Avon Old Farms Hotel, situated at the junction of routes 44 and 10 in Avon, is one of Connecticut's most elegant hostelries. Oriental rugs, antiques, fine moldings, and a marble-and-oak fireplace decorate the Georgian colonial lobby. Original watercolors of Farmington Valley scenes, moldings, poster beds, and bathrooms with marble-like sinks and full-length mirrors enhance each of the 39 new guest rooms completed in 1982 (adding to the original 44 rooms). Ornate conference rooms, a coffee shop designed to appear like a trellis gazebo, a beauty salon, and a health club and sauna are available for guest use. Situated on 12 acres of landscaped grounds, the site includes a large outdoor pool and pool house, playing field, and playground. Brick walks, colonial antique copper lanterns, and extensive landscaping all provide a resort-like setting.

Avon Old Farms Hotel was established by Jack Brighenti, his wife Charlotte, and their two sons, Stephen and Silvio, in 1958 through Jackson, Inc., a family-owned holding corporation. Jack Brighenti had emigrated from Castion Veronese, Italy, in 1909 and settled in Avon in 1928. As a skilled cabinetmaker he soon found employment with a prestigious Avon family—the Alsops—and later in the construction of Avon Old Farms School. Like many of the Italian immigrants he brought with him the philosophy of hard work and saving for a better future for his family. He implemented this by investing in hundreds of acres of inexpensive land in Avon when it was a farming community. His business involvements grew with a town that was soon to become the most affluent suburb in the greater Hartford area.

Jack built Avon's first housing development, Jackson Heights. With his son Stephen he opened an appliance store and electrical contracting firm in 1948. With his other son, Silvio, Jack opened a plumbing and heating firm.

In 1958 ground was to be broken on the Brighentis' largest project yet, a 24-room motel that was one of the most luxurious in the greater Hartford area. The motel was leased to and operated by Elmer and Belle Young, owners of the The Avon Old Farms Inn restaurant across the street. The motel was an immediate success, and Jack and his sons in the early 1960s added on an additional 20 rooms.

Jack Brighenti's sons followed in their father's footsteps after his death in 1974. Stephen's three sons, Stephen, Michael, and Gary, and Silvio's three sons, John, Jeffrey, and James, in 1977 became directors of Jackson, Inc., with the oldest grandson, John, becoming president. At this point, they began to make plans for an ambitious $2.5-million expansion program for the motel. Stephen Jr. became general manager of the motel in June 1978.

The Brighenti family acted as general contractors with the aid of local architects and a construction management firm and were the electrical, plumbing, and heating contractors, as well. Construction of the complex was completed in June 1982, at which time the name was formally changed to Avon Old Farms Hotel.

The Avon Old Farms Hotel is a fine example of New England hospitality set amid beautiful surroundings. Operated with a strong service orientation, it is the result of the labors and cooperative efforts of a family whose founder believed in hard work, building quality, and taking advantage of the opportunities offered him in his new homeland.

Avon Old Farms Inn

The intersection of routes 44 and 10 in Avon was a stopover for Boston, Hartford, and Albany stages for many years. The passengers stayed overnight at the Marshall Tavern. Today, very near that location, is Avon Old Farms Inn, part of which has stood since 1757. According to the National Restaurant Association it is one of the 20 oldest inns in the country.

The property on which the inn is situated belonged originally to Thomas North, whose father, John, had moved to the area

Avon Old Farms Inn's foyer, lobby, private dining room, and second-floor bedrooms are part of the original structure built in 1757. Erected by Nathaniel North, the property was received by his father, Thomas, as a land grant for his services in King Philip's War. (Drawing by Olive Metcalf.)

in the 17th century. Avon was part of Farmington and later called Northington when Thomas received a land grant as a result of his services in King Philip's War. In turn his son, Nathaniel, settled on part of this property in 1757. The building he erected is now the inn's foyer, lobby, private dining room, and second-floor bedrooms.

The next major addition came in 1832. Nathaniel's great-grandson, Joseph, was the town blacksmith. He decided to build a stone shop next to his house, which has also become part of the inn. When Joseph's neighbor, the Marshall Tavern, was full, the extra guests were sent to the blacksmith for overnight accommodations. The inn gradually evolved after that period and came to include the original house and blacksmith shop. Further additions were made and in 1923 it became the Avon Old Farms Inn.

In conjunction with the inn today, although under separate ownership, is the Avon Old Farms Hotel across the street whose guests are frequently patrons of the

restaurant. Although overnight guests are still accommodated, the inn has become one of the Hartford region's most highly regarded eating places.

One of the major features of Avon Old Farms Inn is its flexibility. Parties of 10, 30, or 100 can be accommodated with ease. The inn consists of six dining rooms, four of them appropriately named the Coach, Forge, Tavern, and Northington rooms, respectively. There are also a private dining room and a conference room. The Forge room, for instance, includes Joseph North's old blacksmith shop and many of the original tools are used in the room's decor.

The innkeepers of this unique and historic country dining facility are Louis and Anne Panagakos. They describe their menu as American but with a Continental flair. Certainly the elegance and hospitality which are offered have succeeded in establishing the inn's reputation, while the historical nature of much of the building and its decor have delighted visitors and natives alike for many years.

Barrieau Moving & Storage, Inc.

During World War II Hartford was deeply involved in the war effort. New and expanded plants had brought numbers of families into the region, making it one of the country's most important defense areas. It was in 1944 that 16-year-old Gerard Barrieau set out on his pursuit of a career in the moving business armed with a single truck and much determination.

Barrieau knew the problems and possibilities involved in his venture. His father, Livain Barrieau, had long been in the same business, having established a moving company in New Bedford, Massachusetts, in 1917. That city remained the family home until 1928, when the Barrieaus moved to Hartford. For a while Livain worked at Royal Typewriter until it became obvious that hard times would bring layoffs. As a result he returned to his former pursuit. This time he transported oil as well as furniture under the name of Barrieau Express.

Gerard Barrieau, today the president of Barrieau Moving & Storage, was continuing in his father's footsteps in 1944. By age 18 he had purchased E.J. Martin Company, a Hartford furniture mover, merging it with Barrieau Express. As the postwar years brought new industries to Hartford, the business continued to grow. In 1957 Barrieau took an important step when it obtained an operating authority from the Interstate Commerce Commission and also purchased a Belmont Street brewery for conversion into a storage facility. In 1961 a building on Brown Street was added to the firm's property, which then included four vans. Finally, in 1966, Barrieau bought the present site of the company's headquarters at 301 Murphy Road in Brainard Industrial Park.

Almost 100 people are employed in the organization today, which offers diversified and specialized services. Customers have multiplied over the years because Barrieau Moving & Storage has emphasized those services.

Today the third generation of the family is highly visible in all aspects of the com-

pany's operations. Shipments now go far afield of Hartford and one may see a Barrieau truck in Paris, Mexico City, Los Angeles, or Miami. While personal effects remain an important part of the business, electronic equipment, trade displays, and other commercial items are moved and stored, reflecting the varied industrial

One of the Barrieau moving vans used in the 1950s.

One of the modern Barrieau fleet in front of the firm's storage facility and office building.

nature of the Hartford region. Barrieau Moving & Storage uses the latest technological advances to increase efficient and speedy transportation. Gerard Barrieau notes that, while conditions have changed since his father was in the furniture business, the firm's commitment to provide the best possible service for its customers remains the same.

Chase Enterprises

Chase Enterprises does not have roots that go back to the 18th or 19th centuries as many other Hartford firms do. Nevertheless, even though it is a relatively new business, its effect on the city has been important even beyond the changes it has brought to Hartford's skyline. Chase Enterprises' story is very much the story of one man, David T. Chase, who, with a dedicated staff of skilled businessmen, has created a modern American success story not unlike that of the founders of industries in an earlier time.

When David Chase arrived in America in 1946 under the auspices of the United Jewish Appeal, he was determined to obtain an education. He had been born in Poland in 1929 but had lost most of his family during World War II and the Holocaust, only narrowly escaping himself.

Finding Hartford to be the right place to live, Chase obtained his first job washing cars and went on from there to other endeavors working in a nursery, or as a busboy, and finally becoming a salesman. It was when he began selling prefabricated garages that he hit upon the idea of erecting them himself. Gradually the jobs multiplied and became more complex. David Chase found himself in the business of remodeling and building.

Throughout this period Chase had grad-

The Parkview Hilton Hotel, overlooking Bushnell Park in Hartford.

David T. Chase, founder and head of Chase Enterprises.

uated from Weaver High School in Hartford and had studied at Hillyer College and the University of Connecticut. But construction was to be his profession, particularly in sales and management of properties.

Starting with home improvements, the business expanded in the mid-1950s into commercial work, primarily in the new shopping centers that were beginning to develop in suburban areas.

Meanwhile, Chase had opened his first office on Albany Avenue, from which he ran the home improvement and remodeling operations. Today, however, Chase Enterprises occupies the 18th floor of "The Gold Building" at One Financial Plaza, a Chase structure. The years in between have brought phenomenal success to Chase both in and outside the Hartford area.

Chase Enterprises has made its presence felt in its home city. In 1975 it completed One Financial Plaza. With 26 floors and 650,000 square feet of space, it has readily become a Hartford landmark. Its major tenants, besides Chase, include United Technologies, The Travelers Insurance Companies, Peat, Marwick, Mitchell & Co., and the State Bank for Savings. In 1981 Chase completed construction of One Corporate Plaza, a 16-floor building containing 400,000 square feet of space which is today occupied by such businesses as Aetna Life and Casualty and Arthur Young & Company. In 1982 a former hotel was renovated and opened as the Parkview Hilton which,

as its name implies, overlooks Bushnell Park. Its plant includes 402 units and 32 suites with conference facilities for approximately 2,000 people.

The third major structure in downtown Hartford will be completed in 1983 and will be known as One Commercial Plaza. It is a 27-story building and will include 750,000 square feet of space as well as a 540-car parking garage. These buildings are the first skyscrapers erected in downtown Hartford for many years and each one has lent its unique presence to the central city.

Chase Enterprises, however, has consistently maintained a policy of diversification. As early as 1973 it purchased WTIC-AM & FM, Hartford's oldest and most popular radio station. In a somewhat different area Chase has a major interest in Tele-concepts, a firm based in West Hartford. The corporation designs, manufactures, and markets telephone models and accessories through telephone company stores across the United States.

These are only a part of Chase Enterprises' activities in the Hartford area. A full description of the organization would have to include such other investment building services as financing, interior design, leasing, and management.

Chase has expanded outside of the city in the communications field, the electronics industry, and manufacturing. Its interests range from Sabin Industries, Inc., of Mount Clemens, Michigan, a manufacturer of pottery and glass, to Apollo Cablevision in South Hillsborough County, Florida, a partnership that owns and operates a cable franchise.

The phenomenal growth of Chase Enterprises has brought major physical changes to Hartford. But it has benefited the city in other ways that have an important effect on the life of the community. Many

of Hartford's cultural, educational, and medical institutions have received strong support from the firm and from David Chase himself. Also, the problem of much-needed middle- and lower-income housing has been of concern for some time, and efforts have been made to work with local government to find ways of overcoming the financial problems inherent in inner-city housing development.

David Chase has always believed that problems are only temporary, that they can be overcome with effort and determination. His accomplishments as well as those of the

organization he has built are an example of how he has put that belief into action. Chase Enterprises has grown in 30 years from a small company into a multimillion-dollar corporation. In that respect it is a 20th-century version of a story that has been repeated many times throughout American business history. Above all it is evidence of the financial and industrial vitality of Hartford as that century draws to a close.

One Commercial Plaza, Hartford.

One Financial Plaza, "The Gold Building," in Hartford.

The Collinsville Company

For 200 years Yankee artisans and entrepreneurs have worked together to improve the quality of life by utilizing the power of the Farmington River in Collinsville. Over the years, that power has been used to manufacture many different products to meet the transient needs of changing times. By 1900 the Collinsville plant had made flour, lumber, edged tools, hammers, ploughs, tool steel, forgings, castings, production machinery, machine tools, adjustable wrenches, hydraulic pumps and motors, molded cow horn products, leather goods, wrought iron work, plastics, portland cement, and concrete blocks. All of these were products created by dedicated, ingenious men using locally available materials and power from the river.

Collinsville's greatest growth came from the manufacture of edged tools: hoes, shovels, axes, chisels, adzes, machetes, swords, bayonets, lances, and knives. These were made in thousands of styles and sizes. For 125 years Collinsville's edged tool factory was the world's largest and most successful. This era ended when it became apparent that most of the interested and discriminating edged tool users had disappeared with the tall trees and the open prairies. In 1967 company management discontinued all tool making in Collinsville.

The factory was Collinsville's only industry and its shutdown created a number of problems for its employees and the town. Both company and town management agreed that everyone's best interest would be served by a new corporation organized to work with the town's many talented people and their splendid water power system to utilize the historic factory buildings as a home for new enterprises.

Thus the Collinsville Company was organized. All of the stock in the venture was quickly bought by local people who wanted to do their part to keep Collinsville an attractive center of innovative manufacturing. Within two years the plant was completely occupied by more than 50 new small businesses whose products include keyless

locks, pipe organs, fasteners, air tools, lubricants, N.C. machine tools, hand-blown glass, inertia measuring machines, ultra-precise gears, and foamed plastic optical polishing materials. One company uses the hydropower facility to design, test, and sell small water turbines of previously unmatched high efficiency. It has also designed the first efficient turbine capable of passing fish without injury.

Of course, some of the townspeople had worked for years operating and maintaining the company's water power system. These people now provide guidance and inspiration to a great many volunteers who have

---

TOP: *Start of construction of the lower Collinsville Dam, March 1913.*
BOTTOM: *Forebay, spillway, and dam of the Collinsville Canal.*

freely donated their services over the years to maintain the company's hydroelectric facility. A major effort of the engineering and legal volunteers has been to find ways to save fossil fuel by using the firm's hydroelectric power without violating the myriad governmental regulations which are so effective throughout the country in preventing the utilization of hydroelectricity.

Collinsville attracts visitors who come to see the village, which has changed little in 100 years, or to look at the exhibits in the historical society's museum. The federal government has declared the center of Collinsville, which includes the factory and hydropower system, a National Historic District. It is certain that as long as Yankee ingenuity and hydropower effectively work together, Collinsville will continue to produce needed goods and will make interesting history.

The Connecticut Bank and Trust Company

The birth of modern banking in Connecticut took place during the 1790s as the result of a long-standing problem for the state's merchants—their dependence on Boston and New York. Commercial leaders in Connecticut believed that that dependence would grow stronger because of the banks being established in those cities. They determined to free themselves by establishing their own. The Connecticut Bank and Trust Company (CBT) was one of the results of that determination.

A New London, Connecticut, inn was the site of a meeting which formed the Union Bank in 1792, CBT's first predecessor and the fourth oldest bank in the nation. Meanwhile, in Hartford, the success of the city's only bank, The Hartford, enticed some citizens to challenge its monopoly. As a result, the Phoenix Bank was established in 1814 by legislative charter which attached stipulations requiring the bank to raise one million dollars, open a branch at Litchfield, Connecticut, and pay the state $50,000 toward the funding of a medical school at Yale. Phoenix grew with the Hartford area, then becoming a home for increasing numbers of manufacturers and insurance companies in need of capital for building and expansion.

Following the Civil War, two other predecessors of CBT were formed: The Hartford Trust Company in 1867, and The Connecticut Trust and Safe Deposit Company in 1871. They lent their financial support to many progressive developments in the late 19th century, including the telephone, railroad expansion, and Hartford's new electricity industry. One innovation at this time was the formation of The Hartford Clearing House, a check-clearing service similar to that in use today, which Hartford Trust joined in the 1880s. In 1919 the two banks merged as The Hartford-Connecticut Trust Company.

Hartford-Connecticut was required to close during the Bank Holiday of 1933 but was among the first to reopen and pioneered in the 1930s by establishing branches in several Connecticut towns. World War II brought additional pressure for capital, and the bank helped meet the critical financial needs of the region's defense industries.

CBT was formed in 1954 by the merger of Hartford-Connecticut and the Phoenix State Bank and Trust Company, itself the result of mergers between the Phoenix Bank, Capital National Bank, and Park Street Trust Company. In 1970 CBT became the major subsidiary of CBT Corporation, a holding company.

The Connecticut Bank and Trust's predecessors succeeded through sound yet progressive management which benefited Hartford and the nation. CBT, today the state's largest banking organization, fills a special obligation to this heritage. Through 95 statewide branches and 3,600 employees, and with total assets exceeding $3.5 billion, it is able to offer the most modern facilities and inclusive services available in banking today.

One Constitution Plaza, site of The Connecticut Bank and Trust Company headquarters today.

Former headquarters of The Connecticut Bank and Trust Company at 760 Main Street, Hartford. Today it is a branch office.

The Connecticut Historical Society

Hartford in the 1820s was taking its first step toward becoming a major industrial, banking, and insurance center. A new vitality was evident. Yet there were some men who were concerned that progress and change would cause people to overlook their debt to the past.

The Reverend Thomas Robbins of East Windsor, in particular, believed that Connecticut would lose sight of its heritage if steps were not taken to preserve the records of the past. Through his urging, and with support from several prominent citizens, a charter was granted by the General Assembly in 1825 establishing The Connecticut Historical Society.

Its birth was followed by 14 years of inactivity until renewed interest and another charter in 1839 revived it. The Society found a home in Hartford at 124 Main Street above a store adjacent to Center Church. Then, in 1843, it acquired space in the Wadsworth Atheneum where regular hours were established by its first librarian, the Reverend Robbins. In 1857 David Watkinson died, leaving among his bequests $100,000 to establish a library of reference. The Watkinson Library was opened in the Atheneum in 1866.

Many individuals, such as James Hammond Trumbull and Charles Jeremy Hoadly, donated their time, efforts, books, artifacts, and manuscripts. Then, in 1892, Albert Carlos Bates became the fifth librarian, a position he held for 47 years. Under his guidance The Connecticut Historical Society grew into a mature institution.

Thompson R. Harlow became director in 1940 and, over the next four decades, broadened the Society's collections, strengthened its financial support, and increased its staff. In 1950 he supervised a relocation to the Curtis Veeder House at One Elizabeth Street, where renovations and additions have resulted in a modern facility containing a museum, library, and auditorium. He organized the Society around three major areas—library, museum, and publications—and, upon his retirement, its membership included people from many states and several foreign countries.

Under the present director, Christopher P. Bickford, the Society offers workshops, seminars, genealogy instruction, and other programs. The museum contains a superb collection of which Connecticut furniture, paintings, clothing, and clocks are a part. The library's holdings include an extensive collection of manuscripts and genealogical monographs to aid researchers, in addition to which are the more than 100 publications the Society has published.

Although it is a privately supported institution, the library and museum are open to the public and membership is offered to all who are interested in Connecticut history. The Reverend Thomas Robbins' belief that the past is worth preserving has resulted in an institution of which Hartford can be proud.

The Wadsworth Atheneum, home of The Connecticut Historical Society from 1843 to 1950.

Connecticut Printers, Inc.

In 1832 Daniel Kellogg established D.W. Kellogg & Co. in Hartford, thereby founding what is believed to be the oldest commercial printing company in America still in continuous operation. The history of Connecticut Printers, Inc., begins with this organization and that of Newton Case's firm which was started in 1836 and known as Case Tiffany.

Kellogg & Co., which subsequently became Kellogg & Bulkeley after the Civil War, produced lithographic prints depicting a wide variety of portraits and scenes from American life. These lithographs were printed first in black ink by carefully pressing paper against an inked stone. A good lithographer, working steadily, produced about 100 prints a day. The colors were then applied by hand, with one worker responsible for each color. Kellogg also made signs, labels, and calendars. Case's firm, which became Case, Lockwood & Brainard in 1868, was a compositor and letterpress book manufacturer.

Both firms, which were hugely successful, continued to adopt the latest improvements in their craft. In the late 19th century Kellogg & Bulkeley installed electric-powered presses, and increased output to 1,000 prints per hour. The lithographic stones used to make the prints were gradually replaced by zinc and aluminum plates, and in 1908 an offset press was introduced. Two years later the firm was using a photomechanical process which further increased production and lowered costs. Hartford was a major publishing center in the late 1800s.

Case, Lockwood & Brainard, with its own bindery, concentrated on book printing and manufactured 350,000 volumes a year, including *The Cottage Bible, Webster's Unabridged Dictionary,* and works by Mark Twain. However, as Hartford's commercial life expanded, the firm became more involved in servicing insurance companies and other businesses.

The merger of these two firms which established Connecticut Printers, Inc., took place in 1946 and the plant site in Bloom-

The Old Jail, erected in 1793. It later housed a tavern and eventually the company's printing facilities. This location at the corner of Pearl and Trumbull streets was the firm's headquarters for many years.

field was purchased. In 1973 the company became a wholly owned subsidiary of The Robertson Group. This strengthened the financial position of Connecticut Printers and led to greater diversification.

The company maintains sales offices in New York and Hartford, serving customers throughout the northeastern United States. Today it manufactures a wide selection of educational and children's books, special-interest magazines, catalogs, and many materials for insurance companies and other business concerns. Connecticut Printers, celebrating its 150th anniversary in 1982, is justly proud of both its modern facilities, its long history in the Hartford community, and its ability to help its customers be successful.

James L. Freeman, president of Connecticut Printers, Inc.

The Connecticut Printers plant at 55 Granby Street in Bloomfield.

Connecticut Natural Gas Corporation

When lighting was proposed for Hartford's streets in the 1840s, some citizens were concerned that it would encourage people to stay out late at night, thereby making them susceptible to criminal activity and illness. Night and day, they said, were part of the natural law and should not be tampered with by artificial devices such as gas lamps. However, other Hartford citizens wanted Connecticut's second largest city to install gas lighting as other eastern cities were doing at that time. The result was that several of the city's leading men were granted a charter by the Connecticut General Assembly under which they formed the Hartford City Gas Light Company, one of the community's first public utilities and a forerunner of the Connect-

The main office of the Hartford City Gas Light Company, occupied from 1905 to 1928 at 565-67 Main Street in Hartford.

The firm's interior, 1915.

icut Natural Gas Corporation.

The founders' original investment of $100,000, a very large amount for that period, was used to lay five miles of mains in Hartford and to build a plant on Front Street which could distribute five million cubic feet of manufactured gas. As Hartfordites changed their lighting habits from the use of whale oil lamps and tallow candles to gas lamps, the new company expanded steadily and throughout the 19th century added property and new facilities to meet the increasing demands of both individual and industrial consumers in Hartford.

The 1890s, however, introduced electricity as a competitive source of lighting. Hartford Gas realized the need to develop new markets and uses for gas. While expanding its fuel distribution system into West Hartford and Wethersfield in 1899 and East Hartford in 1907, the firm successfully promoted gas as an efficient fuel for water heating and cooking. Thus, even though its primary market was changing, Hartford Gas was able to maintain uninterrupted growth throughout the period as illustrated by the move in 1905 of its main offices to larger spaces at 565-67 Main Street. There the latest gas appliances were displayed for the potential buyer.

The new century brought the acquisition of the South Manchester Light Power and Tramway Company, the construction of a large service building, the extension of gas lines into Glastonbury and Bloomfield, and another move of corporate offices to 233 Pearl Street in 1928. They would remain there for more than 50 years.

A major change for Hartford Gas had taken place by 1959, when conversion from supplying manufactured gas to that of natural gas was completed. This was accomplished by piping the natural gas to Connecticut from the fields of Louisiana and Texas. The construction of a steam and chilled water plant in 1961 was also a significant step in the firm's expanded service as well as an early effort to enhance the environment. This facility, the first investor-owned plant of its kind in the world, provided year-round climate-control service to downtown Hartford's buildings, eliminating the need for construction of several

boiler plants with their resulting pollution. Ten years later another first was accomplished when the company introduced an experimental natural gas fuel cell home; this also reduced pollution and saved natural resources at the same time by using natural gas to produce electricity as a power source. The next year marked the completion of a liquefied natural gas plant, which provided storage for over one billion cubic feet of fuel in a liquefied state ready for use when needed during cold weather periods. The company's supply capability was greatly enhanced by this, making it one of the best for any utility in the country.

In 1968 the New Britain Gas Light Company, a utility founded in 1855, merged with Hartford Gas to form the Connecticut Natural Gas Corporation. Six years later the Greenwich Gas Company was added to the firm, thus completing the structural outline of the present corporation.

Connecticut Natural Gas now serves over 124,000 customers in 21 Hartford-New Britain area communities and Greenwich and supplies almost 25.5 billion cubic feet of gas. Dividends have been paid for 131 consecutive years, longer than any other utility on the New York Stock Exchange, which has listed its common shares since 1978.

The organization continues its close ties to downtown Hartford. In 1980 it began occupation of a modern, attractively designed central office building at 100 Columbus Boulevard. The chairman and president is Robert H. Willis, who oversees the operations of a corporation which now includes the important subsidiaries, Hartford Steam Service Company and Fuels, Inc. The former heats and cools most of the major Hartford downtown buildings through the system of underground piping described earlier and Fuels, Inc., is a specialized company supplying propane for residential, industrial, and commercial customers in the Hartford and Greenwich areas.

One of the company's latest innovative steps indicative of the future involves the use of radio telemetry and computers. An automatic device attached to the individual meter records the usage and transmits the information to a receiver located at 100

An appliance display at the Hartford City Gas Light Company in the 1920s.

LEFT: *The new home of Connecticut Natural Gas Corporation at 100 Columbus Boulevard.*

Columbus Boulevard. There the signal is decoded to computer language, which in turn calculates and prepares the proper charge.

The present strength and importance of Connecticut Natural Gas has been accomplished by pioneering in areas unimagined in 1848. Space heating, air conditioning, and a variety of industrial and commercial innovations using gas are examples of the way in which the utility has improved and progressed over the years. Today pioneering in new technology continues in order to provide the most efficient service possible for the customers of Connecticut Natural Gas.

Cushman Industries, Inc.

Simon Fairman, an iron worker from West Stafford, Connecticut, developed a crude, hand-operated chuck. A chuck is a device for centering and clamping work in a lathe or other machine tool. Fairman received a patent, signed by President Andrew Jackson, for his chuck in 1830. The invention of the chuck was to be of great importance to the future of industry.

One of Fairman's daughters married A.E. Cushman, a patent maker at Colt Fire Arms in Hartford, who eventually acquired his father-in-law's patent. Cushman began producing chucks in his home at Spring and Church streets, using a single lathe run by a foot treadle. He would go to New York City, sell his product, and return to Hartford to resume work. The popularity of his device required a move to larger quarters and by 1885 he, with his son and A.P. Sloan, the factory superintendent, incorporated the firm.

Foreign markets accounted for much of the sales and Cushman chucks became so popular that the name Cushman became a generic term. In 1914 Cushman moved to its present location on Windsor Street, and in 1923 A.P. Sloan became president. Cushman proceeded to expand its facilities and introduce new designs and equipment. This was particularly important during World War II, when the company worked

around the clock to answer the demand for chucks required by defense plants.

In the postwar era Cushman opened operations outside the United States through affiliations in England and South America. Between 1962 and 1963 alone, under president Richard Banfield, the firm doubled its size through acquisition.

This growth—in combination with the development of improved products—is being given new emphasis today. Edward J. Shages, president between 1963 and 1976, and John L. Way II, president since that time, have brought Cushman into the era of modern technology. The corporation's long experience has made it the largest manufacturer of chucks in the world. It continues to develop more sophisticated chucks because of its strong technological capabilities and its willingness to invest in the best equipment available. A new flexible machining system

will result in a greater product range, with computers being used in all facets of the business. Presently Cushman is determined to capture a larger share of the foreign market, which, as president Way points out, "can be done if you manufacture the best product at reasonable cost."

Cushman Industries works closely with the Hartford Board of Education to establish programs in the metal trades and provides training for young people and the handicapped. It believes that a skilled work force in the future will ensure workmanship of the highest quality. Cushman Industries' commitment to improvement has been the life blood of the organization since Fairman turned his idea into a reality.

An aerial view of Cushman Industries, Inc., as it appears today.

The early home of the Cushman Chuck Company, around 1862.

The Dexter Corporation

Windsor Locks was known as Pine Meadow in 1767, when 22-year-old Seth Dexter began his clothier business there. Seth's family had come to Massachusetts with the first Puritans, but early in life he had chosen to move to Connecticut and be on his own. He had no idea that in establishing his trade he was founding the forebear of The Dexter Corporation, which has been under the direction of members of the Dexter family ever since. It is the oldest manufacturing firm operating in Connecticut today and the second or third oldest independent manufacturer in the country.

Seth, with his son, Seth II, opened his clothier works to other interested young men who were trained in the trade and then moved on to open their own shops. Dexter also introduced the art of cloth dressing. His other properties included a saw and grist mill, the latter becoming a feed mill and store which operated until 1928. In his basement Seth's grandson, Charles, developed a handmade wrapping paper made from manila rope and eventually produced as much as 200 pounds per day. With the need for continuous process he moved his operations to larger quarters and used the name of C.H. Dexter and Company. In 1867 he was joined by his son, Edwin, and two sons-in-law, B.R. Allen and Herbert R. Coffin, in C.H. Dexter and Sons.

Paper manufacturing was undergoing a period of such growth that a new paper machine was installed and a large addition was made to Dexter's original mill.

As happened so frequently in the 19th century, fire destroyed a large part of the mill in 1873. The owners of the company since the death of Charles Dexter, Edwin and Herbert, rebuilt while leasing other properties in order to continue paper production. The fire had been beneficial in one sense, for the new mill, constructed of brick, housed the newest equipment in the paper-manufacturing field.

The firm was constantly striving to produce a better paper and its success was evidenced by the growing popularity of its

Offices of The Dexter Corporation, on the site of the original clothier works.

products. Another addition was constructed in 1881 and more equipment was installed which gave Dexter the capacity to manufacture white and colored French tissues.

After Edwin's death in 1886 Herbert Coffin retained control until 1901, during which time the company expanded its product line, increased sales, and continued to improve its plant. His two sons joined in a partnership to run the organization until it was incorporated, at which time Arthur D. Coffin became president. The facility was yet again expanded with the construction of a new administration office, a boiler plant, and production buildings. In 1929 a mill was purchased in Manchester, Connecticut, and it was at this site that successful experiments were conducted which developed long-fiber papers, a product Dexter continued to manufacture at Windsor Locks after the Manchester mill was sold.

The success of any business depends in part on product development. Beginning in the 1930s Dexter became a major innovator in the industry. Porous, long-fiber tea bag paper, fibrous meat casings, and mimeograph stencil base were among many items introduced.

Dexter Coffin succeeded his father as president in 1936 and proceeded to change company output from short- to long-fiber products. After World War II the domestic market for Dexter products returned and the plant hummed with activity. In 1947 the last short-fiber paper was manufactured and with new production capacity available, product development included successful efforts with microglass fiber webs and expanded use of man-made fibers such as polyester and rayon.

In the mid-1950s Dexter launched an acquisition program to diversify its product line away from the capital-intensive nature of paper manufacturing. This diversification program placed the company in new markets with numerous new products, and, as the 1980s began, what is now called The Dexter Corporation had a total of 55 manufacturing plants in the United States and 15 in foreign countries. The business is currently comprised of four groups which manufacture and market liquid and powder materials for industrial coatings, electronic chemicals, and engineering adhesives, as well as tissue culture and microbiological products used in medicine, research, and biotechnology. Chemical compounds are produced for energy conservation, corrosion, and microbiological control as well as sanitation and maintenance uses. What was

An old picture of a grist mill, the building where handmade papers were first manufactured.

originally a paper mill in Windsor Locks is now called the Nonwovens Group, manufacturing products for applications as tea bags, surgical disposables, and sailcloth.

Dexter became a public corporation in 1967 but remains under the direction of seventh-generation Dexter descendant David L. Coffin, chairman. The corporation he oversees is far different from Seth's clothier mill or Charles Dexter's basement paper factory. The tradition of innovation in product development, however, is still just as important for the organization's success as it was for its predecessors. The Dexter Corporation, a Fortune 500 company, is proud of being the oldest firm listed on the New York Stock Exchange. Its technical services, research laboratories, and other offices now range well beyond the Hartford area, but after 215 years, Windsor Locks remains its home.

Ensign-Bickford Industries, Inc.

For early 19th-century miners, maiming and death from blasting accidents were frequent occurrences. William Bickford, who invented the safety fuse and thereby greatly helped to alleviate that peril, was the founder of a company that still bears his name today. Ensign-Bickford Industries, Inc., continues to manufacture commercial blasting products but has expanded into aerospace, fiber, and other industries.

Bickford, a Cornwall, England, leather merchant, patented his invention in 1831 and established the partnership of Bickford, Smith & Davey to produce the "Miner's Safety Fuse." It consisted of twisted threads of hemp into which black powder was inserted. The strands were countered and waterproofed to produce a slow-burning fuse which would reduce the chance of a blasting accident. Word of the manufacture of this device soon spread and drew the attention of Richard Bacon of Simsbury, Connecticut. Bacon was superintendent of the Phoenix Mining Company, which had revived the old Simsbury Newgate copper mine. He visited the small Cornwall factory and was made the firm's American agent. Under the name of Bacon, Bickford & Eales, a Simsbury factory was opened by 1836.

Competition was intense and the infant company showed little growth. In an

William Bickford, inventor of the original safety fuse.

The main office of Ensign-Bickford Industries, Inc.

attempt to revive their venture, the English partners sent over Joseph Toy, a bookkeeper. Before he could succeed, the factory was totally destroyed by fire in 1851. Toy, however, was determined to carry on. A year later he had acquired Bacon's share and built a new factory on the banks of Hop Brook, site of the present Simsbury plant. By 1859 the new firm of Toy, Bickford & Co. had been able to overcome most of its competition by manufacturing a more efficient and reliable fuse. Another example of Toy's courage came when the new factory also went up in flames. He rebuilt again and sent his son-in-law, Lemuel Ellsworth, to open a California branch of the company in 1867.

A son-in-law, Ralph H. Ensign, joined the firm in 1863. When Toy died in 1887 Ensign and two other of Toy's sons-in-law were left a thriving enterprise, which was renamed Ensign-Bickford Company. The firm continued to develop new and better products, including a lead detonating cord in 1913, a textile detonating cord in 1936, and an oil and static-resistant safety fuse some years later.

Following World War II, Ensign-Bickford took a major step with a decision to diversify. Darworth, a subsidiary firm, was founded in 1947 to produce Cuprinol® wood preservative. In 1970 Darworth moved to Avon, Connecticut, acquired other products, twice expanded its plant,

and built a facility at LaGrange, Georgia. Today its products include caulking compounds, paint sundries, and several types of wood preservatives and stains.

Ensign-Bickford's expertise in commercial explosives was extended to government work in the 1950s. This resulted in the formation of an aerospace division for the production of components and devices for rockets, missiles, and space vehicles. The company also bought land in Louviers, Colorado, in 1957, which now contains a branch facility serving the western mining markets. Another production and distribution center was established in 1968-69 at Graham, Kentucky, in the midst of extensive coal fields. Ensign-Bickford has continued to grow and includes subsidiaries and affiliates in Canada, Chile, and Mexico.

The company's steady growth led to reorganization in 1971 when E-B Industries, Inc., was formed. Under this parent organization Darworth became a division and Ensign-Bickford a subsidiary with two divisions: blasting products and aerospace. Finally, in 1981, the parent firm took its present name and now includes the domestic subsidiaries: Darworth Company, Ensign-Bickford Company, and Ensign-Bickford Realty Corporation. The latter has developed an industrial park in Avon and renovated factory buildings which now house the town's municipal offices. In addition, employee housing originally owned by the firm has been renovated and sold. New single-family residences in Avon and luxury apartments in Simsbury have been constructed to provide comfortable and attractive places to live.

The corporation maintains not only its foreign branches, but has created two new domestic divisions. One of these is the research division, which provides technical support for the entire organization. Its goal is to develop new products and ensure their safety, high quality, and reliability. The other new division, film fibers, carrying on a long history of textile involvement, manufactures a film which is converted into fibers, tapes, and yarns for use in a wide variety of products such as carpets, identification tapes for the cable industry, and stuffer yarn for power cable.

Ensign-Bickford Industries, Inc., is under the direction of David J. Andrew, who suc-

ceeded John E. Ellsworth as president in 1970, and Joseph Ensign Lovejoy, chairman of the board of directors since 1979. Traditionally Ensign-Bickford has been characterized by its strong commitment to the community through a policy of corporate social responsibility reflected in its support of many cultural and educational endeavors. The Ensign-Bickford Foundation, for example, funds summer positions in several agencies by which students are provided meaningful employment and training within the community. Another highly popular program, the symposium series for adults and students, is an effort to increase public awareness and knowledge of important contemporary issues in American life.

Ensign-Bickford Industries, Inc., whose original product was designed to enhance blasting safety, begun by a man whose invention saved countless lives, continues to work for improvement in the safety and quality of life today and in the future.

Reproduction of early fuse machinery using some original American parts and a reprint of the original safety fuse patent and drawing.

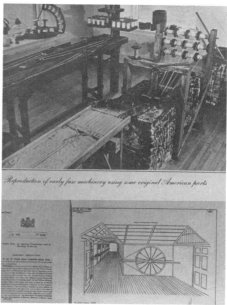

Piping and water-control gates at the site of the original dam on Hop Brook. The boiler room is in the background.

Finlay Brothers Company, Inc.

Mark Twain published *The Adventures of Tom Sawyer* in 1876, the year in which Finlay Brothers Company, Inc., made its start in the printing world. The founders, of course, had no idea that almost 90 years later their firm would publish a historical biography of the world-famous author.

James and William Finlay came to America from Scotland in 1874 and settled in Manchester, where they were employed in the Cheney Brothers Silk Mills. Their first love, however, was printing and, on a part-time basis, they worked at that trade. The mill placed some of its printing jobs with them and, with other business thriving, James decided to venture out on his own.

By 1876 he had purchased the Lang Printing Company's equipment and had set up shop at 96 Asylum Street in Hartford. This attempt did not succeed and he returned to Manchester, although remaining in the printing business. Local contracts, again primarily from the mill, increased to the point that William joined his brother in the firm.

The Finlays decided to try Hartford again and in 1890 established a shop at 28 Temple Street. From that time to the present the company was closely tied to the develop-

J. Herbert Finlay, Jack Findlay, and Kenneth Finlay *(left to right) — the two brothers and their cousin headed Finlay Brothers Company through most of the 20th century.*

Malcolm G. MacKenzie, president of Finlay Brothers Company, Inc.

ment of industry in the Hartford region. As manufacturing came of age at the turn of the century, Finlay Brothers served the needs of businesses by printing brochures, lists, folders, and mail-order catalogs.

The growth of Finlay Brothers in the 20th century, however, was achieved by James' sons, Kenneth and J. Herbert, and a nephew, Jack Findlay (his Finlay mother had married a Findlay). They ran the company until recent times. The need for more space, the result of a growing enterprise, meant constant moving to ever-larger quarters. Finally, in 1960, Finlay Brothers settled into its present home at 390 Capitol Avenue. It was at this time that the company gradually began to augment its letterpress with offset and started to expand its services for customers.

Today Finlay Brothers Company, Inc., is a full-service printer headed by Malcolm G. MacKenzie, president. MacKenzie, also a native of Scotland, came to Finlay Brothers in 1962, bought an interest in 1970, and took over ownership from Jack eight years later. He has led the firm through a period of remarkable growth and modernization. Between 1978 and the present employees have increased from 35 to 65 while computerization has developed greater flexibility and broader service capability. Today Finlay Brothers is the largest commercial printer in Hartford, its success the result of dedication to quality and performance.

Greater Hartford Consortium For Higher Education

Traditionally, Hartford has taken great pride in its many institutions of higher learning. In 1972 its six independent colleges formed the Greater Hartford Consortium for Higher Education, enabling their students to use the resources and take many courses offered by each. The schools maintain their own identity but their programs are strengthened and broadened by this cooperative effort.

Trinity College, founded in 1823, is the second oldest independent, liberal arts college in Connecticut. With an enrollment of 1,700 men and women and a full-time faculty of 135 members, Trinity attracts a national student body. Its 86-acre campus is distinguished by some 50 buildings of both traditional gothic and modern architecture, including an outstanding library of more than 650,000 volumes. Over 600 courses are taught annually in 27 majors, along with special options such as independent study, internships, and exchange programs. Long committed to high-quality education in the liberal arts and sciences, Trinity offers degrees at both the bachelor's and master's levels.

The 200-acre campus of the University of Hartford is located in the suburb of West Hartford. The university was chartered in 1957, though parts of it date back to the later 19th century. It accommodates 11,000 students in a total of eight colleges. They include schools of engineering, art, music, business, and education, as well as a college of arts and sciences and a technical college. A new computer center is under construction. Between 1977 and 1981, the university's operating budget rose from $17 million to $40 million.

Saint Joseph College in West Hartford was founded in 1932 by the Sisters of Mercy to provide women the opportunity to obtain liberal arts degrees in an environment which also would cultivate their spiritual lives. Although the college is in the Roman Catholic tradition, members of all

The long walk at Trinity College was designed by the English architect, William Burges, and is one of the best examples of collegiate Gothic architecture in the country. Founded in 1823, Trinity is the second oldest liberal arts college in Connecticut.

faiths have always been welcome. A coeducational graduate division, initiated in 1959, has expanded into a program designed for many specialists including teachers, scientists, and social workers. The college continues to develop programs to meet the needs of its students in today's diverse society.

Now located on a 13-acre campus in Hartford's west end, Hartford College for Women was founded in 1933 as "Mount Holyoke in Hartford." The venture flourished and six years later Hartford Junior College opened as an independent, two-year, liberal arts transfer college for women. The present name was adopted in 1963. In 1968 the college established Connecticut's first counseling center, providing a range of programs and services for adult women. Hartford College offers courses in

25 fields of study and continues to be dedicated to academic excellence in a close personal environment.

Hartford Seminary resulted from a merger in 1913 of the Theological Institute of Connecticut, founded in 1834; the School of Christian Workers, organized in 1885; and the John Steward Kennedy School of Missions, begun in 1911. Known as the Hartford Seminary Foundation until the present name was adopted in 1981, the school offers M.A. and D.Min. degrees and provides continuing education and consulting services for clergy, laity, and churches. Important religious issues are explored through research projects and programs conducted with industry and the professions. The seminary includes a highly respected center for the study of Muslim-Christian relations.

The critical need for technological experts in Hartford's industries led to the founding of The Hartford Graduate Center in 1955. The school was originally part of Rensselaer Polytechnic Institute of Troy, New York, and is still affiliated with it although now independent. The school was located in South Windsor until 1971, when it moved to its present campus at 275 Windsor Street, Hartford. The curriculum has greatly expanded beyond the early emphasis on engineering. Students from more than 800 companies and institutions attend courses in business administration and health care management, as well as engineering and computer and information sciences and other technologies.

Rising fast on the southwest side of Dana Hall is the university's new computer center, which will also house the academic administration offices.

The Hartford Courant

The French and Indian War had been over for more than a year when on October 29, 1764, Hartford citizens were introduced to the first edition of a weekly newspaper, *The Connecticut Courant*. The history of its successor, *The Hartford Courant*, the nation's oldest continuously published paper, thus encompasses much of the history of Hartford and the nation. The founding publisher, Thomas Green, guided the newspaper through its first three years. In 1777 the second owner, Ebenezer Watson, died and left control in the hands of his widow, Hannah B. Watson. The *Courant* was one of the few newspapers in the country supporting the patriots' cause and Mrs. Watson continued to publish it through the Revolution despite the disastrous loss by fire of its paper mill and warehouse.

Following the war the *Courant* was on a sound financial basis, unusual for newspapers of the day, because the owners, Hudson & Goodwin, had expanded into book publishing and had succeeded in producing several early best sellers, including John Trumbull's *M'Fingal* and Noah Webster's *Blue-Backed Speller*.

Charles D. Warner (d. 1900), editor of the Courant *for many years and coauthor, with Mark Twain, of* The Gilded Years.

The home, for many years, of The Hartford Courant *on State Street (here shown to the right of the Princess Theatre). These buildings have since been torn down; the* Courant *moved to Broad Street, near the state capitol, in 1950.*

The *Courant* became a daily paper in 1837 and through mid-century experienced rapid growth in circulation resulting in relocation to larger quarters at 14 Pratt Street in 1867. At this time the paper merged with the *Evening News* and Joseph R. Hawley and Charles D. Warner became editor-in-chief and literary editor, respectively. Hawley, who became a governor and a senator, and Warner, an author who would write *The Gilded Years* with Mark Twain, remained with the paper for over 20 years.

The *Courant* moved to a new building on State Street in 1880, and by the end of the century had acquired typesetting machines and a new press that could produce 12,000 sixteen-page papers an hour. Editorial cartoons were introduced, color appeared in advertisements, photographs were tried (although not used on a regular basis until 1920), and in 1913 the Sunday edition was first issued.

A final relocation was made in 1950 to Broad Street, where further additions have expanded the paper's facilities. Keith L. McGlade is the publisher and chief executive officer and Mark Murphy is the editor and vice-president under the ownership of The Times Mirror Company, which purchased the paper in 1979. Thomas Green would not recognize *The Hartford Courant* plant today. The use of offset printing, process color, computer typesetting, and video-display terminals are all a major part of publishing the paper. Eleven news bureaus are maintained in the state and another is located in Washington, D.C. Over 900 full-time and 350 part-time employees are involved with this modern newspaper, custodian of a long and prominent heritage in Hartford.

Hartford Despatch & Warehouse Company, Inc.

The history of Hartford Despatch at 225 Prospect Street, East Hartford, begins in 1906 when Everitt V. Eldrige commenced operations at the company's first office at 105 Albany Avenue in Hartford. Business consisted of moving families and hauling freight from the New Haven Railroad, although when wagons or trucks were not in use they carried meat and produce or were rented for hayrides and outings.

Arriving in Hartford from Springfield, Massachusetts, E.G. Mooney, formerly of the Boston-Springfield Despatch Company, purchased control and became president in 1919. One of Mooney's first acts was to erect the area's first public warehouse in East Hartford in 1920. At that time the present company name was adopted. A division was formed under John G. Hyland which specialized in the distribution of national brand products such as Procter & Gamble and Borden. By 1940 the company ran terminals and warehouses in several cities including a Hartford warehouse at 410 Capitol Avenue. During World War II Hartford Despatch was involved in household storage for servicemen and transportation of defense products to east coast ports.

Mooney and Hyland were dynamic members of the Hartford business community. The former was one of the founders of Allied Van Lines, Inc., in 1928 and served as a director and member of its executive committee for 25 years. Allied was the first van line and has become the largest moving organization in the world. Hartford Despatch is one of its largest booking and hauling components. Hyland, as executive vice-president, was long active in the Motor Transport Association of Connecticut and served in East Hartford town government.

Robert K. Mooney, E.G.'s son, joined the firm in 1950 and became its president in 1962. After purchasing control in 1971 he led Hartford Despatch through a period of vigorous expansion of its freight and moving operations. Believing that impend-

Moving van No. 18—an example of the Hartford Despatch fleet from earlier times (circa 1922).

ing deregulation of the trucking industry would prove harmful, Hartford Despatch sold its interstate franchises and freight equipment in 1978. It now concentrates on its public warehouse and its moving operations. The latter includes total worldwide moving with door-to-door service, important to Connecticut's many international corporations and families working overseas.

Robert Mooney has also been active in community affairs such as the Greater Hartford Chamber of Commerce, including ser-

vice as chairman, and the Hartford Foundation for Public Giving. He recalls that when the Friends of Mark Twain restored the author's Hartford home, they found that Twain had removed the paneling and mantle to Redding from the family library. These pieces were eventually found intact in a Hartford Despatch warehouse and returned to their original home—a unique example of Hartford Despatch's success at providing bonded warehouse storage and complete customer service.

One of the modern-day moving vans which serve Hartford Despatch customers today.

Hartford National Bank and Trust Company

Hartford National Bank and Trust Company is the city's oldest bank, dating from 1792 when the General Assembly granted a charter for the Hartford Bank. The need for it was evident. Hard money was scarce and citizens, such as Jeremiah Wadsworth, Noah Webster, and John Trumbull, felt that if Hartford's trade and commerce were to survive, a bank was a necessity.

When Hartford Bank opened just off Main Street, its resources consisted of $100,000. Its first president, John Caldwell, was one of Hartford's leading citizens as were the other individuals who directed the bank well in the years ahead.

The first major test came with the War of 1812, when Hartford commerce stood still. Hartford Bank trembled, as did others, but survived. Once the war ended small industries and insurance companies blossomed and Hartford Bank helped to finance many of them.

Hartford Bank became part of the national banking system in 1865. Economic uncertainty and inflation followed the Civil War and culminated in the Panic of 1873. Hartford National's directors, however, had invested soundly and avoided the lure of speculation which ruined many other financial institutions. By 1892 the bank's capital was well over one million dollars.

The early 20th century brought major changes through mergers: in 1910 with

The present headquarters of Hartford National Bank and Trust Company at 777 Main Street, Hartford.

John Caldwell, president of the Hartford Bank from its inception in 1792 to 1819.

Farmer's and Mechanic's Bank of Hartford, in 1915 with Aetna National Bank which created the Hartford-Aetna National Bank, and in 1927 with U.S. Security Trust Company which had specialized in trust work. The latter merger formed Hartford National Bank and Trust Company, and a year later its Main and Pearl Street headquarters was opened.

The Depression was banking's greatest challenge. Hartford National closed its doors (as did all Connecticut banks by state order) after New York City banks were closed, but only to protect its depositors. It reopened at the earliest date following the federal Bank Holiday and qualified for membership in the new Federal Deposit Insurance Corporation without the need for further capital.

Since 1933, and particularly after World War II, Hartford National has expanded statewide by merger and consolidation. With headquarters at 777 Main Street, it maintains 64 offices and is the second largest bank in Connecticut.

Hartford National Corporation, the parent bank holding company, was formed in 1969. Hartford National Bank, under chairman and chief executive officer Robert L. Newell, is the corporation's major subsidiary. Today the bank provides comprehensive individual, commercial, and corporate services. Its founders had wanted to develop Hartford's economy. Hartford National Bank and Trust still performs that task.

Heublein Inc.

Longtime residents of the Hartford area pronounce it "Hi-bline." Linguists say "Hoy-bline." Most of its customers around the world call it "Hugh-bline." But no matter how it's pronounced, the name has been associated with fine foods and beverages for more than a century.

Today's Heublein is a multibillion-dollar company with an impressive array of products—including Smirnoff Vodka, Kentucky Fried Chicken, A.1. Steak Sauce, and Inglenook Vineyards Wines—that are enjoyed by people around the world.

It all began quite modestly in 1862, when Austrian immigrant Andrew Heublein established a small hotel in downtown Hartford. Heublein had an unstinting dedication to quality and his establishment soon became widely known for the excellence of its food and drink.

The tradition of quality was continued by Andrew's sons, Gilbert and Louis, who in 1875 formed the partnership of G.F. Heublein & Bro. Starting as importers and distributors of foods and beverages, the brothers branched out into the production of beverages. Their most notable innovation was the introduction in 1892 of "The Club Cocktails," the world's first bottled cocktails. They gained wide popularity and today, almost a century later, prepared cocktails continue to be one of Heublein's best-selling products.

Heublein became the U.S. agent for A.1. Sauce from England in 1906. In 1918 it acquired the U.S. manufacturing rights for A.1., a timely transaction that enabled the company to remain in business through the Prohibition era.

Another significant step was the purchase in 1939 of U.S. production and marketing rights for a little-known spirits brand called Smirnoff Vodka. Today, thanks to Smirnoff's quality and Heublein's astute marketing, Smirnoff is the world's most popular brand of distilled spirits, with sales of more than 12 million cases a year.

Heublein grew rapidly in the years after World War II, winning recognition for its ability to anticipate and to respond promptly to changes in the consumer marketplace.

TOP: *The original home of what was to become Heublein Inc. was in this building at Gold and Mulberry streets in downtown Hartford, Connecticut. It was opened in 1875 as G.F. Heublein & Bro., importers, producers, and marketers of fine spirits, wines, and foods.*

ABOVE: *The new corporate headquarters of Heublein Inc. is located in Farmington, Connecticut. The building covers 1.5 acres on a 20-acre hillside site.*

Reflecting the company's growth, Heublein was listed on the New York Stock Exchange in 1962. It has continued to expand since then, partly through internal growth and partly through acquisitions. The two largest additions were United Vintners, Inc., a leading producer of California wines, acquired in 1969, and Kentucky Fried Chicken Corporation, the world-famous convenience food chain, in 1971.

Heublein's corporate headquarters in Farmington, Connecticut, is the nerve-center for an international network of plants and offices. But the firm's roots are still in the Hartford area, and Heublein continues to be a strong supporter of numerous civic, cultural, educational, and health-service organizations that enhance the quality of life in greater Hartford.

A.C. Hine Company

A.C. Hine Company has sold its products for more than 67 years, always under the ownership of the Hine family. It is the oldest Pontiac dealership run by one family in the United States.

Albert C. ("A.C.") Hine, Sr., opened his dealership in 1915 at Allyn and High streets. A.C. sold Fords in his spare time. His ability to best the company's full-time salesmen brought him to the attention of the Oakland Motor Car Company of Pontiac, Michigan, which offered him a Connecticut franchise. After moving to Pearl Street in 1916, his enterprise settled into its permanent home at Washington Street in 1918.

Selling automobiles then was quite different from today. Often car salesmen had to instruct the buyer how to drive and even spend a night on the farm in order to do so. Sometimes cars were bartered. For many years A.C. Hine's showroom displayed a huge oriental rug exchanged for an automobile.

Under his franchise, A.C. established dealerships all over the state, traveling throughout Connecticut encouraging garage owners to purchase one or two cars for local

A.C. Hine, founder, at his desk in the new building at 189 Washington Street about 1919.

The Pearl Street showroom of A.C. Hine Company as seen about 1918. The car displayed is an Oakland.

sale. Meanwhile, in Hartford, Oaklands were at first brought by rail to the Albany Avenue railhead where the cars, delivered in two parts, were off-loaded, transported to the company, and assembled for display in the downtown showroom, a "store" separate from the service center. When A.C. moved to Washington Street he consolidated all operations under one roof.

A.C. Hine Company sold Oaklands but added lines such as Chalmers, Locomobiles, and Krebs trucks. In 1924 Oakland introduced four-wheel brakes and Hartford residents were treated to a display of their efficiency. Part of Washington Street was hosed down by the fire department and the Oakland's brakes were tested on the slippery surface to show their superiority.

In 1932 Oakland was discontinued by General Motors, giving way to its successor, Pontiac, which was first produced in 1926.

A.C. Hine sold that car exclusively until 1973, when it also acquired a Honda franchise. During World War II auto servicing continued but the rest of the building was rented to the War Department.

A.C. died in 1944 and the business passed to sons A.C. Jr. and Thomas, with A.C.'s brother, Harry C. Hine, acting as treasurer, a position he held for 26 years. Today Tom Hine is president, a veteran of World War II and of 42 years in the automobile business. A.C. Hine Company employs about 50 people and new cars are delivered directly by trailer truck. Two things, however, have not changed since 1915: the firm's reputation for quality and service, and its original Connecticut dealer's license number four.

Kaman Corporation

In 1945, at 26 years of age, Charles H. Kaman established the original Kaman Aircraft Company with a $2,000 passbook loan, a handful of employees, and a groundswell of small investments from local residents, businessmen, and Connecticut factory workers who had faith in "Charlie's" ideas.

A magna cum laude graduate of Catholic University, Kaman had distinguished himself as wartime chief of aerodynamics at Hamilton Standard Propeller Company where his work as a pioneer helicopter inventor led to servo flap control for improved helicopter reliability—and the foundation for his new company.

Through the years, Kaman helicopters established a long series of records and firsts. Kaman produced the world's first jet turbine helicopters and the first twin engine helicopters. Kaman's Air Force "Husky" established world altitude records flying to over 37,000 feet, and Kaman's Navy "Seasprite" and "LAMPS" helicopters, still produced here as of 1982, are noted for their reliability, durability, and superior performance. Kaman also ranks as a major supplier of high-technology components for aircraft built by other makers. Products designed and made in Connecticut include

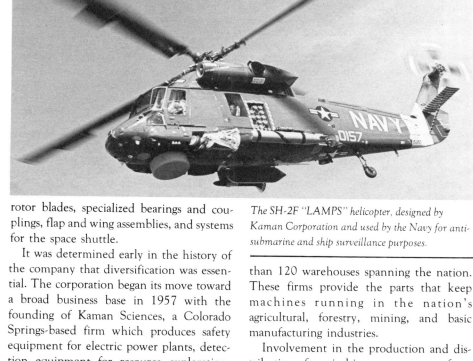

The SH-2F "LAMPS" helicopter, designed by Kaman Corporation and used by the Navy for anti-submarine and ship surveillance purposes.

rotor blades, specialized bearings and couplings, flap and wing assemblies, and systems for the space shuttle.

It was determined early in the history of the company that diversification was essential. The corporation began its move toward a broad business base in 1957 with the founding of Kaman Sciences, a Colorado Springs-based firm which produces safety equipment for electric power plants, detection equipment for resource exploration, and performs high-technology studies for national defense agencies.

In the '60s and '70s Kaman diversified further, building four strategically balanced business groups: Aerospace, Sciences, Bearing and Supply, and Music.

By 1982 Kaman's largest business was its group of Bearing and Supply distribution companies, which stock over 50,000 industrial necessities in a system of more

than 120 warehouses spanning the nation. These firms provide the parts that keep machines running in the nation's agricultural, forestry, mining, and basic manufacturing industries.

Involvement in the production and distribution of musical instruments stems from Mr. Kaman's interest in state-of-the-art technology—and his well-known skill as a guitarist. When technologies shifted from wood to metal helicopter rotor blades, Kaman Corporation was able to redirect the efforts of vibration specialists, engineers, and workers (who otherwise might have lost their jobs) to the task of enhancing vibrations in the same materials to produce a revolutionary new guitar. The introduction of Ovation guitars in 1966, using existing plant and skills, launched the Music Group. Used by a large roster of top performers, Kaman's Connecticut-made guitars account for more than 50 percent of the nation's production of acoustic guitars. The company is also a major factor in musical string production, and ranks as the nation's largest distributor of musical merchandise.

Kaman Corporation grew through technical preeminence, fiscal conservatism, and people dedication; today Charles Kaman presides over one of Connecticut's major industrial employers with sales approaching $.5 billion per year.

Charles H. Kaman, founder and chairman of Kaman Corporation, with a prototype of his first helicopter, circa 1945.

Industrial Risk Insurers

Electricity, the telephone, the automobile: These were just three of the major innovations that dramatically changed the landscape and life of America in the 1890s. As new industries developed, it became necessary for insurance companies to keep abreast of new technology so they could adequately insure emerging enterprises. As a response to these needs, on February 13, 1890, 11 insurance companies formed the Factory Insurance Association (FIA) to specifically write property insurance on large, sprinklered facilities.

FIA's first office was a single room on the second floor of the Goodwin Building, which survives today in downtown Hartford on Asylum Street, opposite the civic center. In 1891 the Western Factory Insurance Association (WFIA) was started in Chicago to underwrite midwestern properties. Within a few years the FIA and WFIA became founding members of the National Fire Protection Association, whose origins began with a group appointed to develop a sprinkler standard.

As the country grew, so did FIA. Inspection service was expanded and insurance

The antique sprinkler head collection on display at Industrial Risk Insurers' home office in Hartford.

coverage broadened to include business interruption, sprinkler leakage, and windstorm. FIA inspectors became famous for their thoroughness and their meticulous attention to detail, which benefited industry in terms of improved protection, fewer losses, and lower rates. When World War I erupted, the FIA's reputation among its policyholders and other insurance organizations came to the attention of the War Department, which retained association inspectors on a "dollar-a-year" basis as fire protection specialists for the department's installations.

During this period, the Oil Insurance Association, similar to the FIA and including many of the same member companies, was founded to offer coverage and inspection services to the oil industry.

When the war ended in 1918, America emerged as the most highly industrialized nation in the world. With the return of peace and a surge in demand for automobiles, appliances, and other consumer items, factories continued to expand, thus increasing the need for insurance. The FIA kept pace with this business and industrial activity by opening additional field offices and introducing new package policies for fire, sprinkler leakage, riot, vandalism, and molten material. These innovations provided the policyholder with the broadest insurance coverage possible.

The stock market crash of 1929 and the Depression which followed brought new problems and challenges for property insurers. Empty and/or strike-bound plants were susceptible to fire by accident and arson. Industries faced with financial losses or, at best, very low profits, often cut their maintenance funds, which enlarged the risk of fire. During this bleak period, the FIA made a major effort to help its insureds maintain proper levels of protection by increasing its inspections and advising plant management on methods of protection.

Despite the Depression, the association continued to open new field offices. The Pacific FIA was founded in 1932 and within three years the insurance in force of the three associations — FIA, WFIA, and PFIA — totaled more than $6 billion. Again, keeping up with the times, coverage was broadened to include sprinklered occupan-

This view of the fire safety laboratory shows a portion of the many sprinkler systems used in the training of fire protection personnel. All of these systems are actually functional and are routinely demonstrated for lab attendees. This unique training lab maintains the largest and most diverse collection of modern fire protection equipment in the world.

cies beyond purely industrial risks, and such perils as explosion, aircraft and vehicle accident, riot, civil commotion, and malicious mischief.

In 1940 Europe again went to war. American industry retooled and within the year was exceeding the combined output of Germany, Italy, and Japan. To accommodate this surge in production, huge plants with automated assembly lines were constructed and again the FIAs were there to provide their expertise in loss prevention and control. The demand for services from the FIA, WFIA, and PFIA finally led to their merger in 1943. The newer, larger association opened several more offices, formed an engineering council to coordinate nationwide loss control activities, and founded a fire safety laboratory for training purposes.

The postwar period spawned the development of nuclear energy. Again the FIA was in step with the times, as it assumed management of the Nuclear Energy Property Insurance Association in 1956 and

trained key engineers in nuclear physics so they could effectively analyze and safeguard nuclear facilities. During this year the FIA moved into its current quarters at 85 Woodland Street, Hartford.

In the early 1970s a new underwriting organization, formed in Canada and called Canadian Industrial Risks Insurers (CIRI), became affiliated with the FIA. In 1975 the Factory Insurance Association and the Oil Insurance Association merged to form Industrial Risk Insurers (IRI). This seemed a logical marriage as both served many of the same insureds, worked with many of the same insurance agents and brokers, and were backed by many of the same member

companies. The consolidation provided policyholders and insurance agents and brokers with a broader base of operations, greater underwriting experience, expanded engineering services, enlarged capacity, and enhanced financial stability.

Today IRI numbers some 1,200 employees around the world, with 300 located in Hartford. International liability-in-force, covering some 50,000 risks in more than 60 countries, exceeds $700 billion. Under the stewardship of Jack W. Cates, president, IRI's premium volume has

The present office building of Industrial Risk Insurers, at 85 Woodland Street, Hartford.

The Goodwin Building in Hartford (circa 1890) was the first office of Industrial Risk Insurers, then known as the Factory Insurance Association.

increased 36.5 percent over the past five years. New marketing efforts have included the introduction of Difference in Conditions coverage in 1977 and the formation of IRI Corporation in 1979 to spearhead international services. In addition to an existing engineering services office in Brussels, Belgium, new offices have been opened in London (Hitchin Herts), England; Frankfurt (Neu-Isenburg), West Germany; and Sydney (Crows Nest), Australia.

Since loss prevention is at the heart of every IRI policy, new engineering activities over the past few years have included an improved impairment handling program, known as RSVP (Restore Shut Valves Promptly); a pre-emergency planning program, titled PEPlan; and OVERVIEW, a total management program for loss prevention and control.

For nearly a century Industrial Risk Insurers has delivered what the industrial insurance buyer needs most—a world of experience in preventing loss and unquestioned financial protection when it occurs. Backed by the resources of its 45 member companies (some of whom are headquartered in Hartford), IRI plans to continue this kind of total insurance commitment during the 1980s and beyond.

Lux Bond Green & Stevens

No better example of the recognition enjoyed by Lux Bond Green & Stevens can be cited that when an order from the Fiji Islands arrived at Hartford addressed simply to Lux Bond and Green, USA. Often referred to as "the Tiffany of Connecticut," the present company evolved from three separate jewelry firms.

M.A. Green entered business in Waterbury in 1898, concentrating on gold frames for eyeglasses and pocket watches, later expanding into fine jewelry. Now known as M.A. Green, Inc., this firm is a wholly owned subsidiary of Lux Bond Green & Stevens.

The second firm, Philip H. Stevens Company, was formed by Stevens in 1902-03 and first operated a small store on Asylum Street before moving to 65 Pratt Street in 1912. It was later taken over by Arthur Terwilliger. This new jewelry store featured departments for giftware, glass, and china. A West Hartford branch was opened in 1947.

Lux Bond & Green, begun in 1908 in Hartford, was the third venture. Harry E. and George Lux, together with Austin

The Pratt Street store of Lux Bond & Green as it appeared in the '40s and '50s.

The Lux Bond & Lux store located at 859 Main Street, as it appeared in the early 1920s.

Bond, opened their business on Main Street, moving to 70 Pratt Street in 1928. In 1933 M.A. Green's son, Irving G. Green, who had worked in his father's Waterbury company, moved to Hartford and purchased the store under the name of Lux Bond & Green.

These Hartford firms remained competitors until 1963, when Lux Bond & Green bought Stevens. The stores, however, were run independently until 1968, when they merged and moved into a handsomely redesigned building at 15 Pratt Street under the current company name.

Lux Bond Green & Stevens is one of the largest firms of its kind in New England and, as a full-line jewelry company, also offers a fine selection of giftware, crystal, china, and silver. Its 95 employees include engravers, polishers, and other craftspeople who are highly trained in the art of fashioning quality merchandise.

Robert E. Green, president since 1972, grandson of M.A. Green, has now been joined by his two sons, Marc and John. He points out that the jewelry business is now much more dynamic than in the days of the company's forebears. Jewelry then consisted of certain standard items such as watches and bar pins with styles that remained unchanged from year to year. Today styles change constantly and the variety of merchandise offered has expanded considerably. Furthermore, new methods of manufacture and modern equipment have improved the final product.

By also providing repair and other service facilities, Lux Bond Green & Stevens combines a tradition of concern for the needs of its customers with the kind of expertise that can only be developed by a firm which has conducted its business successfully for over 80 years.

J.M. Ney Company

James Madison was President and war with England was approaching when in 1812 Marcus Bull opened his gold-beating shop at 14 Gold Street. He hoped to produce a quality gold leaf that would compete with New York imports. Bull would be astounded at the success of his venture, now represented by the J.M. Ney Company.

In 1847 John M. Ney, for whom the business is named, came to Hartford from Lorraine, France, and joined the firm of Ashmead & Hurlburt, successor to Bull. By 1867 he had become sole owner and president. Although gold from the company was used in a variety of ways, such as that which graces the state capitol dome, the first products for dentistry were made under William Johnson, who had worked with Bull. This became the firm's major occupation well into the 20th century. J.M. Ney produced gold plate, gold solder, and in 1913 introduced casting gold for use with dentures. This important step in the development of gold alloys led to the establishment

Jerry Norton, employed by J.M. Ney from 1926 to 1963, is shown working on gold foil (which is no longer produced by the company).

of a research department in 1914 to study the relationship between metals in alloys.

In 1921 the National Bureau of Standards and the firm developed a method for testing gold alloys, which resulted in the J.M. Ney Company testing laboratory for monitoring quality control and standardization. A year later courses were instituted to instruct dentists and technicians in the uses and improvements of new products.

The development of alloys for dentistry

had broader implications. In World War II Ney alloys were used in radar instruments, and soon an electronics division was manufacturing alloys for a wide range of equipment. This included scales, radios, and gyros, and now encompasses computers, guided missiles, and space satellites. By the mid-20th century the company had considerably diversified its products.

The firm occupied property at 265 Asylum Street until 1917, when it moved to 71 Elm Street. The present plant in Bloomfield was opened in 1956. The Barkmeyer Company of Yucaipa, California, was purchased in 1966 and produces high-temperature furnaces for use in dental offices and laboratories. A further expansion came in 1975 with the purchase of the Chayes-Virginia Corporation of Danbury, Connecticut, which was moved to Bloomfield and manufactures mounted wheels for use in shaping metals. Finally in 1977 the All-T Company of Redmond, Washington, became the Precision Machining Division.

Today the organization is led by its chairman and president, Frank S. Wilson and, in keeping with its tradition, remains one of the most prominent developers and manufacturers in the dental field as well as a major supplier of precision products for business, space, electronics, and other industrial instruments.

The J.M. Ney Company was located at 265 Asylum Street in Hartford until 1917.

Northeast Utilities

In 1881 Hartford was a thriving commercial, industrial, and cultural community of 42,000 people living along 80 miles of gas-lighted streets. Thomas Edison had developed the first commercially practical incandescent lamp, and participants in the scramble to be first with electric lighting service in Hartford included existing gas light and steam heating companies. However, a small group of prominent businessmen, including Mayor Morgan G. Bulkeley, believed that Hartford would best be served by an independent electric company. Their petition for a charter of incorporation for

tenure was his revolutionary contract in 1901 to provide the Billings and Spencer factory in Hartford with hydroelectric power at the manufacturer's cost for steam.

Austin C. Dunham (right), first president of The Hartford Electric Light Company, and Robert W. Rollins, general manager, in the single-story office at 266 Pearl Street, about 1901-02.

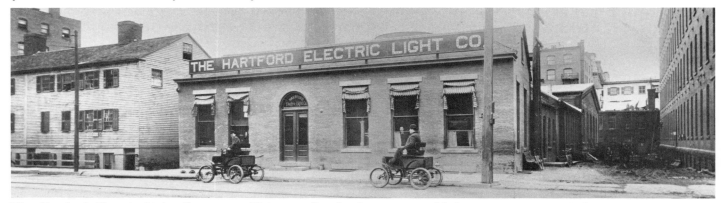

The Hartford Electric Light Company (HELCO) was granted by the Connecticut General Assembly on April 12, 1881.

A textiles merchant named Austin C. Dunham was elected president of the fledgling company, which began operations on April 7, 1883, with a display of 21 arc lamps at the old New Haven and Hartford railroad depot. *The Hartford Courant* editorialized, "The push and enterprise of the new company promises well for the early use of electric lights on the principal business streets of the city." By 1886 Hartford was considered the best-lighted city of its size in America and by 1890 the city had the first all-electric streetlighting system in New England.

The electric industry developed rapidly, Dunham's inventiveness and willingness to try new ideas attracted manufacturers eager to have their equipment tested, and HELCO's reputation for pioneering grew. Prominent among the company's many industry "firsts" during Dunham's 30-year

This was a first for the country and led to conversions by many industries in the Hartford area.

By 1902 the electrical inspector for the Hartford Board of Fire Underwriters had declared Hartford "far in the lead of any other city in the world in the use of electricity for light and power per capita."

HELCO also developed electricity for home use. In 1908 it staged the equivalent of an all-electric home demonstration, half of the appliances featured having been designed by Dunham himself. Electricity's future seemed limitless. The firm's expansion into the towns around Hartford necessitated the building of additional generating stations at Dutch Point (1904) and South Meadow (1921).

In 1925 HELCO helped create the Connecticut Valley Power Exchange, a pioneering power pool which enabled participating utilities to coordinate power plant operation on a single-system basis for greater fuel economies and reliability of service. Its suc-

HELCO's original office at 266 Pearl Street, about 1902. The alley at right was widened and extended in 1922-23 to form Ann Street.

cess inspired the formation of similar pooling arrangements throughout the United States and in many other countries.

In the Depression year of 1933, HELCO received the electric industry's prestigious Coffin Award for such accomplishments as reducing rates and improving service quality, maintaining employment at the 1929 level without reductions in pay and paying regular dividends—as it had since 1897.

Prudent planning enabled HELCO to carry heavy power loads during World War II, when peak annual output exceeded one billion kilowatt-hours—13 times that in World War I.

The 1950s brought new demands. A final generating unit was added to the South Meadow Station and a new coal-fired plant was built on the Connecticut River below

Middletown. In 1954 HELCO joined other New England utilities in forming the Yankee Atomic Electric Company to bring the benefits of nuclear power to fuel-poor New England.

Northeast Utilities Created

HELCO affiliated with The Connecticut Light and Power Company (CL&P) and Western Massachusetts Electric Company to form Northeast Utilities (NU) in 1966. Holyoke Water Power Company joined the new system the following year. This new venture made possible the operation of these companies on a single-system basis for maximum reliability of service at the lowest practicable cost for the benefit of NU's then nearly one million electric and gas customers. NU promptly took over construction of the first unit of the Millstone Nuclear Power Station and proceeded with plans for the million-kilowatt pumped-storage hydroelectric power facility at Northfield Mountain in Massachusetts.

On June 30, 1982, HELCO slipped quietly into history when it was merged into CL&P. However, NU continues the tradition of pioneering and innovation characteristic of HELCO. In 1968 it became the first utility in the nation to establish an environmental department at the vice-presi-

The Millstone Nuclear Power Station in Waterford in 1982, showing Units I and II in operation and Unit III, at left of complex, under construction.

dential level. In 1981 it launched NU 80s/90s, a comprehensive energy conservation program to reduce oil dependence—and costs—in both NU's generation of electricity and the ways its customers use energy in their homes and businesses.

The principal element in NU's effort to reduce the region's dependence on costly foreign oil is nuclear power. NU's farsighted investment in the Connecticut Yankee and Millstone nuclear power stations have made the system one of the most nuclear-intensive in the nation. Its technology has established an enviable record for safety as well as economy.

Today NU provides electric and natural gas service to more than 1.2 million customers in Connecticut and western Mas-

sachusetts. More than 40 percent of its 200,000 shareholders live in its service territory, as do nearly all of its approximately 8,300 employees.

Austin Dunham once expressed HELCO's philosophy as "the steady and determined adoption of the newest and most improved methods known ... the effort being made constantly to give the public their full share in the advance of the art."

That philosophy continues at Northeast Utilities.

The Hartford Electric Light Company began operations April 7, 1883, with an Armington-Sims steam engine powering a display of railroad depot arc lamps.

Peat, Marwick, Mitchell & Co.

Peat, Marwick, Mitchell & Co. has played a key role in the growing participation of the accounting profession in American and world business. Today some 26,000 professionals and staff in 348 offices around the globe serve more than 50,000 clients, ranging from small family businesses to giant multinational corporations. Peat Marwick has clearly stated its fundamental objective as being the foremost professional accounting firm involving commitment to professional excellence in constructive, innovative, and cost-effective service to clients.

With the increasing number of clients located in Connecticut, Peat Marwick opened its Hartford office in 1958 at 750 Main Street with 10 employees. These employees represented a firm spanning the 20th century.

Two Scottish accountants, James Marwick and Roger Mitchell, formed the original partnership in 1897. It was a time when American business leaders saw no practical need for skilled accountants. The first real opportunity to prove otherwise came during the Panic of 1907. Hartford-born J.P. Morgan asked Marwick and Mitchell to apply their banking expertise to assess the solvency of the old Knickerbocker Trust Company. Their efforts during a time of economic crisis demonstrated the value of an independent accountant to the business community and gained recognition for the firm.

In 1911 the partners joined the respected English firm of W.B. Peat & Co., forming an international copartnership. The vigor of the newer American firm and the prestige of the English one provided a solid base for a worldwide practice. Evidence of this is found in the fact that today Peat Marwick is comprised of more than 2,000 partners in 68 countries.

The stock market crash of 1929 and the resulting Securities Acts of 1933 and 1934 challenged all public accounting firms. Peat Marwick met the challenge and has since experienced phenomenal growth. An office in Waterbury, Connecticut, was opened in 1950 followed by the establishment of the Hartford office eight years later.

Expansion at Hartford came in 1963 as Peat Marwick and Knust, Everett & Cambria (KEC) merged, maintaining offices at 100 Constitution Plaza. In 1975 Waterbury was consolidated into the Hartford office. At that time the staff numbered 62 and the growth and addition of clients has further increased that number to 170, including 15 partners. Hartford is one of the most diversified offices in the firm, counting Aetna Life & Casualty, Timex Corporation, Kaman Corporation, and numerous other businesses and individuals as clients. These are serviced by accounting and auditing, tax, management consulting, and private business departments.

In its quarter century in Hartford, the firm's partners and employees have involved themselves in the community. As needs have been identified, Peat Marwick has donated certain consultation and analytical services to state and city government and the Hartford Civic Center. Personnel have participated and held offices in the Chamber of Commerce, such as the Foreign Trade Zone Committee, several hospital boards, and numerous civic, charitable and professional organizations.

The managing partner of the Hartford office is David J. Kirkpatrick, who believes that the future is bright in Hartford for a firm like Peat Marwick that is willing to make the commitment of resources and involvement in the community. As the global business community becomes increasingly interdependent, there is greater need for more sophisticated communication, better data management, and unfettered capital formation. Peat Marwick will play a significant role in the future as it has in the past quarter of a century, with a highly skilled staff of professionals who have kept pace with industrial specialization and technological developments.

Rourke-Eno Paper Company

Although America was at war with Mexico in 1847, most Hartford citizens were going about their business as usual. That year, however, Erastus Tucker, a grocer, changed his business and founded E. Tucker & Sons on Chapel Street. The new company manufactured paper boxes but soon included wrapping paper, grocery bags, fancy writing paper, and straw board among its products.

The Rourke-Eno Paper Company is a direct descendant of Tucker's firm with much of its history revolving around the leadership of William H. Rourke. Rourke, who had worked at the Platner & Porter papermill in Unionville, Connecticut, joined Tucker & Sons in 1907. He and L.F. Heyward purchased control of the firm in 1910. A year later Frank H. Eno bought Heyward's interest and in 1915 Tucker & Sons became the Rourke-Eno Paper Company.

The former Rourke-Eno plant on Allyn Street in Hartford.

The late William H. Rourke, a major figure behind the growth of Rourke-Eno and chairman of the board from 1947 to 1956.

The following years under Rourke's guidance were marked by continued growth as the company became a distributor for the products of many printing and industrial mills. In 1924 Bulkeley Van Schaack bought Eno's interest and Rourke-Eno became a stock corporation, opening its first branch in 1929 at New Haven.

During World War II the firm was known for its expertise in handling contracts in the specialized field of defense papers, and Rourke's goal of gaining wide recognition for the company was attained. After the war Rourke-Eno underwent rapid expansion, opening branches at Springfield and Boston, Massachusetts; Cohoes, New York; and Bridgeport, Connecticut, the latter merging in 1971 with the New Haven branch, and acquiring the Narragansett Paper Company of Providence, Rhode Island, in 1952.

A major step for Rourke-Eno was its 1970 merger with Alco Standard Corporation, Valley Forge, Pennsylvania, through which it became a member of Unisource Corporation, a division of Alco Standard. Shortly after this merger Macadam Associates, Inc., of Danielson, Connecticut, was made a division of the organization. Whalen Fine Paper of Rochester, New York, also became a division, although later transferred to another Unisource company, and in 1977 a division was opened in Worcester, Massachusetts.

Rourke-Eno, located for many years on Allyn Street in downtown Hartford, moved to its present site at 261 Weston Street in 1957. During 1981 this plant was expanded and a new office building was constructed. That same year John H. Oakley became president and chief executive officer. Through its several branches Rourke-Eno can ensure customers rapid delivery of its many products, which now include a wide range of packaging materials, printing paper, and shipping supplies. As one of the largest paper-distribution companies in Connecticut and New England, Rourke-Eno, now well into its second century of operation, has long been an important part of Hartford's commercial and industrial development.

185

Sage-Allen & Company

For almost 100 years Sage-Allen has been one of the most important businesses on Hartford's Main Street. The original store was opened at Main and Pratt streets in April 1889 by the partnership of Normand F. Allen, Jerome E. Sage, and Clifford Moore. Sage-Allen then had a total of 15 employees and offered such items as fine linens, silks, hosiery, and multi-buttoned gloves, then a highly popular item.

The first major event in the company's history occurred in October 1898 when the store was relocated across Main Street in a new and larger building. A fire in 1896 had destroyed the Hart & Merriman store. Sage-Allen bought this property and in a single night moved into its new permanent home. The eight-story building had the distinction of being the tallest in Hartford and one of the first to be fireproof.

Several significant changes followed during the next years. Upon the retirement of his partners in 1903, Normand Allen became sole owner of Sage-Allen. The need for expansion was evident as the firm continued to prosper. In 1910, 1929, and later with the purchase of the Kohn building, adjacent property was acquired, enabling the store to add considerably to its floor space.

The first Sage-Allen store, at the corner of Main and Pratt streets.

Normand F. Allen, one of the founders of Sage-Allen.

Mrs. Normand Allen became president of the firm in 1922 after the death of her husband, a position she held until her own death in 1940. She was widely respected in the Hartford community as was her son, Edward N. Allen, who succeeded her as president. Long active in Republican politics, Allen served as state senator, mayor of Hartford, and lieutenant governor of the state from 1951 to 1955.

Under the leadership of William Haine, president from 1960 to 1965 and chairman of the board from 1965 to 1970, Sage-Allen began a program of expansion which has resulted in 12 suburban branch stores throughout Connecticut. In 1972 Sage-Allen became a public company but remains under the direct control of the Allen family, thus being the largest independent department store in Connecticut.

Representing the family today are Lafayette Keeney, former president and now chairman and chief executive officer; Charles Haine, president and chief operating officer; Normand Allen, divisional merchandise manager and assistant corporate secretary; and Allen Westphal, corporate secretary.

Sage-Allen offers a wide variety of medium- and higher-priced quality wearing apparel and accessories as well as giftwares and domestic merchandise. Its successful growth continues to be accompanied by dedication to customer service, a hallmark of Sage-Allen & Company since the little one-room store opened on Main and Pratt streets in 1889.

Sage-Allen's largest branch at Westfarms Mall, West Hartford.

Security Insurance Group

Even though Security Insurance Group is relatively new to Hartford, having moved from New Haven in 1965, its origins, in part, can be traced to the city that became its home. Security began operations as the Mutual Security Insurance Company under an 1841 Connecticut charter granted to Jehiel Forbes and other New Haven merchants who wanted to obtain marine insurance without the delays experienced in dealing with companies in Hartford or more distant cities.

While the young enterprise also wrote fire policies, marine insurance remained centrally important to it, particularly as shipping increased to California during and after the Gold Rush years and as vessel traffic grew on the Great Lakes. In 1873 the firm became the Security Insurance Company of New Haven.

In 1905 a general agency was established in San Francisco, an event that was to have serious consequences. After the great earthquake and fire of 1906, many insurance companies faced bankruptcy. Security saw its resources severely strained but, in the tradition of Hartford insurers, met its obligations through a major bank loan for which the company's board members personally pledged repayment. By 1917 Security had expanded into auto insurance with the Connecticut Indemnity Company.

The 1950s began a long period of expansion through corporate acquisitions and formations which included entering the life insurance market by establishing the Security-Connecticut Life Insurance Company, now an independent firm. Notable among other additions was the acquisition of the Fire and Casualty Insurance Company of Connecticut, allowing the development of commercial multi-peril and homeowners business, and the acquisition of the New Amsterdam Casualty Company of Baltimore and its subsidiary, the United States Casualty Company of New York.

Developments of the 1960s included a new name, the Security Insurance Company of Hartford, adopted with the move

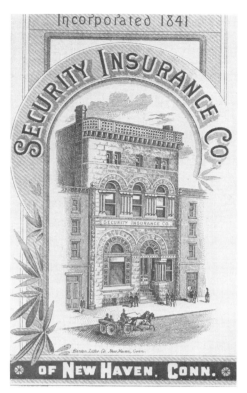

A notepad showing the New Haven office of Security Insurance Company in 1890.

from New Haven, and a 1968 reorganization of Security's new companies into one operating group.

In 1973 Textron purchased Security but sold it five years later to Orion Capital Corporation, an insurance holding company based in New York which continues as Security's parent company.

Recent years have seen Security occupy

a striking new headquarters building in Farmington and the firm's expansion into the reinsurance field through Security Reinsurance Company, Massachusetts Reinsurance, and Security Reinsurance Underwriters, Inc. It has also entered the worldwide insurance market via Security Insurance Company (U.K.) Ltd. of London.

Today the operations of Orion Capital, Security and Employee Benefits, Inc., another Orion subsidiary, are directed by Alan R. Gruber, chairman, and Edward J. Hobbs, president. Security is entering a new era of development as the insurance operations of these companies are consolidated, again increasing the scope and impact of this long-established Connecticut firm.

Herbert Mason, second secretary (1872 to 1904) of Security Insurance.

An interior photograph of the Security Insurance Company office about 1897, when it was located at Center Street in New Haven.

Stanadyne, Inc.

Stanadyne, a worldwide corporation located on Deerfield Road in Windsor, has claimed Hartford as its home for over a century. Its beginnings involve two separate but related developments. The first concerns a Manchester, Connecticut, inventor, Christopher M. Spencer, who developed and manufactured the Spencer seven-shooter at his Spencer Repeating Rifle Company during the Civil War.

With the arrival of peace Spencer moved to Hartford where he established a firm for the production of drop forgings, sewing machine shuttles, and other industrial items. At this time Spencer built an automatic turret screw machine which served as the basis for his new venture with George Fairfield, the Hartford Machine Screw Company.

The Connecticut General Assembly chartered this firm in 1876, describing it as a manufacturer of screws, hardware machinery, and other wares. Success was almost immediate and within six years the venture expanded into the western market with the purchase of the Elyria Tap and Screw Company in Ohio which was granted Connecticut incorporation as the Western Automatic Machine Screw Company, a subsidiary of the Hartford firm.

The second part of Stanadyne's story revolves around Walter B. Pearson of Chicago. He foresaw the need for precise metal fasteners which, if produced in large quantities, he believed would find a ready market among American manufacturers. Thus in 1900 Pearson and others formed the Standard Screw Company with the purchase of the Chicago Screw Company, the Detroit Screw Works, and the Worcester (Massachusetts) Machine Screw Company, firms that accounted for 50 percent of the nation's output of metal fasteners.

Illinois Screw Company was added to Standard, and in 1905 the very prosperous Hartford Machine Screw Company and its western subsidiary were bought. As a center for the manufacture of sewing machines, bicycles, and machine tools, the Hartford area provided a solid base for the growth of Hartford Machine Screw, offsetting the loss

An aerial view of Stanadyne, Inc., offices at 100 Deerfield Road.

of the automobile industry which had begun its shift to Detroit.

With the advent of World War I, the Hartford division of Standard underwent further expansion in order to meet urgent defense needs, particularly time fuses and parts for the new Liberty aircraft engines. Its efforts, officially and gratefully acknowledged by Great Britain, entailed operating 24 hours a day, seven days a week and, for the first time, the employment of a large number of women.

Following the end of hostilities the company, like many others, experienced a period of stagnant production. This was followed by the boom of the mid- and late-1920s which ended in the Great Depression. The Hartford company survived the difficult years of the 1930s by concentrating on efficiency in its manufacturing process and constant improvement of its product line. As World War II approached the business again found itself deeply involved in full-time defense work, putting its expertise in precision products to use in manufacturing vital parts for tanks, planes, bulldozers, tractors, and other equipment needed for military purposes.

With the belief that American manufacturing would enjoy continued prosperity by meeting domestic needs after the war, Standard Screw began a program of modernizing plants and equipment in all its subsidiaries. The company also acquired the services of

Vernon Roosa, a designer of a delicately machined fuel injection system made especially for diesel equipment. By the late 1950s the growing market for this product more than justified the several years of designing and testing invested in the system.

Another new concept was that of a single-handled faucet, developed and patented by Alfred M. Moen at the Ravenna Metal Products Company in Seattle, Washington. Lacking sufficient capital to underwrite the manufacture of the faucet, Ravenna applied to Standard which purchased the company in 1956 and moved the faucet's production facilities to Elyria. Today this faucet line and the diesel fuel systems are dominant in their respective markets, and together with the Western Cold Drawn Steel division (the sixth largest independent producer of cold-drawn steel in the United States) and the mechanical and hydraulic tappets and valve train automotive parts of the Chicago division comprise the principal components of Stanadyne.

In order to reflect the growing diversity of the corporation's products, the board of directors in 1970 voted to change the firm's name to Stanadyne, Inc. Another result of diversification was the creation of an Advanced Products Center at Windsor for testing engines and other equipment as well as for developing new products through close consultation with Stanadyne's customers.

A further acquisition was made in 1973 with the purchase of the Zeigler-Harris Cor-

poration of Pine Grove, Pennsylvania. As a manufacturer of stainless steel sinks, Zeigler-Harris expanded Stanadyne's line of plumbing products. In 1977 Supermet division, a leader in powered metal technology and manufacture with plants in Ohio and Illinois was acquired. In 1980-81, with the dissolution of the Stanscrew division, the company left behind the fastener product line of its origins. The Stanadyne Diesel Systems Group consolidated all diesel operations at its Hartford plant and three new plants in North Carolina. An international division was established to take advantage of the opportunities for sale of Stanadyne products on the world market.

The vision of men like Christopher Spencer and Walter Pearson, along with others who have worked at Stanadyne over the years, has resulted in one of the country's largest organizations involved in the design, manufacture, and distribution of complex metal products and components used by industry and the individual consumer. The present chairman, president, and chief executive officer, Paul A. Mongerson, oversees a corporation of 6,000 employees with sales and service agencies in over 74 countries including branch offices in Paris and Tokyo, subsidiaries in Connecticut, Mexico, Canada, and Brazil, and distribution and manufacturing locations throughout the United States.

Stanadyne has been a leader for many years in seeking solutions to environmental problems. An acid neutralization plant at its Chicago facility, a waste treatment plant at Hartford, and conversion from coal to gas furnaces are examples of its continuing concern for clean air and water. Because of the pride taken in its products and employees, Stanadyne has encouraged its workers, as a matter of corporate policy, to advance their education, has established scholarships and programs at technical schools and colleges, and has contributed liberally to advance local health and cultural projects. Although international in scope, Stanadyne remains an important member of the Hartford industrial and commercial community as it begins its second century of operations.

The Hartford Machine Screw Company, circa 1890.

Taylor & Fenn Company

The production of interchangeable parts and machine tools, originally spurred by the needs of clock and firearms factories, has long been of basic importance to American manufacturing. For nearly 150 years Taylor & Fenn has been supplying castings to meet the special needs of industry.

Taylor & Fenn's story begins with Levi Lincoln's purchase of an old woolen mill on Arch Street in Hartford in 1834. There he opened a business for the manufacture of his invention, a cast-iron faucet for molasses barrels. By 1841 he had built his own foundry where he also made machine tools. That year his two sons, George S. and Charles L., entered the business which became George S. Lincoln & Company.

The success of this firm was related to the textile, firearms, and paper industries which relied on Lincoln for specialized quality tools. Another significant part of the company's production was architectural and

The present plant of the Taylor & Fenn Company at 22 Deerfield Road, Windsor.

The Arch Street Foundry in 1906. Then the Phoenix Iron Works Corporation, the firm became the Taylor & Fenn Company a year later.

ornamental iron work such as that on the state capitol dome in 1878 and replaced by Taylor & Fenn a century later when the building was renovated.

Following two more name changes the business was incorporated by Charles L. Taylor in 1901 as the Phoenix Iron Works Corporation. Six years later the current name was adopted when Wilson L. Fenn joined the company.

The 20th century found Taylor & Fenn increasingly involved with defense work. In World War I it produced several specialized machines for arms manufacturers and during World War II it developed a versatile

machine for milling gun parts which was highly sought after by American and Allied defense industries.

The present facility at Windsor was built and occupied in 1950-51. This plant contains the most modern equipment in metallurgy, including computers, and an electric melting process which provides strict quality control in a pollution-free environment. More than 300 employees, headed by Edgar B. Butler, Jr., president and direct descendant of the founder, are involved with customer consultation and design, analysis, and production of the precision castings required by today's industry. In 1981 T & F Alcast, a new subsidiary, was added for the production of aluminum castings.

Taylor & Fenn is unique in the variety of metals poured and in the fact that every method of sandcasting is carried out at the Windsor site. Its sales territory now extends over the northeastern United States, Pennsylvania, and Ohio. Taylor & Fenn emphasizes that its success is due to a highly developed industrial art taught to each new generation of employees ensuring that skill and quality in metallurgy will continue to be as vital a company asset as it has been since 1834.

Thomas Cadillac, Inc.

Although Thomas Cadillac, Inc., is a recent arrival in Hartford, it represents the fourth generation in a direct line of Cadillac dealerships.

Originally, Cadillacs were sold in Hartford at Brown Thomson & Company until General Motors, unable to induce them to build separate facilities, looked elsewhere. The franchise was awarded to Russell P. Tabor, who built the present plant at 1530 Albany Avenue just before the 1929 stock market crash.

The physical layout of the Tabor Cadillac Corporation was far ahead of its time. It was designed as a series of one-story adjoining buildings which allowed ample space and efficient lateral traffic flow. As dealer and distributor for both Cadillacs and Oldsmobiles, Tabor off-loaded cars at the company railroad siding and distributed them to dealers throughout the Hartford area. During the Depression Tabor Cadillac was located in what is now the used-car area of the plant, while a First National food store occupied the present new-car showroom.

In 1959 after Tabor's death, the firm was sold to Richard C. Daniels, a former Ohio Buick dealer, and became the Richard Daniels Cadillac Company. The Oldsmobile franchise was discontinued in the 1970s and the volume of Cadillac sales continued to increase. The present company is the largest Cadillac dealership in New England.

The franchise became Thomas Cadillac,

The Thomas Cadillac showroom at 1530 Albany Avenue.

Inc., in early 1978, when it was purchased by Calvert Thomas and his son, Calvert Bowie Thomas. Calvert Thomas had been tax counsel, assistant general counsel, and secretary for the General Motors Corporation. Thomas Cadillac is a close-knit family organization. Calvert Thomas serves as president and general manager; his wife, Margaret Berry Thomas, is secretary and treasurer; Calvert Bowie Thomas is vice-president and assistant general manager; and a second son, Douglas Mackubin Thomas, a West Hartford attorney, is a director. Calvert Thomas, a graduate and trustee of Washington and Lee University and a graduate of the University of Maryland Law School, is a member of five state bar associations, including Connecticut. He is a trustee of the Connecticut Opera Association and belongs to the Greater Hartford and the West Hartford chambers of commerce. His son, Calvert Bowie, holds B.S. and M.A. degrees in education from Michigan State University, and is a former Lansing, Michigan, school teacher and principal.

With a heritage spanning most of the century, Thomas Cadillac currently employs 60 people and extends over more than

seven acres. Its extensive facilities make it an important and leading transportation center in the community. It was recently selected by a national survey of General Motors dealerships for service satisfaction, being one of three Cadillac dealers so chosen and the only one in the eastern United States. In Thomas' words: "We constantly try to achieve the best in quality service. It is our responsibility and obligation to those who purchase their cars from us."

Calvert Thomas, president of Thomas Cadillac, Inc.

Calvert Bowie Thomas, vice-president and assistant general manager of Thomas Cadillac, Inc.

The Travelers Corporation

With home offices now on the site of the historic Sanford Tavern, The Travelers has been a landmark since 1864. As Hartford has grown, so has The Travelers. Together, the city and the people at The Travelers have shared a rich and colorful heritage. Today The Travelers ranks among the largest diversified financial institutions in the United States.

1864: Founded by James G. Batterson, The Travelers becomes the first company in America to insure against travel accidents.

1865: Begins offering life insurance.

1865: Publishes initial issue of first industrial magazine.

1884: Introduces first retirement income contract.

1889: Begins offering liability insurance.

1889: Begins offering employers' liability insurance, precursor to workers' compensation.

1892: Introduces "double indemnity" policy.

1897: Issues first automobile insurance policy.

1902: Establishes branch office system.

1903: Opens first school to train insurance agents.

1904: Organizes first engineering department in insurance industry.

1904: Introduces first life insurance policy with waiver of premium in the event of total and permanent disability.

1907: Begins writing property damage forms.

1913: Begins offering group life insurance.

1913: Introduces first cash settlement life insurance policy.

1919: Offers first aircraft liability insurance.

1922: Offers first salary allotment plan.

1925: Offers fire and inland marine insurance.

1928: First company to offer lab services as a part of engineering.

1936: Pioneers retrospective rating in which final premium is figured after losses are known.

1938: Combined assets pass one billion dollar mark.

1939: Begins issuing fidelity and surety bonds.

1956: Establishes first weather research center in insurance industry.

1957: Introduces first premium budget (all-lines monthly payment) plan.

1958: Begins offering life insurance to women at lower rates than to men.

1962: Combined assets pass four billion dollar mark.

1965: Pioneers the concept of providing commercial package policies for most types of businesses.

1965: Combined assets pass five billion dollar mark.

1967: Initiates the Minority Office Skills Training Program.

1968: Enters the field of variable annuities and offers participation in mutual funds.

1968: Opens Hot Lines phones for prompt claims handling.

1969: Issues first accident policies for space flight and lunar exploration.

1969: Pioneers standard, discount, and surcharge method of pricing.

1971: Establishes first Office of Consumer Information in the insurance industry.

1973: Launches the PEP (Physical Exercise Pays) Program.

1973: Issues accident policies for space flight in connection with three manned Skylab missions.

1975: Insures the American crew of the first international space flight, the Apollo/Soyuz Program.

1977: Sponsors the 1977 National Figure Skating Championships.

1978: Pays over $14 million in claims to the City of Hartford after roof col-

LEFT: *In 1901 nearly the entire personnel of The Travelers could be posed on the steps of the home office. Today the company employs over 10,000 people in Hartford and nearly 30,000 across the country.*

BELOW: *Apollo 11 astronaut Neil A. Armstrong, mission commander, prepares to salute the American flag in one of the century's most historic photographs. The Travelers insurance covered the lives of the crew on this and other important space missions.*

lapse of Hartford Civic Center Veterans Memorial Coliseum (largest individual claim payment in Travelers history).

1980: Adopts "space-age" approach in electronic communications through Interactive Agency/Company Computer System and ties with Satellite Business Systems communications satellite.

1980: Inaugurates Travelers Older Americans Program.

1981: Insures the crew of the flight of the space shuttle Columbia.

1982: Introduces a Universal Life Insurance policy.

1982: Unveils plans for expansion of Group Department to new multimillion-dollar complex in Wallingford.

1982: Combined assets pass $26 billion mark.

Veeder-Root Company

Following the Civil War America was entering the first stages of the Industrial Revolution. Steam power was still the major source of energy but electricity and oil were soon to play a role in manufacturing. One area that was to become a basic element of industry the world over was developed in those postwar years—the counter. Veeder-Root, at 28 Sargeant Street, Hartford, is the largest manufacturer of counting, controlling, indicating, and recording devices in the world.

It started with piano hinges. That was what Joel H. Root set out to make in his small Bristol, Connecticut, shop in 1866. When he passed the business on to his son, Charles J. Root, in 1885 he had not expanded much beyond them. But soon after, Charles added a counter of his own design.

Meanwhile in Hartford, Curtis H. Veeder, an engineer, had become wealthy from his many inventions. He was also an ardent bicyclist and over the years had tried to make a workable cyclometer. In 1894 he finally achieved success and sales skyrocketed. Through Root's and Veeder's plant, counters of all kinds were being produced by the end of the century.

The Veeder Manufacturing Company as it appeared in 1906 at its present site on 28 Sargeant Street in Hartford.

The Veeder-Root complex at 28 Sargeant Street and Homestead Avenue.

The future of this new industry was best indicated in 1903, when the Wright brothers used a counter on their first flight in order to measure the number of propeller revolutions. World War I brought a further need for counters in aircraft and as measurers of ammunition rounds.

Industry after the war became a major user of the devices, leading to the 1928 merger of the two companies as Veeder-Root Inc. The Depression hit but the introduction of the gasoline pump computer in 1933 reversed the company's fortune. Soon the instrument was being used all over the world. Consumer production was halted during World War II while Veeder-Root turned to defense needs.

The importance of counters in American life was evident once peace had returned. Automation, whether in the voting booth, the factory, or in space research, required some sort of sophisticated counter. Veeder-Root formed its own research and development group in order to manufacture new and better products for use in modern technology.

In 1966 the firm became Veeder Industries Inc., which became a wholly owned subsidiary of Western Pacific Industries in 1976. President Dennis A. Kennedy directs the operations which include facilities in Europe, Canada, Brazil, and Australia. Now employing more than 2,700 people, Veeder-Root manufactures almost 7,500 product lines in its field, including the newest version of its first product—the gasoline pump computer. A Bristol manufacturer and a Hartford inventor are responsible for it all.

WVIT-Channel 30 TV

WVIT-Channel 30, Connecticut's NBC affiliate, serves the 24th largest television market in the United States. Owned since 1978 by Viacom International Inc. as part of its communications and media division, WVIT is well-known for its news and sports coverage and its community-oriented programming.

Much has changed since Channel 30 went on the air in 1953 as the second new station in the country following a freeze in 1948 on further licensing. Julian Gross, operator of a Hartford advertising agency and a New Britain radio station, was its owner. Although it was a CBS network affiliate until 1955, local programming constituted most of the broadcast day which began at 4:30 p.m. and ended at 1 a.m.

A major event occurred in 1955, which tested the new station and its personnel. That year flood waters had devastated many Connecticut towns. Channel 30 presented a two-day telethon featuring many entertainment personalities and was able to raise over $350,000 for relief. Today telethons are a tradition at WVIT.

The transmitter was located at Rattlesnake Mountain in Farmington. Live broadcasting originated at Bishop's Corner and Rockledge Country Club before the present studio was occupied in 1954 at 1422 New Britain Avenue in West Hartford. NBC owned the station between 1956 and 1959, a period in which movies became available for television and syndicated programs gradually replaced many local productions.

Connecticut Television purchased the station in 1959 and ran it as WHNB-TV until the sale to Viacom. During these years television came of age. The Hartford-New Britain station was able to offer extensive network programming, which included live national news and sports events made possible by rapid technological advances within the industry. Channel 30, for instance, was the first all-color station in Connecticut.

As WVIT approaches its 30th anniversary, station management has emphasized

A view of WVIT's control room, which features the latest electronic technology.

innovation and comprehensiveness. WVIT is strongly committed to serve the community. Expanded news coverage has included the reopening of the Civic Center, the ceremony following the death of Governor Ella Grasso, and a live broadcast lasting more than five hours of the Pope's visit to Boston. It was the only non-Boston station to cover the event.

WVIT has become the Whalers' hockey team television home and Red Sox games have been added to the station's expanded roster of sport's coverage. News and public affairs programming such as "Connecticut Newsmakers" and "The Public File" now provide a more balanced format between sports, information, and entertainment.

The station has received several UPI and public service awards. Thirty News was the first Connecticut station, in 1979, to receive an Emmy for "Outstanding News Program." A 1981 Emmy for "Outstanding News Reporting" as a result of its coverage of Ku Klux Klan activities in Connecticut and four nominations for sports, documentary, and news programming indicate that WVIT is a station on the move.

WVIT's news trucks used for on-the-spot reporting. The station's satellite antenna is in the background.

YMCA of Metropolitan Hartford, Inc.

The Young Men's Christian Association of Metropolitan Hartford has always been committed to Christian principles and ideals. It has sought to enrich the lives of people by utilizing its resources in developing human potential and shaping character.

The YMCA has played an important role in the life of Hartford and surrounding towns. This role has continued to grow over the years.

At the time of its founding in 1852, Hartford was experiencing a major influx of young men who were seeking employment in its factories and businesses. The YMCA was organized specifically "to seek and assist young men who came to reside in the city."

The YMCA not only provided housing, it also provided cultural, educational, recreational, and spiritual opportunities. It has continued to provide these opportunities through good times and bad, through depressions and world wars, through changes in neighborhoods, in towns, in politics, and in governments. The YMCA has witnessed many social changes and the YMCA, too, has changed. It has changed as people's needs have changed, but it always has sought to help people grow and develop.

Parent-child programs at the YMCA emphasize quality time together.

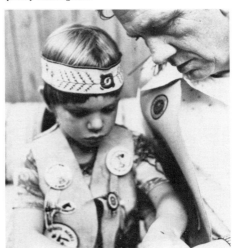

YMCA camp experience brings smiles.

The organization faced many problems in its early days, but prominent Hartford citizens, such as Colonel Charles A. Jewell, and General Charles T. Hillyer, among others, were determined that the YMCA should succeed. It was incorporated in 1886 and, with broad support from the community, built a permanent home in 1892 at the corner of Pearl and Jewell streets, where it was long a landmark.

In 1892 manual and academic training was extended through Hillyer Institute, which became Hillyer Junior College, an independent school after 1947 and now the University of Hartford.

A separate Hartford County YMCA was founded in 1918 and together the two organizations served the 28 towns of Connecticut's capital region for the next 50 years. In 1972 the two merged to form the present YMCA.

Over the years many activities have been provided. In 1939 an Industrial Management Club was begun in order to provide industrial workers an opportunity to develop leadership and management potentials. With the cooperation of industry and business, classes were held, seminars conducted, and visits made to Hartford plants.

Another program, called Friends of Boys, organized young shoeshine and newspaper boys into territories in order to reduce the problem of bullying competition and street fighting. The Hartford YMCA was one of the first YMCAs in the United States to do work such as this in an urban area.

In 1943 new services began, including educational testing, job referrals, and family counseling.

In recent years the Hartford Association has been more active than ever in helping meet the needs of people in today's environment. Responding to current social needs, the YMCA developed parent-child clubs called Indian Guides and Indian Princesses, established before-school and after-school child-care centers called Latch Key, and is helping encourage achievement of potential among minority teenagers with a Black and Hispanic Achievers Program. A collaborative effort with the city of Hartford and the United Way has provided a comprehensive community center program under YMCA management at the Stowe Village Housing Project.

Health enhancement programs, including early calisthenics classes, then sports such as basketball, volleyball, gymnastics, and swimming, to today's corporate fitness and cardiovascular health programs, all have been YMCA innovations. Today's wellness movement can also be traced to the YMCA.

Camping programs pre-date the turn of the century and led to the founding of Camp Jewell in 1901 and Camp Woodstock in 1922. In 1955 the first comprehensive, year-round outdoor center in the country was opened by the YMCA in Colebrook.

Besides these two camps, where thousands of youngsters and families enjoy good fellowship in an outdoor, recreational setting, the YMCA operates nine community-based branches: Farmington Valley, Glastonbury, Hartford Central (with an extension at Stowe Village), Indian Valley, South Regional, Tobacco Valley, Wheeler Regional, East Hartford, and West Hartford, the latter two located in buildings constructed by both the YMCA and the YWCA.

In 1972, when the Hartford County Association merged with the Greater Hartford YMCA, the certificate of consolidation stated that the purpose was "to build, through spiritual, intellectual, social, and physical activities, a worldwide fellowship

united in loyalty to God and primarily concerned with the development of Christian personality and attitude throughout our society." As a major force and an active partner in building and strengthening the human resources of the capital region, the YMCA of Metropolitan Hartford has lived up to this commitment.

Proud of its past, it looks to the future with confidence and excitement as it seeks to help young people and families develop self-confidence and self-respect. The YMCA encourages all people to build a

Group activities are fun at the YMCA Stowe Village Center.

faith for daily living, based on the teachings of Jesus, which will help them to be responsible citizens and family members. It also emphasizes that health of mind and body are sacred gifts and physical fitness and mental well-being are conditions to be achieved and maintained. By recognizing the worth of all persons, it has worked for interracial and intergroup understanding as well as the development of world peace. It is this concern for the total person that has been the hallmark of YMCAs everywhere, a tradition which the Hartford YMCA has exemplified since 1852.

One of the goals of the YMCA is physical fitness for all people.

197

Patrons

The following individuals, companies, and organizations have made a valuable commitment to the quality of this publication. Windsor Publications and The Connecticut Historical Society gratefully acknowledge their participation in *Hartford: An Illustrated History of Connecticut's Capital.*

AAA Hartford
American School for the Deaf*
The Associated Construction Co., Hartford, Connecticut
Avon Old Farms Hotel*
Avon Old Farms Inn*
Barrieau Moving & Storage, Inc.*
Charter Oak Bank and Trust Company
Chase Enterprises*
C.I.G.N.A. Corporation, Contributions and Civic Affairs
The Collinsville Company*
The Connecticut Bank and Trust Company*
Connecticut Lighting Center, Inc.
Connecticut Natural Gas Corporation*
Connecticut Printers, Inc.*
Cushman Industries, Inc.*
The Dexter Corporation*
Ensign-Bickford Industries, Inc.*
Finlay Brothers Company, Inc.*
Greater Hartford Consortium for Higher Education*
The Hartford Courant*
Hartford Despatch & Warehouse Company, Inc.*
The Hartford Graduate Center
Hartford National Bank and Trust Company*
Hartford Office Supply Company
Hartford Technical Institute
The Harvey & Lewis Co.
Heublein Inc.*
A.C. Hine Company*
Industrial Risk Insurers*
Kaman Corporation*
Lux Bond Green & Stevens*
Mr. & Mrs. John S. Murtha
J.M. Ney Company*
Northeast Utilities*
Peat, Marwick, Mitchell & Co.*
Mr. and Mrs. Robert Pedini
Rourke-Eno Paper Company*
Sage-Allen & Company*
Security Insurance Group*
Sheraton-Hartford Hotel

Stanadyne, Inc.*
Taylor & Fenn Company*
Thomas Cadillac, Inc.*
The Travelers Corporation*
Veeder-Root Company*
WVIT-Channel 30 TV*
YMCA of Metropolitan Hartford, Inc.*

*Partners in Progress of *Hartford: An Illustrated History of Connecticut's Capital.* The histories of these companies and organizations appear in Chapter 12.

Index

Numbers in italics indicate illustrations.

204

This Book Was Set In
Grecian,
Printed On
70 Pound Warrenflo
And Bound By
Walsworth Publishing Company
Halftone Reproduction By
Robertson Graphics